The Cinema
of Feng Xiaogang

Hong Kong University Press thanks Xu Bing for writing the Press's name in his Square Word Calligraphy for the covers of its books. For further information, see p. iv

To My Parents

The Cinema of Feng Xiaogang

Commercialization and Censorship
in Chinese Cinema after 1989

Rui Zhang

香港大學出版社

HONG KONG UNIVERSITY PRESS

Hong Kong University Press
14/F Hing Wai Centre
7 Tin Wan Praya Road
Aberdeen
Hong Kong

Hardback ISBN 978-962-209-885-5
Paperback ISBN 978-962-209-886-2

British Library Cataloguing-in-Publication Data
A catalogue record for this book is available from the British Library.

Secure On-line Ordering
http://www.hkupress.org

Printed and bound by Condor Production Co. Ltd., Hong Kong, China.

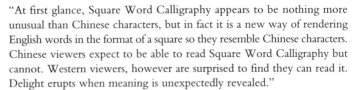

Hong Kong University Press is honoured that Xu Bing, whose art explores the complex themes of language across cultures, has written the Press's name in his Square Word Calligraphy. This signals our commitment to cross-cultural thinking and the distinctive nature of our English-language books published in China.

"At first glance, Square Word Calligraphy appears to be nothing more unusual than Chinese characters, but in fact it is a new way of rendering English words in the format of a square so they resemble Chinese characters. Chinese viewers expect to be able to read Square Word Calligraphy but cannot. Western viewers, however are surprised to find they can read it. Delight erupts when meaning is unexpectedly revealed."

— Britta Erickson, *The Art of Xu Bing*

Contents

Acknowledgments

This project would not have resulted in the present form without the generous support from many sources. First, I wish to thank Ronald Green for his tenacious dedication and help offered during the course of my graduate studies at The Ohio State University. The example he has set in his own scholarship, as well as in the various graduate seminars, has been a major influence in my approach to film studies. I also would like to acknowledge the various critical suggestions by Kirk Denton, who contributed very valuable feedbacks to my project. I appreciate the generous support by Julia Andrews, whose fascination with Contemporary Chinese art inspired me to further my career in a new field. I am grateful to the Alumni Association of The Ohio State University, Department of History of Art, and the John C. and Susan L. Huntington Archive of Buddhist and Related Art for research grants and graduate assistantship in 1999–2005. I also want to thank Colin Day, Ian Lok, and Dennis Cheung of Hong Kong University Press for bringing this book through the review, editing and production processes.

Lastly, much of the work on the book could not have been finalized without the encouragement of my parents, Zhang Jie and Yu Zhengmei, and my husband, Wang Weiguo.

1

Introduction

Since *Party A, Party B* (Jiafang yifang, 1997), *Be There or Be Square* (Bujian busan, 1998) and *Sorry Baby!* (Meiwan meiliao, 1999), a series of light-hearted romance comedy films released for the New Year holidays, to his recent film, *The Banquet* (Ye yan, 2006), a court-drama dealing with more serious themes such as desire and power struggle, Chinese film critics and audiences have been impressed by Feng Xiaogang's ability to make highly profitable films. Some of his films are so popular with moviegoers that they have even surpassed imported Hollywood blockbusters at the box office. So, it is perhaps easy to assert that Feng is the most successful commercial film director since the middle of the 1990s. Few Chinese critics, however, have shown respect for Feng's work, and most would agree with Yin Hong, who wrote in *History of New China's Cinema* (Xin Zhongguo dianying shi, 2002) that Feng's works lack depth, sincerity, and passion, and that his films manipulate audiences in order to maximize profits. Yin summarizes his criticism with the statement "buqiu zuihao, zhiqiu zuizhuan" (不求最好，只求最赚 not aiming for the best, but aiming for the most profitable).[1] Many essays and articles on the subject tend to agree with Yin, including works by Ni Zhen and Sha Hui.[2] It is clear that there is something about Feng's work that invites critical disdain. Anyone who has seen Feng's works and are also familiar with Chinese Fifth and Sixth Generation cinema will understand this response. Feng's films seem shallow and playful when compared to the astonishingly exquisite visuality, exotic autoethnography and relentless criticism of the dark side of Chinese history, society and politics in films by Fifth and Sixth Generation filmmakers. Feng's "inadequacies" are obvious to anyone who assumes the criteria of these filmmakers.

However, if we take a closer look at Feng's works and career, and contextualize the popularity of his films against the background of Chinese film history and evolvement of Chinese popular cinema in the past two decades, we would find that Feng Xiaogang's films are far from the mindless escapist productions of a dream factory. Rather, his films provide a particularly graphic demonstration of the "doubleness" of popular culture, exemplifying a "double movement of containment and resistance."[3] The significance of his films is not necessarily a result of awards and acclaims they received from international film festivals and scholars, but rather reflects the degree to which his films represented China's national cinematic trends and exerted influence on China's burgeoning yet vulnerable national film industry. Feng's films not only reflect the changing social-political context of Chinese cinema since the mid-1990s, but also demonstrate the nation-wide growth of popular cinema, a cinema that meets the needs of domestic audiences instead of serving as political propaganda or catering to the demands of international film festivals.[4] Using Feng's career, as well as his "New Year" films as examples, this book presents that these transformations are a result of changing film policies after 1989, the rapid pace of film industry reforms and Chinese filmmakers' negotiation and compromise with film authorities and profit imperatives. In Feng's case, despite working under the constraints of official film ideology and the pressure of profit-making, he has striven to retain in all his films a distinctive and personal imprint, characterized by his sense of humor and cynical commentary on problems of Chinese society. However, he has also had to make compromises. He has avoided conflict with film officials by providing a more implicit rendering of social commentary, and he has answered the demands of investors by inserting into his films as many commercial logos as possible. The resulting ideological and political ambivalence of his films has become something of a hallmark, and, arguably, one of the distinctive characteristics of contemporary Chinese popular cinema in general.

This chapter begins with an introduction to Feng's career. This is followed by a review of studies of Feng's cinema in both English and Chinese publications, summaries of the research methodology and general structure of the work.

Biographical Backstory

With little professional training in script writing or film directing, Feng has succeeded in creating an impressive legacy in the burgeoning, yet unpredictable field of popular cinema. In the process of making himself into one of the most influential film directors in contemporary China, he has utilized various modes of film production from independent production to foreign investment, and has been forced to deal creatively with challenges ranging from censorship, a lack of stable financial resources, and competition from Hollywood blockbusters. His four earliest productions, one film and three TV dramas, were either censored or failed to attract much attention from critics and audiences. These failures led to the bankruptcy of the production company, Good Dream TV and Film Production and Consulting, co-founded in 1993 by Feng and the famous Chinese writer, Wang Shuo. However, since 1997, his films have been among the most popular at the box office and Feng himself has become one of the most active and prolific filmmakers in China. In fact, he is unique among modern Chinese filmmakers for his combination of productivity and popularity: he has produced one film every year since 1996, surpassing most other Chinese filmmakers, including international film prize winners such as Zhang Yimou and Chen Kaige. At the same time, his films, including *Party A, Party B* (1997), *Be There or Be Square* (1998), *Sorry Baby!* (1999), *Sigh* (2000), *Big Shot's Funeral* (2002), *Cell Phone* (2003), *A World Without Thieves* (2004) and *The Banquet* (2006) have made substantial profits in the domestic film market and have even been more successful at the box office than Hollywood blockbusters such as *Saving Private Ryan*. How did he manage to achieve this degree of success?

Feng Xiaogang

Feng was born in Beijing in 1958. Living with his mother and older sister, Feng grew up in a military base referred to as a "grand courtyard" (or, as it is known in the Chinese vernacular, *da yuanr*), a compound containing not only offices and apartments but also other facilities such as a cafeteria, movie theater, grocery store, day care center, post office and even medical clinic. The apartments in this compound, as in many others, were given free of charge to employees of "working units" (*danwei*), i.e. government and military departments, research institutes, etc. These self-contained grand courtyards, enclosed by four high walls and guarded sometimes by armed soldiers at each gate, were relatively isolated enclaves yet, in many ways, miniatures of the larger social infrastructure of society. Because the neighbors in the grand courtyard were at the same time colleagues, the hierarchy in the workplace was also inevitably extended into life after work hours.

As the son of a low-ranking clerk and a resident in the grand courtyard, Feng became very familiar with the living conditions of the so-called "little characters," the insignificant people situated at the bottom of the power hierarchy, who later became the main protagonists in his films. His colorful childhood memories of the grand courtyard clearly influenced his later filmmaking in other ways as well: he chose, for example, to locate many of his productions, such as *Chicken Feathers on the Ground* (Yidi jimao, TV drama 1995), *Elegy of Love* (Qing shang, TV drama, 1995), and *Gone Forever with My Love* (Yongshi wo ai, film, 1994) in such grand courtyards. As a result of China's rapid economic reform beginning in the early 1980s, many of these Maoist era complexes were torn down and replaced by city highways, shopping malls, and luxurious hotels. The resulting nostalgia for a lost youth and past permeates the mise-en-scene of Feng's films. Feng's retrospective and critical view toward commercialization and modernization can also be attributed to this early experience.

During the Cultural Revolution (1966–1976), Feng, younger than the Red Guards generation, experienced neither the iconoclasm, which destroyed almost all the well-established values of Chinese culture and tradition, nor the disillusionment when the Cultural Revolution was redefined as a Ten Year Disaster (*shinian haojie* 十年浩劫) at the end of the 1970s. Feng's experiences in this period are in contrast to those of many Fifth Generation filmmakers. Chen Kaige (1952–), the leading figure of the Fifth Generation, for example, was forced to publicly denounce his father, the once-director of the Beijing Film Studio, who was labeled a traitor and spy because of his experience as an underground Communist in Shanghai during the Republican Era.[5] In 1968, Chen lost all the privileges he enjoyed as the son of a high-ranking official and was sent to a remote village in Yunnan Province where he worked in a tree plantation. Similarly, Zhang Yimou (1951–) was not allowed to take the college entry exams due to his bad "class background" and left his hometown as a teenager. Working as a schoolteacher in a small village, he used to live in such poverty that he had to sell his blood in order to buy himself a camera. Their painful personal experiences during the Cultural Revolution became the major source of inspiration for their filmmaking. Feng, who stayed in Beijing throughout this period, writes in his autobiography that he remembers the Cultural Revolution as a time of peace and quiet. It was also during this time that he developed an interest in art, starting to learn painting.[6] Therefore, the Maoist era is portrayed in Feng's cinema with a great sense of nostalgia and sentiment, rather than criticism and disillusionment.

In 1978, when Chinese universities and colleges re-opened after ten years of closure, Feng passed the entry examination of the Department of Art Direction at the Beijing Film Academy, the only professional film academy in China. Zhang Yimou and Chen Kaige were accepted into the departments of cinematography and directing, respectively, the same year.[7] If Feng had accepted the offer of admission he would probably have became a member of the prestigious Fifth Generation, most of whom were members of the class of 1978. However, because his single-parent family could not afford the cost of the requisite art supplies, he had no choice but to give up this opportunity.[8] Instead of entering the academy he joined the army where he worked as a set designer in a Military Art Ensemble based in Beijing. In 1985, after being discharged, he began to work as a staff member of the All Beijing City Construction Workers Union (Beijing chengjian kaifa zong gongsi gonghui) and then joined the Beijing TV Drama Production Center (Beijing dianshijü zhizuo zhongxin) and worked as a set designer/art director for several TV shows, including *Returning in Triumph at Midnight* (Kaixuan za ziye) and *Plainclothes Police Officer* (Bianyi jingcha). From the early 1990s, he started to write screen scripts for TV dramas and films.[9]

Feng's filmmaking career can be divided into three periods: the formative stage from the early 1990s to 1996, the New Year film period from 1997 to 2000, and the post-New Year film period after 2000.

The Formative Stage

It was during the formative stage of Feng's filmmaking that he first gained notice as a scriptwriter and made his debut as a film director. His scriptwriting during this stage was done in collaboration with Wang Shuo. Wang also joined

Feng in the establishment of a production company named Good Dream TV and Film Production and Consulting (Haomeng yingshi cehua gongsi 好梦影视策划公司). A detailed discussion of the influence of Wang Shuo's writing on Feng's filmmaking as well as the fate of their production company will be provided in Chapter 3.

In 1991, in collaboration with Zheng Xiaolong, the director of the Beijing TV Drama Production Center, Feng wrote his first screenplay, *Unexpected Passion* (Zaoyu jiqing, 1991), a tragic story of the love between a young unemployed urban man and a mysterious girl he meets in a bar. When the young man finally attempts to start a new life and a serious relationship with the girl, he discovers that she has been diagnosed with leukemia. The film won four Golden Rooster nominations, including Best Screenplay. In 1993, Feng wrote another film script, *After Separation* (Da sa ba, 1993), based on Zheng Xiaolong's personal experience. The script provides a vivid and humorous depiction of a man's life after his wife goes to live abroad. This script was also awarded a nomination for the Golden Rooster for Best Screen Script. Although Feng was a very successful scriptwriter and TV drama director during this period, because the study of scripts and TV dramas involves an entirely different methodology, these will only be used to provide background information to his career or as counterparts that help to reveal the meanings of his filmic works. A detailed discussion of his scriptwriting and TV directing is beyond the scope of this study.

Period of New Year Films

The period of New Year filmmaking began with the end of Feng's production company Good Dream, which collapsed because of several unpleasant encounters with official censorship. In order to avoid direct conflict with the censorship board, Feng decided to change his style from "social conscience" to a safer alternative, comedy, where he found other ways to deal with the issues he wanted to expose. In 1996, inspired by a suggestion from Han Sanping, the director of Beijing Film Studio, Feng decided to adapt the popular Hong Kong New Year film (*he sui pian*) genre for a Mainland audience (these were comedy films meant to be released in theaters specifically during the New Year holidays). Based on Wang Shuo's short story "You Are Not a Common Person" (Ni bushi ge su ren), Feng wrote and directed his first New Year film, *Party A, Party B* (1997). The film achieved box-office earnings as high as RMB 15,000,000 (around US$ 2 million) in Beijing, the highest earnings of any film that year. From 1997 onward, he made several other New Year films, including *Be There or Be Square* (1998), *Sorry Baby!*

(1999), and *Big Shot's Funeral* (2001). All these films are light comedies focusing on the lives of ordinary people in various odd situations and circumstances. By infusing stories of ordinary people with deliberate satire and cynicism, his films both appealed to the general public and supported mainstream official ideology. Starting in this period, Feng's films began to demonstrate the "doubleness" of popular culture, in which he expressed his concerns for social problems in implicit or explicit ways, but also endorsed the current social order by providing solutions from within the system for the problems. A detailed analysis of the themes, characters, and the social/cultural context of Feng's New Year films will be the main focus of Chapter 4.

Period of Post-New Year films

In 2000, when many filmmakers were racking their brains for a successful model for New Year films, Feng cleverly exposed the myth that only New Year comedy films could return profits and shifted his focus from comedy to more serious subjects. This act foreshadowed the arrival of the third stage of Feng's career. In this stage, while his films still had traces of witty and humorous dialogue, there was a definite turn toward dark and cynical themes. Dealing with the devastating consequences of an affair, *Sigh* (Yisheng tanxi, 2000) can be seen as Feng's cautious attempt to test the waters of censorship and the Communist Party's ideological control. Although the ending of film was changed according to the censor's requirement, the fact that the film passed at all signals a loosening of the ideological restrictions circumscribing the Chinese film industry, which enabled a shift in emphases from the victory of the "small characters" to the unhappy "big shots," and from light-hearted comedies with hidden criticism to serious examinations of the dark side of the humanity as well as direct commentaries on commercialization and modernization. Starting the early 2000s, Feng began to face more pressing demands for profit-making due to both industry reform and the impact of Hollywood films, which forced him to commercialize his film to satisfy his investors' demands. Chapter 5 features an analysis of Feng's career and changes in his style as well as the situation of Chinese cinema at the turn of the century.

Studies of Feng Xiaogang's Cinema

Despite the recent interest in Sixth Generation films and Chinese films of the late 1990s, Feng Xiaogang's films have remained underexamined by scholars in both the East and the West. Only a handful of scholars have touched on Feng's films in their works. One of the earliest is "Interview with Feng Xiaogang," by Michael Keane and Tao Dongfeng in July 1997 and published in *positions* (7.1, Spring, 1999, pp. 193-200). This interview, focusing primarily on Feng's two TV dramas, *A Dirty Life*, or *Chicken Feathers on the Ground* (Yidi jimao) and *The Dark Side of Moon* (Yueliang beimian), introduced Feng's approach to filmmaking before he became known for the new genre of New Year film. At this stage, he wanted to depict "real life" or even put "real life" under a microscope to show "how the realities of life change a person's desire and … how the desire can change a person's life."[10] This informative interview also accurately reveals the constraints under which Chinese filmmakers work. According to the interview, in the 1990s, a filmmaker had to please the "three olds (san lao 三老): *laoganbu, laoban, and laobaixing*" (老干部、老板、老百姓), i.e. "officialdom, investors and audience."[11] Among these, "officialdom" is the most difficult to deal with. Although providing valuable first-hand information on Feng's early career, this interview mentions neither the deviation of Feng's style toward popular comedic film, nor the success of his early popular films. This interview portrays Feng as a suppressed and frustrated Chinese filmmaker who is searching in vain for a middle path to please the "three olds." While containing detailed discussions of the relationships between Feng and his investors, and Feng and his audiences, the interview lacks a similarly elaborate discussion of Feng's encounters with officialdom that played a significant role in influencing his later career. Other articles either provide background information on Feng's career or introduce the making of his particular films are Xu Ying and Xu Zhongquan's article "A 'New' Phenomenon of Chinese Cinema: Happy-New-Year Comic Movies" (*Asian Cinema* 13 (1), Spring-Summer 2002: 112-27); Kong Shuyu's article "*Big Shot* from Beijing: Feng Xiaogang's He Sui Pian and Contemporary Chinese Commercial Film" (*Asian Cinema* 14 (1), Spring/ Summer 2003: 175-87); Wang Shujen's "*Big Shot's Funeral*: China, Sony, and the WTO" (*Asian Cinema* 14 (2), Fall/Winter 2003: 145-54); and Zhou Shaoming's "Making Money Can Be Funny" (*Cinemaya* 52, 2001: 13-18).

Feng Xiaogang's films have also been briefly mentioned in several books on Chinese cinema. In the postscript of Cui Shuqin's book *Women Through the Lens: Gender and Nation in a Century of Chinese Cinema*, by categorizing Feng's films as "an important component of official mainstream," Cui attributes the success of Feng's commercial cinema to his ability to engage the "audience in a transnational fantasy," especially evident in *Be There or Be Square*.[12] It is true that Feng's commercial cinema is a major component of contemporary Chinese cinema, but it is questionable whether his films can be considered part of the "official mainstream." At first, Feng's films were sponsored by semi-private production company, owned by private investors and reliant on state film institutions only for distribution and exhibition. Without a fully guaranteed recovery of investment or access to channels of exhibition, but with more pressure to return a profit, this production mode is dramatically different from that entirely under the auspices of the government. Secondly, the subjects of his films are far from the positive depictions of lives or stories of China and Chinese people that are the main feature of the official "main melody" film (zhu xianlü). Another serious study of Chinese cinema that spends several pages discussing Feng's cinema is Zhang Yingjin's *Screening China: Critical Interventions, Cinematic Reconfigurations, and the Transnational Imaginary in Contemporary Chinese Cinema*. In the conclusion, Zhang indicates that the unexpected popularity of New Year films, together with "new alliances among filmmakers, government, and the market" and the "proposal for 'the New Mainstream Film' by a group of young Shanghai filmmakers," are the three new developments that "merit special attention" in the development of Chinese cinema of the late 1990s.[13] Zhang summarizes several characteristics of Feng's New Year films. By drawing on *Dreams Come True* (or *Party A, Party B*) and *Be There or Be Square*, as examples, Zhang indicates that "one distinguishing feature of Feng's films…is their 'all-too-apparent reliance on transnational cultural imaginaries.'"[14] This transnationalism, according to Zhang, also became a tendency reflected in other popular films and represented by different ways, such as increasing use of foreign language, and casting non-Mainland/Western actors and actresses. After discussing the latter two new tendencies in a more concise way, Zhang returns to Feng's New Year films with an original idea by demonstrating that, as opposed to Rey Chow's theory of "self-exoticization and autoethnography," the two alleged hallmarks of Chinese cinema of the mid-1980s, Feng's works exhibit a "writing the 'others' within the self," which is realized through the presentation of stereotyped images of the West. He sees this as a transnational imaginary designated to appeal to the local, rather than the international, audience.[15] Due to the limited space, Zhang's analysis, like other works dealing with Feng's cinema, although very inspiring, still proves to be too schematic and in need of detailed elaboration. The study of Feng's works from the perspective of a transnational cinema can also be found in a dissertation by Jason Mcgrath, "Culture and the Market in Contemporary China: Cinema, Literature, and Criticism of the 1990s." This work also provides a valuable examination of the relationship between Feng Xiaogang and Wang Shuo in Feng's early career and the cooperation between Feng's

New Year cinema and the Hollywood studios. In addition, this work also accurately identifies "the two countervailing movements"—a deterritorializing movement from heteronomy to autonomy in the relationship between cultural productions, such as literature and cinema, and state institutions and ideology, and a simultaneous reterritorialization as literature and cinema are commodified and subjected to the market mechanism and the profit imperative.[16] These double movements later almost became one of the major themes of the culture in the so-called "post new era" of the early 2000s.

As a director of Chinese popular cinema, Feng also occasionally attracts attention from Western media and press. Interviews, feature articles, and critical reviews regarding Feng and his works can be found in journals or newspapers such as *Variety, Time Asia, New York Times, Los Angeles Times, Washington Post*, and *Business Weekly*.[17] In most of these articles, especially those published in the early and mid-1990s, Feng is depicted as a victim of the ideological control of a totalitarian regime. In his first appearance in the *New York Times* in an article published on December 1, 1996, Feng is used as a counterpart of Xie Jin—while Xie's film *Opium War* (Yapian zhanzheng, 1997) received full sponsorship from the Chinese government on the occasion of the return of Hong Kong to China, Feng's film *Living a Miserable Life* (Guozhe langbei bukan de shenghuo, aborted, 1996) was cut off in the middle of production.[18] In recent years, while some Western media and press have begun to expand their attention to more diverse films, many others continue to focus on films that are banned, censored, or required to undertake excessive cuts. On October 26, 2000, an interview with Feng Xiaogang regarding *Sigh* (Yisheng tanxi, 2000), a film dealing with extramarital affairs, was published on the official website of *Time Asia*. Adapted from the previously banned project *Living a Miserable Life*, but without encountering the same problems during production and exhibition, *Sigh* signals a "loosening up" in the film industry of the late 1990s. It will be clearer in the following chapter of this study that it is also a film that proves to be a turning point in Feng's career—after making this film, Feng's comedy became more and more cynical and fewer positive depictions supporting Communist rhetoric can be found. Despite these areas of significance, the two major questions that are asked in the interview are about sex and censorship—"Sex scenes are still banned in Mainland Chinese movies. If they weren't, is it a subject that you and others would show more of?" and "The subject matter of your most recent film *Sigh* is very controversial. How much was censored?" When dealing with films made under the socialist system, the Western media are especially attracted to political issues and seem to take on the responsibility of advancing freedom and democracy in post-Mao China.

Among Chinese-language publications related to Feng Xiaogang's works, Feng's own autobiography *I Dedicated My Youth To You* (Wo ba qingchun xian gei ni, 2003), despite being aimed at popular rather than academic readers, is a valuable source for studying his career and the stylistic evolution of his films. Although there are no other books on Feng or his works in Chinese, interviews and reviews of his films can be found in both scholarly journals such as *Dianying yishu* (Film art), popular magazines and newspapers such as *Xin dianying* (New cinema), *Beijing qingnianbao* (Beijing youth newspaper), etc.[19] In some of these, Feng's works are taken as representative of a certain trend in commercial cinema. Specifically, for these articles, Feng's films are able to generate good box-office income while also accurately reflecting and commenting on social problems through the utilization of an innovative genre consisting of a comical storyline, humorous dialogue, and occasional satirical comments on current social problems.[20] Others have scorned Feng's films for their pandering to mass audience tastes and obvious concern for profit. As mentioned in the beginning of this chapter, in the recently published *History of New China's Cinema* (Xin Zhongguo dianying shi, 2002), Yin Hong compares Feng's films with Charlie Chaplin's comedy, but indicates that Feng's works lack the depth, sincerity, and passion of Chaplin's films. Furthermore, according to Yin, Feng's films manipulate audiences in order to maximize profits.[21] More recent writings on Feng's films share a similar opinion. In an essay "Dianying xushi leixing he chuanbo kongjian de kuozhan" (Expansion of the genre of film narrative and space of communication), Ni Zhen compares Feng's films with films by Sixth Generation directors, such as Zhang Yang's *Sunflowers* (Xiangrikui, 2005) and Ma Yinli's *We* (Women lia, 2005), and indicates that although Feng's films are more successful in the box office, they are inferior to the films by the young directors in terms of the "depth of reality they reflect and value of the culture they represent."[22] Sha Hui, in "'Tianxia wuzei' he 'zeihan zhuozei': Feng Xiaogang hesui dianying de beilun" (*A World Without Thieves* and "Thieves Crying 'Stop Thief'": A Paradox in Feng Xiaogang's New Year Movies), questions the integrity of the character of Sha Gen in *A World Without Thieves* by contrasting him with the character of Yuan Fengming in *Blind Shaft* (Mang jing, dir. Yang Li, 2004) played by the same actor.[23] Drawing comparisons between Feng's works and those of the Sixth Generation directors, and quoting filmmakers such as Tarkovski and writers such as Susan Sontag, these scholars assume the criteria of independent and art cinema for their analysis of a popular cinema and fail to recognize Feng's depiction of the subtle uneasiness that lies beneath China's superficial stability and his questioning of modernization and Westernization.

Moving beyond these studies, my research will demonstrate that Feng's cinema is neither simply a regressive utopian fantasy reflecting consumer desire in a materialized world, nor a counter-discourse overtly challenging mainstream official rhetoric. Rather, it is a product of negotiation between the hegemonies of Party art policy in the 1990s and consumerism in the early 2000s, as well as the director's own obsession with "social conscience" throughout his career. Associating Feng's films with their socio-political context, and thus emphasizing the subtle specificities of Chinese cinema, this work will not only address the significance of Feng's own work, but will also begin to undertake a study of the history of Chinese film since the early 1990s.

Methodology

The image of Feng that will emerge in this study is that of a filmmaker working under political and economic pressures in a post-socialist state while still striving to create works with a personal socio-political agenda. Taking this reality into consideration, this study approaches Feng as a special kind of film *auteur* whose works must be interpreted with attention to the specific social and political context of contemporary China and whose success lies in his ability to capture the very essence of a popular culture in which massive industrialization, urbanization, and Westernization have accelerated social change.

Is the mid-20th century theory of authorship, a notion that has been criticized by scholars who have declared the "death of author", too out-of-date for a study of a director active at the turn of the 21st century? The answer to this question depends on which theory of authorship is adopted. Feng Xiaogang, a director whose works are inevitably impacted by commercialization and ideological control, is by no means an *auteur* in traditional sense. In traditional film studies, *auteur* has often regarded as the center and source of inspiration in the production of a significantly personal cinema; thus, his/her work has always carried very unique personal imprints. As Andrew Sarris points out, "meaningful coherence is more likely when the director dominates the proceedings with skill and purpose…"[24] or as John Caughie puts it, "[an *auteur*] film is more than likely to be the expression of [the director's] individual personality; and…this personality can be traced in a thematic and/or stylistic consistency over all (or almost all) that director's films."[25] The centrality of the *auteur* for these scholars hints at an understanding of film as an elitist form of art similar to painting, theater, and music. In the case of Feng Xiaogang, his films have some hallmarks of a traditional film *auteur*, such as the recurring themes of the victory of little characters, unhappy "big shots," and his humorous and cynical commentaries on current social issues. However, the centrality of an *auteur* during film production is a luxury that Feng, who has had to deal with investors' demands for profit and the film censorship board's requirements for "healthy" content, could hardly afford. In the production of his films, he is far from the only source or center of production, nor has he had any intention of treating his films as a form of "high art," a way of expressing elitist sentiments or feelings. He has commented frequently during interviews and at premieres that his films were made for the "masses", for an ordinary Chinese domestic audience, not for foreign audiences or international film festival juries.

The concept of "authorship" has also been utilized by film scholars such as Andrew Sarris and Janet Staiger as a way of re-thinking the value of commercial films, including Hollywood cinema. For these scholars, authorship indicates an attitude toward filmmaking especially characteristic of those directors who work under certain constraints and pressures while still struggling to express themselves. In elevating certain works of "mindless" Hollywood cinema over those of art cinema, Andrew Sarris suggests that "*auteur* theory values the personality of a director precisely because of the barriers to its expression."[26] This approach reminds us the value of many filmmakers working in a highly commercialized motion picture industry, such as Hitchcock, Hawks, Spielberg and Feng, whom would be easily looked down in an orthodox film studies. These filmmakers, who represent subversive countercurrents within a predominant mainstream, either a commercialized film industry or a politically conservative cinema, are *auteurs* because they could achieve personal expression despite either the pressure from a well-established tradition or industry constraints. This notion is further developed in recent studies where authorship is used to describe alternative and non-mainstream filmmakers. In *Authorship and Films,* David A. Gerstner and Janet Staiger pay special attention to films made by women, minorities, and artisans. In all of Feng's films, even the most commercial, he finds unique ways of evoking the value of the grassroots, while pointing out the decadence brought about by fame and wealth and voicing his concern over the various side effects of the market, commercialization, and globalization. The transformation in Feng's early career from a director of films of social conscience to a director of comedy—directly related to a series of unpleasant encounters with censorship—as well as the return of formerly banned subject matter in his recent films, demonstrate Feng's struggles with the desire for self-expression, the pressures of ideological surveillance, and the imperatives of profit-making. Given these struggles, Feng's experience as a filmmaker in post-socialist China is a good example of a new kind of authorship, which, as David Gerstner and

Janet Staiger indicate, is especially significant to "those in non-dominant positions in which asserting even a partial agency may seem to be important for day-to-day survival or where locating moments of alternative practice takes away the naturalized privileges of normativity."[27] As an outsider to state-supported filmmaking institutions, Feng's often implicit expressions of his agenda—to make the voices of the underprivileged "little characters" heard and to question the rapid paces of globalization and economic reform—reflect the hardships of survival under the constraints of tightened ideological control. His recent endeavor to develop his criticism into explicit commentary, despite the pressures of profit-making, can be considered a form of rebellion challenging the values of the newly reformed film industry.

Therefore, the methodology of *auteur* study can be usefully applied to a textual analysis of Feng's films—that is, the recurring themes, treatment of characters, arrangement of mise-en-scene, etc.—to see how the text signifies his criticism and compromises. Furthermore, if we adopt a theory of popular culture when dealing with the contextual aspects of his film production, i.e. political, social, and economic impacts, the more profound significance of his works will be revealed. Unlike works of the modernist *auteurs,* such as Bresson and Cocteau, who showed an elitist reaction against the hegemonic tradition, and more like Hitchcock and Hawks, *auteurs* who always showed a strong personal control of content or style in the face of, but *within*, that tradition, Feng's films present the dual movements of hegemony and resistance, which, interestingly, echoed characteristics of modern popular culture described in many works of mass-culture theory beginning in the 1970s. In his classic essay "Reification and Utopia in Mass Culture," Fredric Jameson, questioned Western radicals', such as Adorno's, view of mass culture as the antithesis of high culture. For Jameson, this view overlooks certain anti-social, critical, and negative operations of mass culture. He suggests, instead, the adoption of a "dialectical approach" to, for example, the relationship between high culture/mass culture in which "we read high and mass culture as objectively related and dialectically interdependent phenomena, as twin and inseparable forms of the fission of aesthetic production."[28] In this sense, high-cultural modernist works might, in their own way, be as complicit in the working of the dominant culture as popular works are in their way; and popular works might be, in their way, as resistant to hegemony as modernist works intend to be in their way. Also according to Jameson, mass culture could be both "utopian" and "ideological," as "[the works of mass culture] cannot be ideological without at one and the same time being implicitly or explicitly utopian as well: they cannot manipulate unless they offer some genuine shred of content as a fantasy bribe to the public about to be so manipulated."[29] In this sense, Feng's crowd-pleasing aspects may work not just to manipulate, but to keep certain progressive and critical issues before the public.

Although Jameson does call scholars' attentions to the complex nature of popular culture, he seems too pessimistic about how much "genuine content" a work of mass culture could provide to its "easily" manipulated audiences. A more balanced or proportional relationship between these two possibilities is evident in Stuart Hall's studies of popular culture. In his seminal essay " Notes on Deconstructing the 'Popular'," he suggests that the study of popular culture should begin with "the double movement of containment and resistance."[30] Hall indicates that the ruling class's intention to maintain a new order and re-educate the so-called popular class, i.e. the uneducated, the poor and laboring classes, is always at stake, because the "popular class" would always make their culture known to the ruling classes in various unpredictable ways. Popular culture, according to Hall, is not only a site where capitalist power is affirmed but also a site of opposition. Therefore, a kind of "back and forth" of the text can always be found, that one minute capitulates to the dreams of the ruling class and the next minute resists these dreams in some way.[31] Drawing on this concept of the "doubleness" of popular culture, Jane Gaines argues that the "dream factory" of Hollywood, which has been traditionally believed to be "mindless," actually delivers popular culture's "best hope along with the worst tendencies."[32] In a similar way, the predominant sense of ambivalence, a combination of both resistance and cooperation in the face of the predominant double pressures of ideological control and commercialization in Feng's films, provides a particularly graphic demonstration of this support/critique double action.

Feng Xiaogang's popular cinema can be considered as a site where both the hegemonic power of ideological control and non-mainstream culture are struggling for a voice, whether the hegemony is perceived as Communist or as capitalist. Within the current transnational environment of China, as an *auteur* in this context, Feng can only maintain his films' vitality and ensure their continued existence through complex negotiations—involving both resistance and cooperation—with the hegemonic Party's art policy and the pressures of commercialization in the Chinese film industry. Throughout his career, the expression of a political and social agenda in his films has been accompanied by compromises arising out of political or economic pressure, resulting in a recurring doubleness in his films' politics and ideology. When the control over film content tightened in the 1990s, Feng's films made implicit reference to many social problems, but also showed a supportive attitude toward mainstream Party policy. Beginning in the early 2000s, when ideological surveillance was largely supplanted by the demands of industrialization and commercialization, Feng has been able to express his concerns for social problems more explicitly, but has had to offer compromises to the demands of profitability by incorporating commercial elements such as all-star casts, commercial logos, and even farcical comic relief into his films. The give-and-take evident in his dealings with both Communist film policy and the profit imperatives of the commercial film industry has produced a sort of doubleness that points to an underlying process of negotiation. In this process Feng attempts to hold together opposite forces of popular culture and "conceives cultural exchange as the intersection of processes of production and reception, in which overlapping but non-matching determinations operate."[33]

To articulate the specific resistance and cooperation that a film *auteur* like Feng has to make in the context of Chinese cinema at the turn of the 21st century, besides studies of the "text" of his films, I will concentrate on Feng's filmmaking career to explain how he has negotiated with different forces and how the "doubleness" took shape and evolved in his films. Finally, the context of Chinese film history since the early 1990s, including industry reform, the changes in the domestic political climate, and the impact of imported films, will also be explored as the social background in which the driving forces behind Feng's own cinema have been formed and generated.

Structure

Recurring themes such as the portrayal of little characters, satirical mockery of the privileged stratums, and implicit/explicit social commentary are discussed in each chapter. Different cultural and political forces, including ideological control, film industry reform, and the importation of Hollywood films, all underlying factors influencing Feng's films, are important focuses of this work. The interactions between the filmmaker and the film authorities represented by the former's resistance, negotiation, and compromise with the authorities and the latter's attempt to control this medium through both governmental legislation and arbitrary film censorship are another major focus of this work. Feng's experiences with the censorship board are representative of similar experiences encountered by other Chinese filmmakers, and the strategies he employed to survive under this system help to highlight and explicate some of the changes that are under way in Chinese cinema. Another aspect that cannot be neglected in a general portrayal of Chinese cinema at the turn of the 21st century or, more specifically, Feng's filmmaking career, is the impact of commercialization of the Chinese film industry and

Hollywood cinema. Feng' s relationship with commercialization and globalization will be addressed in Chapter 5. Throughout the work, the evolution and survival of China's popular cinema, a cinema that sets as its primary goal communication with and entertainment of the mass audience, are also given special attention. As the counterpart of entertainment films, the pedagogical and propagandistic Party-promoted main melody films will also be covered.

Chapter 2 introduces the situation of Chinese cinema on the eve of the Tian'anmen Incident in 1989, a period characterized by the rise of "entertainment films," early attempts at industry reform, and the first film rating system designed to regulate film content through legislation. In discussing this period, attention will also be paid to the historical background and implementation and perpetuation of Communist art policy.

Chapter 3 begins with a review of Chinese cinema after the Tian'anmen Incident in 1989 through 1996, shortly before Feng began to make New Year films. This period witnessed the unexpected rise of "main melody" (zhu xuanlü) films as the Communist Party, learning lessons from the political turmoil of 1989, tightened its ideological control. Although the previously popular category of entertainment films fell into disfavor among Party and film leaders, these films revived in the middle of the 1990s when the Party began a new round of economic reforms as a way of distracting Chinese people's attention from the anguished memory of Tian'anmen Incident. As the reform was extended into the film industry, the industry faced both profit imperatives from the film studios and a reduction in subsidies from the government. As a result, private or semi-private production companies were legitimized as a way of attracting investors and talent from outside the stated-owned film sectors. It was within this context that Feng Xiaogang, a filmmaker without formal training in either script writing or directing, entered the film industry first as a scriptwriter, then as a director. Chapter 3 also deals with the formative stage of Feng's career from 1991, when he completed his first screenplay for the film *Unexpected Passion* (Zaoyu jiqing; dir. Xia Gang, 1991) to 1996, when he directed as many as three TV dramas and one film and began to be noticed by the film world. This stage is characterized by Feng's collaboration with Wang Shuo in works produced by their enterprise, the Good Dream Film and TV Production Company. Also at this stage, the cynicism of Wang's writing began to be echoed in Feng's own productions. Through a detailed analysis of his directorial debut in *Gone Forever with My Love*, I analyze the ambivalence in themes such as nostalgia for a lost past and love, hidden social commentary, and attention to the fate of "small characters," all of which have obsessed Feng throughout his career, and began to take form at this early stage.

Chapter 4 introduces the emergence of Feng's New Year films against the background of the film authority's indecision regarding the function of cinema in the middle of 1990s, and a deepening industry reform oriented towards market demand. Under this circumstance, Feng's New Year films emerged both as a compromise with the Party film policy and a successful exploration of a genre that appealed to the mass audience. The chapter focuses on Feng's first three New Year films produced between 1997 and 2000, because they share similarities of subject, theme, and narrative. In addition to a brief synopsis of each film, the chapter presents detailed analyses of recurring themes such as the victory of the "little character," mockery of the privileged stratum, the image of the West and America, and hidden social commentary. This analysis reveals the distinctive "doubleness" in the ideology of Feng's films and his negotiations with the predominant powers of film ideology.

Chapter 5 explores transformations that took place in Feng's filmmaking as he gradually abandoned the mode of comedy and returned to his early style of "social conscience" in which the victory of a "small character" is replaced by the failed attempts of legally or morally guilty "big shots" to redeem themselves. As a more democratic atmosphere replaced a tightened ideological control in the early 2000s, the hidden social commentaries in Feng's first three New Year films become more explicit in his recent works, targeting the depravity of human beings, the irrational expansion of commercialization and consumerism, and ethical issues brought about by the burgeoning high-technology. At the same time, even though Feng seems to have taken advantage of a loosening of control over film ideology, he still had to deal with the increasingly demanding profit imperatives brought by the fast pace of industry reforms. This put him in a new situation in which, although succeeding in resurrecting his "social conscience" films, he had to compromise and negotiate with the newly dominant forces of commercialization. Commercialization became the locus at which his resistance and cooperation were at work. These films warned his audiences of the devastating consequences of rapid market development and commercialization—immorality, infidelity, and technological intrusion. But at the same time, his films became victims of these very same forces, as he has to please the audience's expectation for popular cinema and investors' desires for maximum profit.

The concluding chapter focuses on the cultural and historical significance of Feng's cinema. The dual trends of resistance and cooperation co-existing in his cinema also became a distinctive feature of Chinese cinema in the new era. Inspired by the success of Feng's New Year films, in 2000 as many as eight New Year films of similar style were made by different film directors. The phenomenon of New Year films also extended into other forms of arts. Chinese theater and TV productions began to promote "New Year Celebration Drama" and "New Year Celebration TV drama." Furthermore, the rise and fall of Feng's career as a filmmaker outside the government film production system reflected the same trajectory that private film production has experienced in the history of Chinese cinema since the late 1980s, which is heavily influenced by China's film authorities' indecision about how to view the function of cinema, the demand for profit-making from production companies, and the challenges from a commercialized film industry.

2

Chinese Cinema on the Eve of the Tian'anmen Incident

Because the evolution of Feng's career has been heavily influenced and even determined by the changing face of Chinese cinema since the late 1980s, it is important to provide an introduction to the general situation of Chinese cinema in the late 1980s. Although the 1980s ended violently with the Tian'anmen Incident, this did not mean that films made before the Tian'anmen Incident did not cast any influence on Chinese contemporary cinema. In fact, many of the trends in the 1980s foreshadowed the direction the industry would take in the 1990s. For example, the flourishing of entertainment films in the middle of the 1990s echoed a similar tendency at the end of the 1980s. Furthermore, reforms that took place in the three sectors of the film industry—production, distribution, and exhibition—in the 1980s, became a determining factor in the dramatic re-construction of Chinese cinema of the 1990s. Finally, the attempts of film administrative authorities to regulate the film industry by government legislation can find their roots in the initiation of China's first film rating of "Not Appropriate for Children" in 1988.

Rise of Entertainment Films

The term "popular cinema" has seldom appeared in Mainland China, however, after the Cultural Revolution, the term "entertainment film" (*yule pian*) came to be frequently used in referring to the kinds of films that would be labeled as popular cinema in Western film studies. Somewhat like in the West, in China, the connotation of this term is often somewhat derogatory. With an emphasis on their function as entertainment, these films are considered neither political socialist realist films, nor elitist art films; they are situated at the bottom of the hierarchy of film genres. Entertainment films, including crime/detective, martial arts/action, comedy and musical films, are believed to provide audiences with nothing more than sheer mindless entertainment, and their rise is often considered a potential threat to political or art cinema. The question of how to treat entertainment films in state film policy and ideology has been a dilemma that the PRC film authorities have had to tackle. Since the Communist Party came to power in 1949, Chinese cinema has most commonly functioned as a propaganda tool. At the same time, because the Party did not completely deny cinema's more universal function of entertainment, filmmakers dedicated to producing non-political and entertainment films always existed. Their significance, however, had been denied until the 1980s, when a series of entertainment films helped to shore up theatre attendance, saving the shrinking film market in the 1980s.

In 1979, the number of moviegoers reached as high as 29.3 billion, which means an average of 30 films were seen per person in one year.[1] In 1980, the number of moviegoers totaled 23.4 billion, for an average of 29 films per person.[2] However, the prosperity of Chinese cinema in the post-Cultural Revolution era was short-lived. An article published in *China's Film Newspaper* (Zhongguo dianyingbao) at the end of 1988 and reprinted in *China's Film Year Book of 1989*, "1988: Memoir of Film Market," describes the situation of the Chinese film market at the end of 1980s as a crisis: "The number of attendees had declined by one billion person-times annually since 1979 … The cost of making a film has increased from around forty to fifty thousand RMB three years ago to eighty thousand per film this year (1988), while the earnings from selling the rights of distribution have declined to half of those in 1983. Out of 142 films made in 1987, only 34 have been able to make ends meet or earn a profit."[3] Entertainment films seemed to be an antidote to the shrinking film market of the 1980s. These films began to show their potential for resurrecting Chinese cinema in the second half of the 1980s, and by the end of the 1980s they occupied a predominant position in Chinese cinema. The first popular entertainment films after the Cultural Revolution were martial arts, suspense, and crime films. As early as 1981, one such film, *Mysterious Buddha* (Shenmi de dafo; dir. Zhang Huaxin 张华欣, 1980), took second place in the box office, while in 1982 a martial arts film, *Shaolin Temple* (Shaolin si; dir. Zhang Xinyan 张鑫炎, 1982), attracted as many as 300 million persons into the theaters, defeating Xie Jin's *Herdsman* (Mu maren, 1982) at the box office.[4] The mid-1980s witnessed a rapid growth of entertainment films. The article mentioned in the previous paragraph states that "after *Herdsman* achieved second place in film attendance in 1982, since 1983, the top four positions of high attendance films have been occupied by martial art films."[5] Besides *Mysterious Buddha* and *Shaolin Temple*, representative entertainment films of the early 1980s included *Murder Case No. 405* (Siling wu mousha an; dir. Shen Yaoting 沈耀庭, 1981), *Wu Dang* (Wu dang; dir. Sun Sha 孙沙, 1983), etc. This trend reached its culmination in 1988 when China's major studios were vying to produce as many entertainment films as possible. Beijing Film Studio made *Huang Tianba* (Jinbiao Huang Tianba; dir. Li Wenhua 李文化, 1987), *The Mahjong Incident* (Feicui majiang; dir. Yu Xiaoyang 于晓洋, 1987), *The Case of Silver Snake* (Yinshe mousha'an; dir. Li Shaohong 李少红, 1988); Xi'an Film Studio made *Desperation* (Zuihou de fengkuang; dir. Zhou Xiaowen 周晓文, 1987), *Great Swordsman of the Yellow River* (Huanghe da xia; dir. Zhang Xinyan and Zhang Zien, 张鑫炎, 张子恩, 1987), *The Grave Robbers* (Dongling da dao; dir. Li Yundong, 李云东, five parts, 1984-1998); Shanghai Film Studio made *The Tribulations of A Young Master* (Shaoye de monan; dir. Wu Yigong and Zhang Jianya 吴怡弓, 张建亚, 1987); E'mei Film Studio made *Soccer Heroes* (Jingdu qiu xia; dir. Xie Hong, 谢洪 1987). Among 158 films produced in 1988, 80 were martial arts, suspense, crime, or musical films.[6]

The rise of entertainment films was accompanied by the emergence of an urban cinema, centered on the works of Wang Shuo. These urban films formed a new trend in entertainment films of the late 1980s. The year of 1988, labeled as the "Year of Wang Shuo", witnessed the adaptation of four of his works into films—*Samsara* (Lun hui; dir. Huang Jianxin 黄建新, 1988, adapted from *Emerging from the Sea* [Fuchu haimian]), *Troubleshooter* (Wan zhu; dir. Mi Jiashan 米家山, 1988, adapted from the short story of the same title), *Deep Gasping* (Da chuanqi; dir. Ye Daying 叶大鹰, 1988, adapted from *Rubber Man*, [Xiangpi ren]), and *Half Sea, Half Flame* (Yiban shi haishui, yiban shi huoyan; dir. Xia Gang 夏刚, 1988, adapted from the short story of the same title). These films successfully convey the sense of cynicism and disillusionment common among urban youth in the late 1980s. The emergence of these sentiments caused great controversies among film critics and film officials with some viewing these films as a morbid reflection of society, and others arguing that this was a tendency that would enrich the genres of Chinese cinema.[7] Although this so-called "Wang Shuo Fever" was later denounced by film authorities after 1989, its influence on Chinese cinema of the 1990s was far-reaching. As Esther Yau comments that the "profound ideological ambivalence" in these films, which "playfully 'subvert' the hegemony of Maoist ideology by combining absurdity, profanity, even obscenity. On the other hand, the Wang Shuo Fever embraces a new 'consumption myth' engineered by the postsocialist regime without hinting at any other alternatives."[8] In Chinese urban cinema of the 1990s, this ideological ambivalence was not only perpetuated in films such as Huang Jianxin's *Back to Back, Face to Face* (Liangkao liang, bei dui bei, 1994), *Signal Right, Turn Left* (Hongdeng ting, ludeng xing, 1996), and *Surveillance* (Maifu, 1996), but also became the foundation of the most popular genre of New Year comedy films, which both paradoxically questioned the hegemony of official ideology and supported, somewhat reluctantly, the status quo.

This unexpected popularity of entertainment films was, at first, a byproduct of economic reforms extending into the film industry. These reforms, beginning in the second half of the 1980s, first targeted the monopolies in film distribution and then ticket pricing. Before the reform, the only legitimate film distributor in China was the state-owned China's Film Corporation (CFC). It purchased films outright from studios at a flat rate usually based on the length rather than quality of the film.[9] Although the film studio would not be held responsible for the financial failure of a film, it could not gain profits from a successful one either. Therefore, in the first three decades of the PRC, following the guidance of the film administration and relying completely on government financial support, the film production sector was indifferent to whether a film generated profit or attracted an audience. However, this situation ended in the 1980s as the government began to initiate economic reforms that challenged the insufficiencies of the planned economy and promoted a "planned market economic system" (*you jihua de shangpin jingji* 有计划的商品经济).

A Party document, "Decisions on Reform of the Economic System," passed by the Central Committee of the Chinese Communist Party at the 12th Party Congress on October 12, 1984, summarizes the essence of this first wave of reform. It indicates several major tasks to further develop the economy, including: (1) the stimulation of the vitality of industry; (2) the establishment of an appropriate price system; and (3) the separation of government functions from enterprise management.[10] By calling for greater autonomy for enterprises from the previously mandatory government planning, this document encouraged enterprises to increase their profits by addressing market demand. This was expected to result in both increased productivity and efficiency.[11] It was against this background of economic reform, along with more specific problems such as declining attendance and rocketing film production costs, that reform within the film industry became inevitable.[12] In the middle of the 1980s, some studios began to demand more autonomy from the CFC in terms of film distribution and the right to share profit.[13] In response, the Ministry of Radio, Film and Television (MRFT) issued "Document No. 975," which allowed local film distributors to purchase films and the film studios to share box-office profits with the distributors.[14] Partially emancipated from the distribution monopoly of the CFC and stimulated by the profit-sharing potential, the film studios began to show enthusiasm for films that they felt would be most profitable. As a result, Chinese cinema in 1988 showed a stronger emphasis on entertainment films.[15]

In addition to the impact of industry reform, the rise of non-political entertainment films was also a result of a cultural and political liberalization that was supported by film authorities. The predominance of entertainment films caused film critics and scholars to question whether this was the correct direction for Chinese cinema or a betrayal of the longstanding Communist art ideology. However, the supportive attitude of many film authorities helped to legitimize these popular films. Beginning with the first issue of 1987, the journal *Dangdai dianying* (Contemporary cinema), the official publication of the China Film Research Center, invited scholars, critics, and film directors to write articles and essays about this new phenomenon of entertainment films. *Dazhong dianying* (Popular cinema) also devoted a whole issue to a discussion of comedy, which included an open letter asking its readers why the Chinese audience preferred foreign films to Chinese films. The conservative attitude toward entertainment films is represented by an article written by the director of the film bureau, Teng Jinxian, who questioned the "low artistic and ideological quality" of these films and condemned them for their absence of any political messages.[16] This view of cinema as primarily a pedagogical tool, interestingly, was challenged from above. In December 1988, the China Film Research Center organized a conference titled "Chinese Contemporary Entertainment Cinema," at which the newly appointed Vice President of MRFT, Chen Haosu, delivered a talk "On the Dominance of Entertainment Film." In this talk, Chen argues that "cinema functions on three levels. At the most fundamental level is the function of entertainment. Based on this, it can be further developed into the artistic and pedagogical."[17] Contrary to the fate of the first two waves of entertainment films in the early 1950s and 1960s, which either provoked administrative intervention or were suppressed by film authorities through political campaigns, the new round of entertainment films was motivated and stimulated by leaders among the film authorities.

These debates on the value of entertainment films reflect a relative relaxation in film ideology and an intention to reform not only the economic foundations of the film industry, but also the superstructure of film policies and administration. Although these tendencies stagnated in 1989 due to the Tian'anmen Incident, they resumed in the middle of the 1990s and signaled a more thorough transformation in the Chinese film industry.

Chinese Film Policy and Censorship

In communist societies, cinema is considered a powerful medium that has a unique capacity for disseminating ideology in an easily comprehensible and politically effective manner to a large audience. In China, as well as in other communist countries, the Party has always been the major force in controlling the film industry. This control was strengthened by state ownership of the industry's infrastructure—studios, movie theaters, and distribution companies. Because most leaders of these film studios are Party members, when they are scrutinizing a film, they are performing double duty as both filmmakers and Party cadres. For this reason, the boundary between government censorship and industry self-censorship became very blurry. Although in the 1950s and 1960s, Chinese film studios all had editorial departments responsible for censoring film scripts as well as final versions of films, the Party leadership always had the priority to override any decisions made by the studio.[18]

Unlike in Hollywood, where it was the dialectical struggle between the state censorship board and industry self-regulation that determined the path of its film industry, Chinese cinema evolved largely on the basis of the development of government film censorship. In the US, most of the controversial themes suppressed by the state or other forces outside the industry dealt with morality, ethics, race, or religion. In 1917, the New York City Film Commission refused to permit theaters to show *Birth Control* (1914), a documentary film about Margaret Sanger, a nurse who promoted birth control.[19] The notorious case of *Miracle* (1949), an Italian film about a simple-minded peasant girl who is seduced by a bearded stranger she imagines to be St. Joseph and subsequently gives birth to a son whom she believes is the Christ child, caused protests from religious groups and threats from the city commissioner to suspend the theatre's business license because the film was considered blasphemous.[20]

Similarly, Chinese film censorship also has paid great attention to issues of morality. The Tenth Clause of the *Dianying shencha tiaoli* (Regulations of Film Censorship) issued in 1997 specifies that plots containing obscene and vulgar content, such as sex, extramarital affairs, violence, and superstition, or other content that is "abhorrent to morality and virtue", "would need to be deleted and modified."[21] Besides these common concerns, Chinese censors have also paid particular attention to the political and ideological rectitude of films, the criteria for which are derived from Communist art policy and ideology.

Perpetuation of Communist Art Policy

Communist China's art policy is based on talks given by Mao Zedong at the Forum of Art and Literature in 1942 in Yan'an. In these talks, Mao outlines the duties of intellectuals, stating that artists should consider themselves part of the revolutionary force and that the audience for literature and art should be workers, peasants, and soldiers. Mao stated that, "the fundamental task of all revolutionary artists and writers is to expose all dark forces which endanger the people and to extol all the revolutionary struggles of the people" and that "writers and artists who cling to their individualist petty-bourgeois standpoint cannot truly serve the mass of revolutionary workers, peasants, and soldiers."[22] It is very clear that in the new society imagined by Mao there would be no unlimited freedom of artistic expression, especially from the "petty-bourgeois standpoint." Instead, the Chinese artists' major task would be to glorify and idealize the new world and the new people. If they wanted to criticize, the target of their criticism had to be the old society and counter-revolutionaries.

After the establishment of the People's Republic, the essence of Mao's Yan'an talks and theories on art was summarized with the phrase "Two Servings" (*erwei* 二为)—meaning that literature and art should serve the people and socialism (*wei renmin fuwu, wei shehui zhuyi fuwu*, 为人民服务、为社会主义服务). This remains the foundation of art policy in China, regulating almost every aspect of art, literature, fine art, cinema, etc. Even in the new millennium, contemporary art leaders still extol the Yan'an talks as the basis of Communist art policy. In 2002, on the occasion of the sixtieth anniversary of the talks, Chinese art authorities from the Ministry of Culture, Ministry of Propaganda, the State Administration of Radio, Film and Television (SARFT), the China Federation of Literary and Art Circles, and the Association of Chinese Writers, joined together to celebrate this "great" event. China's Chairman Jiang Zemin made a pilgrimage to the "base of revolutionary tradition" at Yan'an, where Mao's talks were delivered, not only to show his respect to this "holy land," but also to deliver a talk reinforcing the importance of the "Yan'an Spirit" (*Yan'an jingshen* 延安精神) in the new era.[23] During the several months of this celebration, music concerts, Peking opera, ballets, dramas, and films featuring the "Yan'an Spirit" produced at the request of art authorities filled the stages, theaters, and screens of Chinese cities.[24] Party cadres and senior art officials also gave lectures and presentations about their experiences at Yan'an.[25]

The doctrines derived from Mao's Yan'an talks—particularly the idea that art should serve politics and socialism—have remained important in the creation of a pedagogical cinema that has, in many ways, withstood the many changes in Chinese society over the last decades. The major force that has ensured the realization of these doctrines in Chinese film is the institution of film censorship.

The First Rating System

The attempt made at the end of the 1980s to create a rating system can be seen as a result of both the previously mentioned industry reform and the tendency toward democratization in film administration. In the face of the rise of entertainment films, especially those depicting violence, crime, and sex, Party authorities became concerned about their pernicious influence on Chinese audiences and suggested that the film administration implement a rating system to protect special group of audiences, especially minors. Unlike the total banning of films deemed inappropriate or problematic and the oppression of filmmakers that was common in the 1950s and 1960s, authorities in the 1980s resorted to legislation to regulate such films. In March 1989, on the basis of a request from the State Council of the PRC, the MRFT issued an announcement promoting the special category of "Not Appropriate for Children" (*shaoer buyi*), to be applied in film distribution and exhibition.[26] The document, "Announcement of the Implementation of Film Censorship and Exhibition Rating System" (*Guanyu shixing dianying shencha, fangying fenji zhidu de tongzhi* 关于实行电影审查、放映分级制度的通知)[27] indicates that the rating can be applied to both domestic and imported films, if a film has a plot:
1. with rape, theft, drug abuse, drug traffic and prostitution;
2. with violence, murder, or action that can easily cause children to be afraid;
3. depicting sex and sexual behavior;
4. depicting abnormal phenomena in society.

The announcement also required not only that a rating of "Not Appropriate For Children" be printed on each copy of the film and shown before the title comes up, but also that the rating should be indicated on movie posters and other promotional materials. In November 1989, the Chinese Film Distribution and Exhibition Company, a subsidiary company of the MRFT, issued a similar regulation designed to implement the policy: "Regulation for Exhibiting Films Rated 'Not Appropriate For Children'" (*fangyin shaoer buyi yingpian de guanli banfa* 放映少儿不宜影片的管理办法). Although the motivation behind these regulations was to regulate entertainment films and protect children under the age of 16 by specifying which films were inappropriate for certain audiences, the institution of the category of "Not Appropriate For Children" actually allowed some filmmakers and distributors to exploit particular audiences and gain box office revenue.

The Case of *The Village of Widows*

The Village of Widows (Guaifu cun; dir. Wang Jin 王进, 1988), a film co-produced by Pearl River Film Studio and Sil-Metropolitan Organization (Hong Kong) and released in early 1989, is one of the notorious cases of a film taking advantage of this rating. Depicting three couples' suffering due to strange marital and sex customs in a remote fishing village in Fujian Province before 1949, the film was promoted by movie theaters as directly dealing with "subjects of sex, love, seduction, etc.,"[28] and soon became extremely popular all over China. During the first two days of its exhibition in Beijing Xuanwu Movie Theater, it was shown twelve times without break.[29] Ironically, according to research by a journalist from *Renmin ribao* (People's Daily), there is no evidence that the film was officially rated as "Not Appropriate for Children." Furthermore, the label "Not Appropriate for Children" was not indicated on film posters or film credits as required by the MRFT's regulations. In spite of this, the film was still promoted as such when it was first exhibited in theaters. For example, when the film was exhibited in the city of Ningde, Fujian Province, a note stating that "The film directly touches upon the previously prohibited subject of sex… It is the first Chinese sex film, first film rated 'Not Appropriate for Children'" was attached to the film poster. The note even uses the film's ticket price on the black market in Beijing and Guangzhou as a means of promotion: "In Beijing, the tickets on the black market are ten yuan, and in Guangzhou, twenty-eight yuan."[30] If the ticket prices listed here are correct, it was, indeed, very sensational at the end of 1989, since the average price for a domestic film in Beijing was around six yuan (RMB 6).

Tempted by the explicit promise of sexual scenes, thousands of people flocked to theaters only to be disappointed when they found only conventional depictions of love and sex and nothing provocative. The audience's disappointment and complaints caused some local municipal governments to put an end to such promotions and eventually resulted in lawsuits between movie theaters and City Industrial and Commercial Administration (CICA). In Ningde, the CICA issued an administrative penalty in which the Ningde Dazhong Theater was required to remove advertisement of the film and pay a fine of RMB 2000 for the "exaggerated content in advertisement and false promotion that misled the audiences."[31] The theater refused to accept the penalties and brought a suit against the Ningde CICA at the Ningde Regional Intermediate Court, claiming that all the descriptions of the film were quoted from magazines and newspapers that were widely published and distributed all over China and were not fabricated and made up by the theater. Therefore, the theater asked the court to cancel the administrative penalties. On August 25, 1989, the court, declaring that the emphasis on sex in the content of Ningde Dazhong Theater's advertisement of the film *Village of Widows* was false and exaggerated, supported the administrative penalties. Finally, the theater appealed to the Fujian Province Supreme Court. On May 17 1990, the Court made a final judgment in support of the claim that the theater's advertisement was exaggerated, but overruled the penalty of RMB 2000.

After the controversy provoked by *Village of Widows*, the MRFT found that this rating system actually caused more problems than protections and this way of regulating entertainment films was not very effective. In December 1995, Tian Congming, the vice minister of the MRFT, indicated that the deletion of this rating category was one of the improvements necessary for the reform of the film censorship system.[32] In 1997, when China's first film censorship law, the *Film Censorship Regulation (Tentative)*, was issued by MRFT, the category of "Not Appropriate for Children" was not mentioned.

Although the primitive rating system was short-lived, it demonstrates the film administration's attempt to systemize film censorship. However, the failure to implement the rating of "Not Appropriate for Children" made the administration lose confidence in the rating system. Also, due to the tightened political and ideological climate after the Tian'anmen Incident in 1989, the former method of regulating the cinema through administrative interference based on the Party's political needs was resumed. Therefore, the rating system, as well as non-political entertainment films fell into disfavor with the Communist Party.

Conclusion

The general picture of Chinese cinema at the end of the 1980s is surprisingly similar to that at the turn of the 21st century. In both periods, a relaxed political and social context allowed emergence of a cinema with diversified subject matter. Non-political films, especially entertainment films, became a predominant force in a domestic film market that had experienced a period of decline due to the dominance of monotonous political films. The discussion of whether a rating system should be implemented as a replacement for film censorship in the early 2000s echoed the authorities' attempt in the late 1980s to initiate the first rating system. When these two trends are put beside the development of non-political films in the 1950s, also the result of a brief relaxed political atmosphere and the film authorities' attempt to rejuvenate the industry by giving more space to non-political films, it is evident that the rise and fall of entertainment films illuminate a recurring theme in the film history of the PRC: the Party's indecision about how to view the medium of cinema, whether as a powerful tool of propaganda under the full control of the Party, or as a medium that should meet the demands of the mass audience for non-political content. Therefore, entertainment films, as the least political genre of film, became a battlefield on which many filmmakers, such as Feng Xiaogang, would struggle. Also starting at this time, a play of give-and-take in the relationship between Party control and filmmakers' desire for free expression began to develop.

3

Chinese Cinema from 1989 to the Middle of the 1990s and Feng Xiaogang's Early Career

Introduction

After the Tian'anmen Incident on June 4, 1989, the Party both strengthened its control over ideology and began to promote a new round of economic reform. The concurrent resurrection of conservative film policy and deepening of industry reform meant that private film production companies were least trusted by film authorities because of the non-political subject matter of their films, but were seen by the film industry as the greatest potential force for sustaining the profitability of Chinese cinema. The first half of the 1990s was the formative stage of Feng's filmmaking career: he started to write scripts for movies and TV dramas and then produce and direct films for private companies. Because of his close collaboration with Wang Shuo, the witty and sarcastic dialogues and images of marginalized and alienated urban little characters that characterize Wang's writing also became hallmarks of Feng's films. Meanwhile, Feng's attempts to explore a new kind of cinema that would at once express social concerns and remain attractive to ordinary filmgoers, rather than film authorities and critics, foreshadowed an endeavor that has obsessed him throughout his career. His experience as an entrepreneur striving to make his privately owned production company profitable in the face of pressure from the censors also reflected the difficult situation of private film production companies in the early 1990s.

Economic reforms in the film industry, as we will see in more detail in the following sections, partially ended the state monopoly of film distribution and ticket pricing.[1] Furthermore, as reforms provided state studios with more freedom to co-produce films with foreign and private film production companies, filmmakers without professional training or state affiliation, such as Feng Xiaogang, were able to find ways to enter the film industry. This unprecedented chance occurred against a larger social context of official emphasis on the deepening of reform in the early 1990s, an emphasis signaled by Deng Xiaoping during the famous talk delivered during his southern tour of the cities of Wuchang, Shenzhen, Zhuhai, and Shanghai. In the so-called "Talk on the Southern Tour" (*Nanxun jianghua* 南巡讲话), Deng said, "If we don't keep a socialist orientation, develop the economy and improve people's living conditions, we will only meet a dead-end."[2] He also admitted that the reason why "our nation still remained stable after June Fourth . . . [was] because we promoted the policy of 'reform and opening to the outside world' (*gaige kaifang* 改革开放), and economic development, which improved people's living condition."[3] After the 14th Party Congress in 1992, the previously promoted "planned market economy" (有计划的商品经济) was replaced by a "socialist market economy" (社会主议商品经济), which was soon extended to many areas of the economy. This strengthening of the policy of economic reform was based on Deng's notion of the need to further promote economic reforms as a way of consolidating the Party's power after the crisis of the Tian'anmen Incident.

Despite these economic reforms, after 1989 the Party's policy regarding ideology and art began to stress the importance of the Party's leadership in every aspect of society. This policy resulted in difficulties for Feng and other private filmmakers as only limited opportunities for development were given to non-state sectors of film production. As Deng Xiaoping said in a meeting with Asian-American Nobel Prize winner Tsung Dao Lee (Zhengdao Li) not long after the Tian'anmen Incident: the Party would not only keep "The Four Cardinal Principles" (*Sixiang jiben yuanze* 四项基本原则)[4]—"adherence to the socialist road, the people's democratic dictatorship, the leadership of the Communist Party of China, and Marxism-Leninism and Mao Zedong's thought"—but would also oppose "bourgeois liberalization"—an ideological tendency of the 1980s that "worships Western capitalist countries' 'democracy' and 'freedom' and opposes socialism."[5] Both the reinforcement of the pre-1989 ideological orthodoxy in the early 1990s and the further encouragement of economic reform had an important influence on Chinese cinema. The former led to a rapid growth in government-sponsored main melody films and relegated entertainment films to the least-trusted category. Entertainment films were forced to compete with main melody films for already limited filmmaking resources. The latter, in the meantime, laid the foundation for the survival and revival of non-political films in the middle of the 1990s. In additional to these two counteracting forces of main melody films and non-political films, the completely unprecedented phenomenon of underground cinema also emerged in the early 1990s. This group of young filmmakers, disillusioned because of their inaccessibility to audiences through official distribution and exhibition channels, chose an "oppositional" position by producing works outside of the system and challenging the well-established communist rhetoric. These underground filmmakers later formed the subversive "Sixth Generation." This chapter first provides a general picture of Chinese cinema after the Tian'anmen Incident as contextual information for appreciating the early career of Feng Xiaogang. This is followed by a discussion of Feng's early career as script writer, film production entrepreneur, and film director. I give particular attention to Feng's collaboration with Wang Shuo, the situation of his private film production company in the early 1990s, and Feng's adaptation and appropriation of Wang's style in his directing debut *Gone Forever with My Love*.

Chinese Cinema after the Tian'anmen Incident

The "Rise" of Main Melody Films[6]

According to the Communist party press, the Tian'anmen Incident was a by-product of the inundation of Western culture, represented by popular songs from Taiwan and Hong Kong, action and martial art films from Hong Kong and Hollywood, and avant-garde art.[7] As a result, Chinese film authorities denounced cinema's function as a medium for entertainment. The genre given the responsibility to carry out the function of helping the Party to advocate its policies was the so-called main melody film（主旋律电影）. Throughout the 1990s, these films became the primary weapon through which the Party held on to and voiced its political message to the rest of society.

First proposed on March 1987 by the vice-minister of the MRFT, Ding Qiao（丁峤）, and the vice-director of the Shanghai Film Studio, Shi Fangyu（石方禹）, at a meeting with directors of major Chinese film studios, the term "main melody" films was understood to refer to films that could "invigorate national spirit and national pride and encourage Chinese people to construct the 'Four Modernizations,'"[8] and that also demonstrated a *"spirit of creation"*（创作精神）.[9] According to Ding and Shi, "Only films that have positive and healthy content and are exquisite in quality can be considered 'main melody' films."[10] Although the notion of main melody films began to be mentioned by certain film leaders at the end of the 1980s, it didn't become an officially sanctioned category until the end of 1989. As we saw in the previous chapter, before the Tian'anmen Incident in 1989, the late 1980s witnessed the burgeoning popularity of entertainment films but very few films that could be considered main melody. In contrast to Chinese cinema in 1988, when 60 percent of the annual film production consisted of martial arts, suspense, and musical films,[11] the second half of 1989 witnessed an unexpected rise in the production of main melody films. In terms of subject matter, main melody films at this stage dealt mostly with the "grand history" of Chinese revolution and Party leadership, showing an unapologetic emphasis on leaders, historical events, and the victory of the Party or national heroes against foreign invaders. Although contemporary stories dealing with anti-corruption, the promotion of education in rural areas, model party leaders and cadres, and patriotism and loyalty to the nation were also included in main melody films, they were in a clear minority. The most typical ones are historical epic films such as *Founding of the Nation* (Kaiguo dadian; dir. Li Qiankuan 李前宽 and Xiao Guiyun 肖桂云, 1989), a portrayal of the days leading to the establishment of the PRC, or *Baise Rebellion* (Baise qiyi; dir. Chen Jialin 陈家林, 1989), a biographical film about a rebellion lead by Deng Xiaoping in his twenties. *Sun on the Roof of the World* (Shijie wuji de tai yang; dir. Xie Fei 谢飞 and Wang Ping 王坪, 1991) tells a story of efforts and sacrifice two generations of engineers dedicated to building a power plant in a hinterland of Tibet. *The Nanpu Bridge* (Qingsa pujiang; dir. Shi Xiaohua 石晓华, 1991) deals with the construction of the Nanpu Bridge in Shanghai; and *Her Smile Through the Candlelight* (Zhuguang li de weixiao; dir. Wu Tianren 吴天忍, 1991) shows a loving school teacher's selfless dedication to her students.

After a year of production, a large number of main melody films burst onto the scene of Chinese cinema in 1991. Later labeled the "Year of Revolutionary History Films with Significant Subjects" (*zhongda geming lishi ticai nian* 重大革命历史题材年), 1991 marked the culmination of main melody films with the appearance of Party leaders and key events in China's revolution. For example, *Decisive Engagement* (Da juezhan; dir. Cai Jiwei 蔡继渭, Yang Guangyuan 杨光远 and Wei Lian 书廉, 1991), a ten-hour epic film with three parts and six series depicts the three major military campaigns between the Communist and Nationalist armies during the Civil War (1945-1949). The story of *Creation of the World* (Kaitian pidi; dir. Li Xiepu 李歇浦, 1991) goes back to the end of the 1910s, when Marxism was first introduced to China. In its introduction to historical figures who played important roles in the creation of the Chinese Communist Party, the film depicts Mao Zedong as a significant co-founder of the Party.

Stylistically, at this stage of their development, main melody films were largely a continuation of the socialist realist films of the 1950s. According to Paul Clark, the scriptwriter-centered socialist realist cinema in the early years of the PRC featured a depiction of "typical" characters and events in a "typical" environment, a high degree of glossiness and glamour, an avoidance of naturalism and social criticism, and an extensive use of dialogues and stage-derived presentation.[12] However, despite the stereotypical and idealized depictions of historical events and leaders, there was an undercurrent that tended to approach subjects from a more humanistic angle. This became the main tendency of main melody films in the middle of the 1990s. These later main melody films either chose to portray Party leaders from a more humanistic and sentimental perspective, or focused on stories of ordinary people dedicating themselves to socialist construction and the Party. *Mao Zedong and His Son* (Mao Zedong he tade erzi; dir. Zhang Jinbiao 张今标, 1991) focuses on Mao's love and care for his son, Mao Anying, his selflessness in sending his son to the front in the Korean War, and his fatherly sorrow when he learns that his son has died in an air raid in Korea. Another film in 1991, *Zhou Enlai* (Zhou Enlai; dir. Ding Yinnan 丁荫楠, 1991), featuring a somber and subdued color scheme in the mise-en-scene, focuses on the last years of Prime Minister Zhou Enlai during the Cultural Revolution—how he effortlessly protects Party officials from Red Guard persecution, but hopelessly fights against his terminal cancer.

The rise of main melody film in the early 1990s was made possible by three forms of government support. First, generous support was provided by the government for the making of "Revolutionary History Films with Significant Subjects." Although specific figures of government investment were never released to the public, the support and privileges offered by the state can be inferred from some directors' essays and memoirs about the making of their films. In an article written by Wei Lian, director of *Pingjin Campaign* (Pingjin zhanyi 平津战役, 1992), the third part of the *Decisive Engagement* trilogy, we learn that the film was shot on 200 locations across the northern part of China. As many as 370,000 soldiers of the People's Liberation Army and Air Force, as well as military academy students, participated in the shooting as extras. In order to capture the grandeur of an important scene in the city of Tianjin, twenty-one streets were blocked to traffic and thirteen bus routes were suspended for ten hours. In this shot, ten thousand army soldiers acted as extras, and 2,000 police officers were on location to maintain order during the shooting.[13] The director also admits that "without support from central and local governments, it was inconceivable that the film could be completed."[14] As the most expensive film of 1992, production of *Pingjin Campaign* cost as much as RMB 20.6 million,[15] while the average cost of making a feature film in that year was only RMB 1.26 million.[16]

Secondly, in order to ensure the successful marketing and widescale screening of main melody films, the government promoted these films by issuing official documents requiring that all government-owned institutions, enterprises, work units, schools, and universities purchase tickets for their members as either a form of "political study" or free entertainment. Such official documents were usually co-issued by several government departments depending on which parts of the mass audience were targeted. The Ministry of Propaganda, MRFT, the Ministry of Education, China's Workers' Union, the Women's Federation, and many others participated in these film promotion efforts. The title of these documents usually read "Notice on Organizing the Viewing of the Film ABC" while the body included two orders: (1) The affiliated and subordinate units must organize their members to watch the film; and (2) All film distribution and exhibition units must guarantee sufficient copies and adequate show times for the film. Three documents issued in 2004 can be used as examples. "Notice on Organizing the Viewing of the Film *Zheng Peimin*," co-issued in September 2004 by SARFT (previously MRFT), the Ministry of Propaganda, the Ministry of Personnel, and the Central Commission for Discipline Inspection of the CPC, promoted a film depicting a model government official who is hard working and refuses to be enticed by bribery.[17] In the same month, "Notice on Organizing the Viewing of the Film *My Years in France*," co-issued by seven government departments including the Center of the Communist Youth League, the Ministry of Education, and the Labor Union of China, requested their subordinate units to organize viewings of a film depicting Deng Xiaoping's early years in France.[18] Two months later, the Ministry of Propaganda and the Ministry of Personnel co-issued another notice "On Organizing the Viewing of the Film *Zhang Side*," a biographical film of a PLA soldier about whom Mao wrote the famous article "To Serve People Wholeheartly."[19] Interestingly, the collective purchase of tickets did not necessarily result in high film attendance—even though film tickets were distributed free-of-charge to workers and employees, many still were uninterested in going to the theater to watch the film. For example, *Long March* (Changzheng; dir. Zhai Junjie 翟俊杰, 1998), also a government sponsored and promoted film, attracted only 1,500 audience members when it was exhibited in the city of Shenyang.[20]

The third method was to elevate the artistic or aesthetic status of main melody films by bestowing on them professional or artistic film prizes. Since the early 1990s, main melody films have been the recipients of numerous Chinese film awards such as the Golden Rooster Awards, an annual award offered by the Association of Chinese Filmmakers for achievements in film production, performance, and technology. From 1981, the first year of these awards, to 1988, only one main melody film appeared as a winner of Best Film at the Golden Rooster Awards (*Sun Zhongshan*, a biography of Sun Yat-sen; dir. Tang Xiaodan 汤晓丹,1987); other awards during these years were won by films from more diversified categories: Scar films like *Legend of Tianyun Mountain* (Tianyun shan chuanqi; dir. Xie Jin 谢晋, 1981), literary adaptations such as *Camel Xiangzi* (Luotuo xiangzi; dir. Ling Zifeng 凌子风, 1983), and Fifth Generation films such as *Red Sorghum* (Hong gaoliang; dir. Zhang Yimou, 1988). Beginning in 1990, the Golden Rooster Awards switched their attention to main melody films. The Best Film Award of 1990 was given to *Founding of the Nation*; in 1991, the recipient was *Jiao Yulu* (Jiao Yulu; dir. Wang Jixing 王冀刑, 1991), and in 1992, *Decisive Engagement*. Another important award, the Huabiao Award, sponsored by the MRFT and the Ministry of Culture, has shown an even more unapologetic preference for main melody film since 1990. For example, on its long list of Best Films of 1991, three of the eleven winners deal with historical events of the Chinese Revolution (*Decisive Engagement*, *Creation of the World*, and *After the Battle*), two are stories of China's great leaders (*Zhou Enlai* and *Mao Zedong and His Son*), and two are depictions of socialist construction (*Qingsa Pu River* and *Sun on the Roof of the World*).

Most of the main melody filmmakers were trained in state film schools in the 1960s, before the Cultural Revolution. This generation of directors was probably the most authentically socialist realist. Most of them had been born at the end of the 1930s, and thus were not deeply influenced by Republican-era cinema, which had included realist films with social criticism produced by private studios in Shanghai. Entering film schools at the end of the 1950s or 1960s and watching more Soviet and socialist films than Hollywood or Western productions, they were more familiar with Eisenstein's montage theory than the classical Hollywood style. Therefore, the cinematic languages and styles they used in their films consisted of the glossy and non-naturalistic style of socialist realist cinema, and the subjects for which they showed the greatest aptitude were those that supported Party rhetoric. For example, Cai Jiwei, the director of one part of the *Decisive Engagement* trilogy, started to make films as a cameraman in *A Sparkling Star* (Shanshan de hongxing, 1974), a quintessential socialist realist film of the Cultural Revolution period, and had made two other war films before *Decisive Engagement*. Another very active director of main melody film, Ding Yinnan, the director of many biography films, such as *Sun Zhongshan* (1989), *Zhou Enlai* (1991), *Li Fuchun* (2000), *Deng Xiaoping* (2001) and *Lu Xun* (2005), graduated from Beijing Film Academy in 1966 and entered the film world after the Cultural Revolution. Filmmakers who either grew out of the tradition of Republican-era cinema, such as Xie Jin, or worked outside the official moviemaking system, such as Zhang Yimou and Chen Kaige, were rarely granted opportunities to work on these films. The filmmakers who were excluded from this system needed to explore alternative ways of filmmaking.

Main melody film was a tool for restoring a positive image of the Party and its leaders in the face of the political turmoil of Tian'anmen Incident. To ensure these films fulfill this function, every aspect of the main melody film was monopolized by the state—from the recruitment of filmmakers to the exhibition of films. These efforts seemed very successful in the early 1990s—from 1989 to 1992, main melody films seemingly succeeded in gaining ground that was lost to "entertainment films" in the 1980s. China's Film Year Book of 1992 triumphantly states that "the previous phenomenon of casting the scum of society as main characters almost disappeared and the images of emperors, concubines, eunuchs, hooligans, and mafia no longer dominated the screen."[21]

However, despite all the efforts of official institutions in creating and supporting them, main melody film did not succeed in reconstructing a cinema of heroic images and pedagogical messages that had dominated in the first three decades of the PRC. Although the main melody films have become a recurring theme in the history of Chinese cinema since 1990, their "triumph" did not last very long. Starting in 1992, the prosperity of main melody film began to decline and the disadvantages it brought to Chinese cinema became more and more prominent. Because of the extravagant cost of production, main melody films drained the industry of already limited state sponsorship in filmmaking and brought the state-owned studios more financial troubles. As the most expensive films in production, the costs of production often exceeded revenues. The previously mentioned *Pingjin Campaign*, costing RMB 20 million to make, earned only RMB 5.4 million at the box office, leaving a deficit of over RMB 15 million. The two films mentioned in the article by Wang Shushun as the representative main melody films in the year of 1992, *Sun on the Roof of the World* and *Qingsa Pu River*, also incurred large losses. *Sun on the Roof of the World* spent RMB 1.9 million in production, but earned only RMB 460,000 during its exhibition. *Qingsa Pu River*, with a production cost as high as RMB 1.6 million ended up RMB 81,000 in debt.[22] The burden of these large debts exacerbated the financial difficulty of many film studios. In 1991, the heyday of the production of main melody films, the sixteen state-owned studios' total box office revenue from main melody films was only RMB 12.6 million, enough to produce only ten films at an average of RMB 1.26

million per picture—far from the amount needed to reach the production target of 120 films per year.[23]

The impact of main melody films on Feng's and other non-state-supported filmmakers' careers was devastating. The Party's guaranteed financial support for main melody films meant little support for non-political films. Far from the extravagant RMB 20 million budget of main melody films, the entire assets of Feng's production company were worth only RMB 100, 000 and the lack of investment was one of the main obstacles threatening the survival of the company. It was against this background, without the secured channels of distribution and exhibition enjoyed by main melody films, yet relying on the state film studio infrastructure for the making of films, Feng Xiaogang, from the very beginning of his career, had to work under the pressures of profitability and to cooperate with the film authorities.

Entertainment Films in the Early 1990s

In contrast to main melody films, which enjoyed enthusiastic support from the government but achieved, at best, a lukewarm reception among audiences, entertainment films were constantly frustrated by the indifference or hostility of film officials, but enjoyed great popularity among their audiences. For officials in film administration, many popular cinematic trends of the 1980s, such as the adaptations of Wang Shuo's works and the popularity of pure entertainment films depicting murder, horror, or violence were viewed as products of the "bourgeois liberalization" of the mid-1980s. Therefore, within the post-1989 social and political context, these officials felt an urgent need to "purify" the Chinese film market and save it from the damages of "bourgeois liberalization." To achieve this end, a number of administrative actions were taken.

The liberal-minded vice-minister of the MRFT, Chen Haosu, who, as we have seen in Chapter 2, enthusiastically promoted "entertainment films" in the 1980s, was dismissed from the position. Consequently, the film policy that he had supported underwent a dramatic change. The orthodox Communist art and literature agenda of the "Two Servings" was reiterated as the fundamental film policy. By declaring that cinema should serve socialism, film officials returned to the former orthodoxy concerning the function of cinema, while the previously promoted entertaining function fell into disfavor. In an article on filmmaking in the *China Film Year Book* of 1990, Liu Cheng, who later produced a main melody film, *Kong Fansen* (Kong Fansen; dir. Chen Guoxing 陈国星, Wang Ping 王坪, 1995), indicated that "bourgeois liberalization" was one of the most significant problems of Chinese cinema in 1989, leading to neglect of the "Two Servings."[24] According to Liu, as a result of this liberalization, "we found more representations of hooligans, enemies, spies, and prostitutes on the screen . . . but less class analysis of characters and . . . fewer positive depictions of workers and peasants."[25] Liu argued that in order to solve these problems, it was very urgent that the "Two Servings" be reinforced and the pedagogical function of cinema be emphasized. Both of these goals could be attained through promoting the production of main melody films. Many other articles on the future direction of Chinese cinema shared Liu's opinion.[26] In the aftermath of the 1989 political crisis, the debate in the mid-1980s over entertainment films finally came to an end, and the Party's emphasis on main melody film signaled the return of a conservative ideological atmosphere among officials in film administration.

The changing face of the official art policy was accompanied by a round of economic reform in the film industry that seemed to contradict the idea of a cinema in service to socialism. Instead of socialism, these reforms placed market demand in the foreground.[27] In the film industry, this reform, like the one in the mid-1980s, first affected the distribution system and ticket pricing. Although the 1987 reform was intended to emancipate studios from the CFC monopoly by allowing provincial or local distributors to participate in film distribution, it, unfortunately, complicated the situation of film distribution for the studios. Whereas they had previously needed only to deal with CFC, now they had to negotiate with more than thirty distributors for a film that was to be distributed nationwide. Regarding this problem, a document issued by MRFT on May 31, 1993, "Suggestions on the Deepening of Chinese Film Industries' Institutional Reform,"[28] specified that film distribution could be taken care of by the film studios themselves, emancipating the studios from the complicated procedures of film distribution. The document also took a further step on the question of reforming ticket prices by allowing film producers and distributors to decide the ticket price together instead of, as previously, having the Chinese Film Corporation set prices in terms of the length rather than quality of the film.[29] The result was similar to that seen in the 1980s—having more autonomy in the process of film distribution and ticket pricing, film studios were more eager to make films that were likely to return profits, rather than following orders to make main melody films.

Moreover, as the whole industry was pushed into the forefront of a market economy, government involvement in the form of financial support was greatly reduced. Once fully supported by the government, the whole film industry now received less than RMB 50 million annually,[30] only enough to produce 30 films at an average budget of RMB 1 million to 1.5 million per film.[31] Facing a film production target of 100 films a year, state-owned studios had to rely on non-governmental investments to complete around sixty films. Given these circumstances, although the film authority strove to keep film ideology under its control, it could hardly refuse to allow investments from non-state institutions. As a result, investments from private domestic and foreign film companies, including many from Taiwan and Hong Kong, were involved in China's domestic film production under the name of "co-production" with state film studios. In this sort of co-production, state studios only nominally participated in the process of production by collecting licensing fees from overseas or domestic producers and/or providing equipment, shooting locations, or extras, while the non-state companies were responsible for the majority of film production.[32] As we will see in the later part of this chapter, Feng's entry into the film world—as an entrepreneur in a private film production company co-producing works with state-owned studios—followed this pattern.

Therefore, despite the burgeoning of main melody film and revival of the conservative view toward cinema among film officials, non-political entertainment films remained an important part of the film market in the early 1990s. Among 151 films produced by the sixteen state film studios in 1992, only three, *Pingjin Campaign*, *The Story of Mao Zedong*, and *Liu Shaoqi's 44 Days*, can be considered "Revolutionary History Films with Significant Subjects." At the same time, out of 22 films bearing licenses from the Beijing Film Studio, two-thirds were co-productions. These films not only occupied a majority of the annual output of the studio, but also generated the greatest profit at the box office.[33] According to the *China Film Year Book* of 1994, co-productions with Taiwan and Hong Kong, such as *Once Upon a Time in China* (Shiwang zhengba; dir. Tsui Hark 徐克, 1992), *Farewell My Concubine* (Bawang bieji; dir. Chen Kaige 陈凯歌, 1993), *Fong Sai Yuk* (Fang Shiyu; dir. Corey Yuen 元奎, 1993), and *All Men Are Brothers—Blood of the Leopard* (Yingxiong bense; dir. Chang Hui-Ngai 陈会毅, 1993) all achieved revenues ranging from RMB 3 million to 6 million per film at the box office, while the average revenue per state-sponsored film was only around RMB 1 million.[34]

In the aftermath of the events in 1989, the situation of entertainment films was paradoxical. In spite of the vital role they played in supporting the Chinese film industry, their importance was not recognized by either art officials or film critics. In the talks and official documents of film officials and at Chinese domestic film festivals, it was still main melody films that attracted most attention, while entertainment films were considered only a useful source for subsidizing film production.[35] Beginning in the 1990s, entertainment films were in an awkward situation: they were relied upon the operation of state film studios and official film institutions, but always viewed by the authorities as the potentially dangerous "other" to which no important status could be ascribed in official rhetoric.

Formative Stage of Feng's Career: Attempt at Popular Cinema (1990–1996)

In the early 1990s, when the main melody films monopolized the government-supported film industry, filmmakers who were either unable or unwilling to be complicit with the mainstream had to choose other ways of filmmaking. The Fifth Generation chose to rely on foreign capital, a way of filmmaking that bypassed government sponsorship and allowed for a certain degree of freedom in subject matter. For example, Zhang Yimou's *To Live* (Huozhe), focusing on the turbulent period of the first years of the PRC, was fully sponsored by Sony Production Company. The Sixth Generation, still below the radar of both Western and Chinese critics at the time, moved toward an independent cinema. Zhang Yuan made *Beijing Bastard* with sponsorship from Cui Jian, a famous Chinese rock star.

Feng's career of this period represented a different mode of filmmaking. He tried his luck in many modes of productions—state-owned studios, a semi-private/semi-state-owned production company, and a private enterprise. The result of his exploration was the establishment of a middle path of popular urban cinema that addressed the cultural consciousness of Chinese people in the face of a rapidly changing society and economy. While without direct association with government rhetoric, the films were not apolitical. Rather, there was always subtle or insightful political commentary for more sophisticated audiences to decipher, a feature which proved later especially attractive to the emerging middle-class urban audience. The early stage of Feng's career is characterized by his success as a script writer, his collaboration with Wang Shuo in the Good Dream TV and Film Consulting Company, and his debut as a director of film and TV drama.

Feng Xiaogang as a Scriptwriter

The first scripts that Feng wrote were all collaborative works: two films, *The Unexpected Passion* (Zaoyu jiqing; dir. Xia Gang, 1990) and *After Separation* (Da saba; dir. Xia Gang, 1992) are co-written with Zheng Xiaolong, the president of Beijing TV Production center; and two TV dramas, *Stories of the Editorial Board* (Bianjibu de gushi; dir. Zhao Baogang and Jin Yan, 25 episodes) and *Beijingers in New York* (Beijingren zai niuyue; dir. Zheng Xiaolong and Feng Xiaogang, 21 episodes, 1993) are co-written with Wang Shuo and Cao Guilin, respectively. Feng's abilities began to be noticed in these works, which won several nominations and awards at Chinese film and TV festivals: *After Separation* was nominated for Best Film Script at the 1992 Golden Roosters, *Stories of the Editorial Board* won the award of Best TV Drama at the 1992 Golden Eagles, the most prestigious TV award in China, and *Beijingers in New York* won the award for Best Long TV Drama at the 1993 Golden Eagles. All these works were products of official filmmaking institutions. The two films were produced by the Beijing Film Studio, and sponsored, distributed and exhibited through government-owned channels; the two TV dramas were products of Central Beijing TV Production, a production sector of the Beijing TV Station.

Although the first to bring Feng Xiaogang to the film world's attention, these works were all collaborations with other directors or writers. In the four projects, the influences of Wang Shuo and Zheng Xiaolong, two well-established and veteran scriptwriters and directors, respectively, overshadowed that of Feng. The relatively minor role played by Feng in the production of these works means that they are not as representative as his later works in terms of portrayals of his own ideology and style. Nonetheless, a study of these works does provide valuable information on the early development of Feng's style (and, of course, on the state of China's TV industry in the early 1990s, and the Wang Shuo phenomenon after the June Fourth incident). With this in mind, these collaborative works are briefly introduced here as a background to the formation of Feng's career and as counterparts to facilitate an understanding of his later films.

Unlike the glorification and idealization of Chinese revolutionary history and Party leaders in the main melody films, these works reveal Feng's concern for current social problems and cultural phenomena and his compulsion to reveal the joys and difficulties in the lives of ordinary Chinese people. For instance, *After Separation*, co-written by Feng and Zheng Xiaolong, is loosely based on the personal experience of Zheng Xiaolong. The film captures moments in the lives of a man and woman, both left behind by their spouses who went abroad, and reflects the "fever of going abroad" (*chuguo re* 出国热) in the early 1990s when travel restrictions for Chinese citizens had been removed and government policy began to encourage them to travel or study abroad.[36] This phenomenon provided material for the TV drama, *Beijingers in New York*. This work, as the title suggests, provides a close examination of

Chinese immigrants' successes and failures in the United States. In relation to Feng's later films, this drama can be seen as the prototype of one of Feng's New Year films, *Be There or Be Square*. A comparison of these two works can be found in Chapter 4. The TV drama, *Stories of the Editorial Board*, a hilarious satire of many issues (but none that seem overtly political), co-written by Feng and Wang Shuo and aired on Beijing TV Station in the winter of 1991, is another work that can be seen as a prototype for Feng's later works.[37] Similar to the structure, narrative, and themes of *Party A and Party B* (about a company organized by four friends, who in the process of running their business, meet different kinds of people), the stories in *Editorial Board*, are associated with the editorial board of a popular magazine, *Guide to Living* (Renjian zhinan), which consists of an experienced chief editor and five editors, all from different backgrounds and with different personalities. In their daily work, they encounter a variety of people and incidents, each of which reveals the humor, irony and absurdity that is part of seemingly mundane daily life. One episode deals with a case of domestic violence that two editors are investigating. Assuming that the victim must be a weak and vulnerable wife, the editors visit the family to interview the victim. However, they are surprised to find out that it is the husband who is abused by his robust and strong wife. In another episode, titled "Artificial Intelligence," a very efficient female secretary "robot" is "delivered" to the editorial board as a gift for the editors to use. Working with great diligence and speed for several days, the secretary disappears one day, leaving a note confessing that she is actually a real person who was just temporally unemployed and has now found a new job. She also admits that she had found it much easier to be a robot secretary than a human one, as she could remained engaged in her work without being distracted by the need to please her bosses and maintain superficial "human relationships" (*renji guanxin*) with her co-workers.

The early experience of script writing gave Feng the ability to interest his audiences with a seemingly simple story while attracting them with unexpected humorous scenes and dialogues. Another significance of this experience is that these works foreshadowed Feng's later attempt to seek a middle ground between the political propaganda of main melody films and the rebellious works of the underground cinema by attempting to register the sentiments and concerns of ordinary Chinese audience. For example, *The Unexpected Passion*, co-written by Feng and Zheng Xiaolong, can be seen as the Chinese version of the Hollywood film *Love Story*. The melodramatic story focuses on the hopeless love between a dying woman and her boyfriend, a freelance stuntman. In his attempt to earn money for the woman's medical expenses, the boyfriend undertakes a series of risky stunts. The seeming pathos of this love story about a couple's physical and mental suffering is actually permeated with the two protagonists' hope that every difficulty, even death, will somehow be conquered. One episode from *Stories of Editorial Board*, in which Feng himself plays a role, is another example. This episode deals with the reactions of the editors and readers after hearing rumors of a large comet that is on a direct collision course with Earth and threatens to bring about total human extinction. Feng plays the role of an amateur astronomer who brings his telescope to the editorial board to persuade them that the rumor is true. As the editors begin to accept the fact that they will die, an announcement from the national observatory ensures the public that the comet will, in fact, not collide with the Earth. The phrase that constantly recurs in this episode is that people should not "believe the rumor" (*xin yao* 信谣) and "disseminate the rumor" (*chuan yao* 传谣), implicitly referring to the same widespread use of these two phrases in Communist official media after the Tian'anmen Incident. The appropriation of these phrases and the pervasive threat of death in the episode echo implicitly the experiences of many Chinese people during the June Fourth Incident, which took place only a year before the broadcast of the TV drama. But, whatever its implicit criticisms, the happy ending seems to support the post-June Fourth Party rhetoric that all news of the incident from sources other than China's official press was only unsubstantiated rumor. These works, although not overtly supporting Communist rhetoric, did not position themselves as "oppositional" or as "rebellious." Rather, they provided the audience with a good entertainment without an explicit political or ideological agenda while still addressing the audiences' concerns.

Feng Xiaogang, Wang Shuo and Entrepreneurship

Feng's early career is closely associated with Wang Shuo. As Feng writes in his autobiography, "Through Wang Shuo's seemingly simple depiction, our ordinary life and ordinary language became so lively and fascinating. His perspective on advancing with the times and adopting different angles in seeing things had a far-reaching influence on my later career as a film director."[38] Feng's attitude toward life also had a great influence on Wang's works. "Feng Xiaogang has a native Beijing 'little character's' wisdom of surviving, which could help him to both protect himself and get what he wants at the same time. Although it sometimes sounds pathetic, it is the only way that a 'little character' can more or less preserve his self-respect under very harsh social conditions."[39] The collaboration between the two, indeed, was reciprocal. Feng's formative years as a script writer overlapped with the mature period of Wang's career, when he began to engage in script writing and TV drama production. According to Feng's autobiography, he was introduced to Wang Shuo by Zheng Xiaolong, and they first met in the summer of 1986 while Feng was still a set-designer in CBTP.[40] In 1992, Feng's first movie script co-written with Zheng Xiaolong, *After Separation* (1992), features Wang's witty dialogues and the portrayal of the lives of "little characters." Feng's directorial debut, *Gone Forever with My Love* (Yongshi wo ai, 1994), is based on Wang Shuo's two short stories, *Flight Attendant* (Kongzhong xiaojie) and *Death after a High* (Guo ba yin jiu si 过把瘾就死). Both stories and films incorporate a sentimental nostalgic love story along with a strong sense of disillusionment toward love and idealism, hallmarks of Wang's style. Although it did not appear in the film credits, Wang's short story *You Are Not a Common Person* (Ni bushi yige suren), about how a company director named Feng Xiaogang is racking his brain to make his company profitable, is actually the prototype of the screen script of Feng's first New Year Film, *Party A, Party B*.[41]

In 1993, Feng and Wang co-founded a television and film production company, Good Dream TV and Film Production and Consulting. Feng worked first as a scriptwriter, then as a director. While working at this private film production company, Feng also began to express more insightful and direct critiques of social and cultural issues in contemporary China. These, unfortunately, caused several unpleasant encounters with censorship. The downfall of the Good Dream company was the lowest period in Feng's career, but was also a turning point. Learning from the failure of his productions in Good Dream, Feng explored the new genre of New Year Film, which brought him to the center of national attention. This section introduces works made by Good Dream and examines the influences of Wang's literary style on Feng's films. The decline of the company will be discussed in the following chapter.

Wang Shuo[42]

In 1980s and early 1990s, Wang Shuo produced numerous best-selling short stories and novels, including *Kongzhong xiaojie* (Flight Attendant, 1984), *Fuchu haimian* (Floating above the Sea, 1985), *Yiban shi huoyan, yiban shi haishui* (Half Is Flame, Half Is Seawater, 1986), *Wanr Zhu* (Master of Mischief, 1987), and *Wanr de jiushi xintiao* (No Fast Heartbeat, No Play, 1988), which feature sentimental love stories, little characters, dark comedies and nostalgic memories of the Maoist era. As a writer popular among college students and young urban professionals, Wang Shuo's fictions depicted a society in a transition from Communist to post-socialist ideology, and people experiencing a cultural and moral crisis. As Geremie Barme writes, "Wang Shuo is not a doomsayer or a pessimist but a witty writer of serious intent who uses the present Chinese cultural order as the basis for a fictional world of great humor and insight: a literature of escape and sublimation."[43] However, the portrayal of violence, sex, the tedium of daily life, and the strong sense of cynicism in his novels and short stories made him very unpopular with the elitist critics and official art authorities, causing his works to be labeled "hooligan literature" (*pizi wenxue*). Since the early 1990s, Wang became especially active as a scriptwriter of TV dramas, soap operas and films, including *Yearnings* (Kewang, TV drama, 1990), *Stories of the Editorial Board* (1991), *Dreams May Come* (Mengxiang zhaojin xianshi; dir. Xu Jinglei, 2006) and others.

Good Dream TV and Film Production and Consulting Company

Registered at the Beijing Industry and Commerce Administration (BICA) on September 13, 1993, with RMB 200,000 as a fixed fund and eight employees, Good Dream TV and Film Production and Consulting Company was established as a subordinate institution of the Center of Beijing TV Art. As an "enterprise owned by all the people" (*quanmin qiye* 全民企业), the company was supposed to be a state-owned enterprise. Although the CBTA might have provided the initial funding, it did not contribute a penny to its later operations—none of the six productions of the company received CBTA investment. Therefore, although registered as a state-owned enterprise, the company actually operated independently and so did not enjoy any priorities in the processes of production or in the distribution and exhibition of its products. As a result, Wang and Feng had to both cooperate with state-owned film institutions and pay special attention to the profitability of their business. The pragmatic need for profitability was obvious in the application form they submitted to BICA. Good Dream's fields of business not only included "planning, consulting, and producing film, TV dramas, and entertainment programs," but also some that are totally irrelevant to the film and television industry, such as "wholesale and retail of home electronic appliances, construction materials, and decoration materials."[44] It seems the founders of the company included as many businesses as possible in order to ensure some degree of profit.

Feng Xiaogang's activities in the company represent his first attempt to explore ways of existing within the system while still maintaining artistic freedom. As Feng recalls in his autobiography, he and Wang Shuo envisioned that the company would not only base its business on script writing, but would also seek cooperation with other popular Chinese writers. If the company could get these writers' authorization for the adaptation of their works into film or TV shows, it could either produce the scripts or sell them to other companies.[45] However, when the two embarked on their business venture with the hope of supporting their company from these "lucrative" businesses, they seemed to neglect one important prerequisite—financial resource. In order to be able to purchase adaptation rights from writers and initiate their plan, they needed at least RMB 1 million of investment, an astronomical figure for a company of this size. In order to attract investors, Feng and Wang had to work like salesmen, soliciting investments from various kinds of businessmen and negotiating with them over dinner, usually, in fancy restaurants in Beijing. In contrast to these extravagant dinners, the company was forced to move their office to a more affordable location due to the difficulty of their financial situation. In the end, they wound up as a "bag company," meaning that the company was without any permanent office and had to keep all its property, from legal documents to seals, in a bag.[46]

Good Dream was not only where Feng got his first training as a businessman, it was also where he began to experiment with different subjects and styles of cinema. When Wang Shuo was later employed in a television and film production company Shishi Company, organized by another Chinese director, Ye Daying, Feng became the central figure at Good Dream. The six productions of the company are all associated with Feng, and he worked in multiple capacities as director, scriptwriter, and actor. During the four years of its existence, the company produced three TV dramas and three films, including *Chicken Feathers on the Ground* (Yidi jimao; TV drama, 10 episodes, scriptwriter and dir. Feng Xiaogang, 1995), *Behind the Moon* (Yueliang bei mian; TV drama, 10 episodes, dir. Feng Xiaogang, 1996), *Elegy for Love* (Qing shang; TV drama, 10 episodes, dir. Feng Xiaogang, ca. 1996), *Gone Forever with My Love* (Yongshi wo ai; film, dir. Feng Xiaogang, 1994), *I Am Your Dad* (Wo shi ni baba; film, dir. Wang Shuo, 1995), and *Living a Miserable Life* (Guozhe langbeibukan de shenghuo; film, dir. Feng Xiaogang, aborted). In 1996, the Good Dream failed to register with BICA and was closed in 1997.[47]

Although prolific, the company's many productions failed to generate much profit. The primary reason for this can be traced to censorship. Among the three films, only *Gone Forever with My Love* passed the censors and reached movie theaters. Although *I Am Your Dad* was completed, it was denied approval for exhibition by the Film Censorship Board. *Living a Miserable Life* was aborted in the middle of production when the script was not approved by the censors. The three television productions had somewhat better luck. Although they had certain difficulties during the distribution process, all finally

Gone Forever With My Love

出品人: 李国林　总监制: 王守琴

Movie poster of *Gone Forever with My Love*

reached audiences. Although these works dealt with popular subjects—love (*Gone Forever with My Love*), corruption (*Behind the Moon*), the generation gap (*I Am Your Dad*), and disillusionment (*Living a Miserable Life*)—they were neither works for pure entertainment nor solely for the purpose of profit-making. Rather, by touching upon subjects such as social problems, the depravity of human beings, and injustice between classes, these works reflect Feng's social conscience and their desire to produce meaningful commentary on problems in contemporary Chinese society.

These experiences of a filmmaker/producer beset by various difficulties are reflected in Feng's later films in the frustrated and unsuccessful "little character" who is trapped in recurrent difficulties. *Party A, Party B* ends when the company organized by former film studio colleagues is about to close its doors and the four friends are faced with imminent unemployment. In *Be There or Be Square*, Liu Yuan, the central character, is engaged in many professions, but the fact that he can only afford to live in an RV indicates that none of them were profitable. In *Sorry Baby*, the male protagonist's boss is unable to even pay his own driver, since his travel agency business is failing.

Feng's career as a film director is marked with his special attention to his films' performance at the box office, his goal to make films on subjects appealing to an ordinary Chinese audience rather than elite film critics or foreign film festivals, and his ability to strike the chords with the Chinese people. This is due to his familiarity with the hardships that ordinary people face in their daily lives, and the pressures of survival that a small business owner has to endure in running a business.

Feng's directing debut—Gone Forever with My Love

Working as both director and scriptwriter and thus having full control of the medium for the first time, in *Gone Forever with My Love*, Feng demonstrates his expertise in rendering a common love story from an unusual perspective and on the basis of an original mode of narration. In this film, he begins his exploration of a popular cinema that is closely associated with contemporary Chinese society, in which massive industrialization, urbanization, and Westernization have accelerated social change and caused the disintegration of previously well-established values without offering anything in their place. Stories in the film are told from a first-person perspective. The storyteller is a deceased man (speaking in a voice-over) who is remembering the last years of his life—how he meets and falls in love with his girlfriend, his pain in breaking up with her after he learns of his terminal disease, and finally, their reconciliation at his death bed. Although it uses the same title as Wang Shuo's short story, *Gone Forever with My Love*, it is only a loose adaptation.[48] Not only is the whole first half of the film an entirely new story which is vaguely reminiscent of another of Wang's short stories, "Flight Attendant,"[49] the film also has a subtext of cynicism toward the reality and nostalgia of a lost past and love, which are all absent in Wang Shou's stories.

Wang Shuo's Short Story

Wang Shuo's two original works, "Gone Forever with My Love" and "Flight Attendant," both written in the 1980s, represent Wang's early style of innocent sentimentalism, and differ dramatically from the mature style of sardonic cynicism in works such as *Wanr zhu* (Master of Mischief) and *Yidian zhengjing meiyou* (Nothing Serious 一点正经没有), and from the "rebellious spirit and absurdist political dimension of his writing," which caused him to be labeled a "hooligan writer" (*pizi zuojia*). [50] Instead of the anti-heroic depictions of idle ruffians and cynical urban youth mocking established traditions, conventions, and moral values, these two early works feature an idealistic romanticism, in which innocent young people's self-sacrifice and passion for love is more predominant than their witty sarcasm. In Wang's story, *Gone Forever*, He Lei (何雷), a cement truck driver working for a construction company, is going to marry his girlfriend, and co-worker, Shi Jing (石静). As the happy couple is preparing for the wedding, He Lei is diagnosed with myasthenia, an incurable disease that causes muscle debilitation. Knowing that he is not only unable to get married, but also has little time left to live, He Lei decides to break up with Shi Jing by making her believe that he has another lover. Naïvely believing that He Lei is cheating on her, Shi Jing breaks up with He Lei and finds out the truth only after she marries another man. The short story is devoid of any indications of social or political criticism. It elaborates the anguished process of how the dying He Lei suffers not only from physical pain, but also emotional torture as he forces the woman he loves to leave him. In Wang's early works, the male protagonists all once belonged to official socialist institutions—the army, government work units, etc. For example, the central figure in *Flight Attendant* is a navy sailor. In *Gone Forever*, He Lei works for a government-owned construction company. Although he shows an unusual sense of witty humor and occasional cynicism, he is by no means similar to the protagonists in Wang's later works—frustrated unemployed youth, doing whatever they please, and showing disdain for law and social order. On the contrary, He Lei is satisfied with all the benefits he receives as a government employee: a free apartment for his new family, free medical care, and even a friendly relationship with his colleagues and boss. Though not a model worker, not in the PRC sense, he is a good citizen who once bravely rescued an old woman from a fire. Without any sarcasm toward sensitive issues in contemporary Chinese society, or traces of hooliganism in the character-presentation, the tragic life of He Lei in Wang Shuo's version of *Gone Forever* signifies not political or cultural critique, but a universal concern for innocent people's suffering in the face of an unpredictable destiny.

However, in the cinematic version of *Gone Forever*, made by Feng in 1994, the innocent citizen and hard-working government employee in the short story are replaced by a fully fledged antihero typical in Wang's later works, who "ridiculed Chinese intellectuals and the traditional and official notion of morality, decency, and integrity" and "mocked the pretentiousness of the intelligentsia as well as the absurdity of the official ideology." [51] Moreover, the pure love story is subverted by sophisticated commentaries on China's cultural condition and politics. These alterations not only echo the sense of disillusionment and pessimism brought on by the Tian'anmen Incident, but also foreshadow Feng's pursuit of a cinema that features antiheros, marginalized outsiders, and little characters, and tackles problems in Chinese society.

Characters

The male protagonist in the book is a blue-collar worker in a construction company, whereas the male protagonist in the film, whose name is Su Kai, does not belong to a state work unit. When he first meets the female protagonist, he is engaged in the odd job of delivering cars from one location to another across the country, a job that he has no intention of developing into a lifelong career. As a drifter, Su Kai is typical of the characters in Wang's mature works and shares nothing with He Lei but the sincerity of his love and doomed destiny.

Instead of making Su Kai an individual who proved his heroism by rescuing a woman from fire, Feng deconstructs the heroic image of He Lei into a rather pusillanimous urban dweller, who ridicules anything holy and serious, but is a coward in front of the authorities. In the film, Su's first meeting with his girlfriend-to-be, Lin Gege, on a flight where Lin works as a stewardess, is far from romantic. After asking for too many free beers, he gets drunk on the flight and throws up before landing. The detailed depictions of He Lei's tenderness and charisma in the short story are replaced by incidents emphasizing the male protagonist's carelessness and irresponsibility. When a group of police officers, mistaking him for a criminal, rush into the hotel room he is staying in with his girlfriend, Su is so scared that he faints as soon as a policeman points a gun at him. In this scene, the first part vaguely alludes to the army's "mistaken" arrest and killing of innocent citizens during the Tian'anmen Incident, but the latter part deconstructs the image of the victim before any specific references to the true event can be made. Here, what is questioned is not only the incompetence of an authority that mistakes innocent citizens for criminals, but also the "heroism" of the people at whom the guns are pointing. As we will see in the next section, this kind of implicit cynicism toward politics evolves into a ploy of submerging the filmmaker's political commentary under a seemingly non-political story.

Hidden Sociopolitical Commentaries

Under the tightened ideological control of the early 1990s and unapologetic state support for main melody films, *Gone Forever with My Love* reveals an ambivalent attitude in its dealings with politics and the social and cultural problems of the early 1990s. Chen Xiaoming's comment that "politics" was the mysterious other in the Fifth Generation cinema of the 1980s was even more true in the early 1990s, and can also be applied to an analysis of many other contemporary Chinese films. Chen writes, "Politics becomes a highly stylized, stereotyped, complicated, and ambiguous symbol, a hallmark of Chinese cinematic narratology. [In Chinese film] everything is political and nothing is political at one and the same time. Politics is everywhere and yet it subverts itself at any moment."[52]

Feng and Wang's cinematic adaptation represents this paradoxical treatment of themes related to contemporary problems in Chinese society and the political background of the story they are telling. In the film, cynical yet sophisticated commentaries on contemporary Chinese society in the early 1990s have been delicately woven into a seemingly conventional love story. A very specific time frame for the story is indicated through a seemingly insignificant detail—as Su watches the evening news on Chinese Central Television, there is a broadcast of Chairman Jiang Zemin and Vice-Chairman Hu Jintao's meeting with a foreign delegation. This detail provides enough information to locate the story in time because Jiang came to power after the 1989 Tian'anmen Incident and Hu was appointed his successor in the early 1990s. Thus, the original love story has turned into a story of the early 1990s; this temporal location becomes the basis for a reading of social and political issues in the film.

Other details like this in the film suggesting economic and cultural conditions also serve to reinforce an identification with the early 1990s. For example, Su Kai's job of delivering cars for buyers is a profession that can be seen as a by-product of the rapid economic development in the 1980s and 1990s, when private cars, for the first time in the history of the PRC, became a luxury that the newly wealthy could afford. Most of these people, who were said to have "plunged into the sea" (*xiahai* 下海, meaning started their own private business), were self-employed and totally independent from state-owned work units. They started their business as Su Kai does and then found ways of making their fortunes. But all the benefits—free housing and full coverage of medical expenses—that He Lei enjoys as a government employee in the literary version are unavailable to the self-employed Su Kai in the film. Instead, he has to depend on himself for everything, from earning a living to building a house for his future family. The difference reveals an irony that the Party's alleged goal of improving people's living conditions, advocated by Communist leaders such as Deng Xiaoping, often had to be fulfilled by people themselves.

These details not only orient the audience temporally, they also express the filmmakers' critiques of social and cultural issues in a relatively implicit way. In other words, the 1994 adaptation broke free from the conventional love story of the earlier literary work and provided the audience with both passionate love and hidden, potentially subversive, political messages.

The film also hints at a nationwide materialistic fever in which any lawful or unlawful act was justified by profitability. Whereas Su Kai has to work day-in and day-out to make ends meet, some government employees are making quick money from selling state property. Su purchases the land to build his house from an old man who seems to be assigned by the workplace to take care of the supposed state-owned land. In the film, not only are individual citizens making their fortunes by breaking the law, the government also spares no effort in making profits through apparently illegal means. When selling his apartment to get enough money for the land, Su recounts the history of the building to the buyer. The audience learns that the building was owned by one of Su's ancestors in the late Qing dynasty, when he was a colleague of the famous official Li Hongzhang. Then Su just brushes over the fate of the building during the 1950s: "Then, you know what happened. Now, what has been left for me is just this living room." The underlying message could not be more obvious for anyone familiar with the history of the PRC. In the early 1950s, when the Communist Party had just come into power, thousands of private entities—factories, shops, restaurants, and houses— became state property in the process of socialist transformation. If this information was only meant to provide some background information on Su's family, then the buyer's reply, making a direct association with China's current situation, expresses a more acute commentary on the commercialization in society. He says that he gets some inside information that the government will soon turn this whole building into a historical site to attract foreign visitors. The reason he wants to purchase Su's living room is that he is planning to remodel it into a first-class restroom for these foreign visitors. Not free, but clean and comfortable in comparison to other public restrooms in Beijing, it would surely be able generate a great deal of foreign money.

These seemingly simple plots can be perceived as both political and apolitical. For many ordinary viewers, the film is a love story and these scenes are likely to be neglected as insignificant transitions or linkages to support the narrative logic. But for more sophisticated audiences, these details are actually loaded with cynical social and political commentaries. They imply that some people's family property has been confiscated by the government and never returned, while government officials make fortunes selling state-owned land. Also, the government renovates historical buildings only to attract foreign money, rather than to preserve Chinese culture. The film reveals the crudity of the early years of the PRC and exposes the pervasiveness of corruption among government officials in contemporary China. But more than this, it demonstrates that the whole nation, from the government to the individual citizen, is urgently turning almost everything into a commodity as they attempt to profit from the transformation from a socialist planned economy to a capitalist market economy. Although hidden under an idealistic and romantic love story, these references in the film are already a grand gesture through which the filmmakers express their concerns about the contemporary conditions of Chinese society after the political turmoil of 1989 and the unprecedented pace of economic reform.

Nostalgia of Love and the Past

One effect of the rapid economic development in the early 1990s was a physical transformation of the Beijing cityscape, where both Wang and Feng grew up. Given this background, the film also articulates a strong sense of a kind of nostalgia that is generated by "social and cultural forces [that] gave many people a means with which to deal with the schizophrenic realities of the nation."[53] As part of a generation who were the younger brothers and sisters of the idealistic, but iconoclastic Red Guards, Wang and Feng neither fully embraced political rhetoric, nor experienced a strong sense of disillusionment. Furthermore, having grown up in Beijing during the Cultural Revolution, their memories of adolescence are closely associated with this city and the heroic images of PLA soldiers and patriotism that dominated the media.[54] However, the materialism and consumerism brought on by the rapid economic development after the Cultural Revolution increased the pace of urbanization. In the early 1990s, the Beijing City Municipal Government issued a document, "Beijing chengshi zongti guihua (1991-2010)" (Overall Planning of Beijing from 1991 to 2010, 北京城市总体规划), which envisioned that within 20 years, the city of Beijing would be transformed into "an international and modern metropolis."[55] At the same time, in order to preserve the traditional architectural style of Beijing, the city also promoted the notion of "Reviving Beijing's Features as a Historical City" (*duohui gudu fengmao* 夺回古都风貌). As the two principles were implemented in new construction of the early 1990s, the resulting products were extremely disappointing, characterized by massive Western-style building with totally inappropriate traditional Chinese-style roofs. For instance, along Beijing's most famous street, Changan Avenue, the buildings of the Department of Transportation, the Women's Recreation Center, and the Museum of

Chinese Art and Craft are all in this style. A Chinese architect's comment on this style is very representative: "a skyscraper topped with a Chinese pavilion, neither fish nor fowl."[56] In this process, the city of Feng and Wang's innocent memories was gradually lost to development. As Wang Shuo writes in the very beginning of his short story, "Furious Animals" (Dongwu xiongmeng 动物凶猛):[57]

> I envy those people who come from the countryside. In their memory exists a hometown that generates endless memories. Although this hometown may in reality be a destitute and not poetic place, if they wish, they still can imagine that something that they lost still could be found in that anonymous hometown...
>
> Everything in the city has changed rapidly—houses, streets and people's dress and conversations...
>
> Nothing is left. Everything is stripped clean.

The literary and cinematic works of Wang and Feng concentrate on the urban life of the city and express nostalgia for the old Beijing of the 1970s. This approach to the past and memory differentiates them greatly from the previous generation of filmmakers, who had a critical attitude toward issues related to China's past, history, and politics. The sense of nostalgia also permeated in films such as *Yellow Earth* (Huang tudi; dir. Chen Kaige, 1984), *King of Children* (Haizi wang; dir. Chen Kaige), and *Red Sorghum* (Hong gaoliang; dir. Zhang Yimou, 1988), but was directed toward remote rural areas of China where these directors had been sent as so-called "educated youth" during the Cultural Revolution.[58] As Dai Jinhua argues, the "Wang Shuo Clan" (filmmakers who worked with Wang Shuo or adapted his works, including directors Zhao Baogang and Feng Xiaogang) demonstrated a "metaphoric imagined nostalgia," which "transpose[s] the space of nostalgia from the rural countryside of the 1980s to the anonymous metropolis of the 1990s."[59] In the film, the strong sense of nostalgia derived from Wang's writing is rendered with Feng's own predilections and later became a recurring theme in his films of the later 1990s.

In *Gone Forever*, beautiful scenes of nature contrast sharply with the disorder and dinginess of the city. Warm tones, high-key lighting, and lyrical music are accompanied by neatly composed long takes of nature. Most of these picturesque scenes are also locations where the two protagonists experienced many beautiful moments—love, reunion, their first kiss, etc. When the two return to the city, the mise-en-scene is always composed of disordered rooms, dilapidated buildings, and the indifferent faces of urban people. In the film, the city, representing reality, is a crude place where only unpleasant things happen—Su Kai's unhappy meeting with his girlfriend's mother; devastating news from an apathetic doctor telling Su about his illness. The city is also a place from which the two protagonists seek to escape. Once the two decide to get married, they buy land far away from the city and build a new house to start a new life.

The sense of nostalgia is also extended to Feng's rendition of the love story. Opening with a male voice-over telling the audience that he is remembering the last years before his death, the whole story is told from the perspective of the already deceased Su Kai—the love is lost forever and the past is irretrievable. The film's last take is a crane shot pulling up from a sweet and harmonious scene depicting the happy life of Lin Gege and her friends; it ends with Su's voice-over, "I love you my dear and I miss the life with you so much…" In many scenes, Su Kai's melancholic voice-over interrupts the narrative and comments on the ongoing action in the film, expressing his happiness or sadness as he tells the story. The whole story is structured as a dead man's retrospective on earthly life. Borrowing the basic storyline of Wang Shuo's literary version but changing its direct, third-person narrative to first-person flashback, Feng accentuates the sense of tragedy and nostalgia experienced by ordinary people in an era of social flux. These sentiments echo with Chinese people's experiences after the bloody night on June Fourth and in the face of a sudden inundation of commercialization and materialism brought by economic transformation.

As Feng's directing debut, the film *Gone Forever with My Love* also foreshadows obsessions that recur in his more mature works: the "little character's" hardships as they strive to survive outside mainstream society; the nostalgia for a lost and innocent time filled with promises, heroism, and peace; and commentary on the side-effects brought by the surging expansion of commercialization and materialism.

Three TV Productions—At the Edge of the Underground

After Wang Shuo left Good Dream, Feng started to work with other writers on new projects. *Chicken Feathers on the Ground* (Yidi jimao, 1995, scriptwriter and dir. Feng Xiaogang) is a ten-episode TV drama adapted from Liu Zhenyun's two short stories, "Work Units" (Danwei) and "Chicken Feathers on the Ground" (Yidi jimao). *Behind the Moon* (Yueliang bei mian; dir. Feng Xiaogang, 1996) is a ten-episode TV drama based on Wang Gang's novel of the same title. *Elegy for Love* (Qing shang; dir. Feng Xiaogang) is also a ten-episode TV drama. Both writers later became the main scriptwriters for Feng's film projects. Liu Zhenyun wrote the script for *Cell Phone*, while Wang Gang was one of the scriptwriters of *A World Without Thieves*. Along with the film *Gone Forever with My Love*, these works either highlight social issues such as government corruption and injustices suffered in an increasingly hierarchical society or feature heightened emotions embedded in ordinary Chinese people's daily life. Although dealing with different subjects, they all tend to convey some classical and grandeur themes such as love, betrayal and redemption. Throughout Feng's career, he has never been so overtly critical to social issues and depravity of human nature, but the failure in gaining approval from the censors for exhibition of these works suggests the impossibility of such works existing in Chinese popular culture at that time; it also contributed to the shift to light-hearted comedy later in Feng's filmmaking career.

Behind the Moon features an ambitious young couple enticed by extravagant materialism and easy profits. The work is permeated by a mood of pessimism and desperation: it begins with a scene in which the husband is about to be executed and ends with the husband's flashback in which we learn that his wife has committed suicide. Reminiscent of *film noir*, the style of *Behind the Moon* features a contrast of bright and dark lighting, great patches of shadow in the mise-en-scène, and a mood of foreboding conveyed by the background music. Rather than portraying the couple as ruthless and greedy criminals, the work casts them in a more sympathetic light. The couple's destiny is blamed primarily on false promises of economic prosperity, on social inequality, and government corruption. The production was sponsored by a private company and, therefore, did not have any problems with censorship in its early stages of production. However, when the completed version was submitted to MRFT, its direct criticism of social problems and sympathetic attitude toward the two criminals led to a ban on its release on Chinese television.[60]

Chicken Feathers on the Ground tells the story of how a recent college graduate, Xiao Lin, who is stuck in a small unit of a government department, is perplexed and disgusted by the bureaucratic routine and power struggles in the office and the trivialness of ordinary life but finally assimilated into it. Although *Chicken Feathers on the Ground* passed the censors, it was still not allowed to be aired on TV stations in major cities such as Beijing.

Unlike the other two stories, *Elegy of Love* does not comment on contemporary social issues; rather, it is a touching story about love and self-sacrifice. A happy couple's life is shattered when the husband, a violinist, is severely injured and passes into a coma. The wife, in order to get enough money to support her husband, accepts a rich businessman's proposition to become his mistress. Another man, also in love with the wife, generously helps her in dealing with her problems, but asks nothing in return. When the husband wakes up, he has lost the ability to play the violin and, sensing the changes in his wife's life, leaves for the remote countryside to become a music teacher for peasant children. Even though the only one of Feng's early productions not to encounter significant trouble with censorship, this TV drama's poetic and lyrical style did not attract much attention from distributors. Assigned to a midnight slot on several local TV stations, this work soon passed into oblivion.

The two film projects, *Living a Miserable Life* and *I Am Your Dad*, which will be discussed in more details in the next chapter, encountered enormous difficulties during production and distribution and were either forced to abort or denied licenses for distribution. The failure of these two works led directly to the collapse of Good Dream in 1995 and forced Feng Xiaogang to abandon films of social criticism and explore a new way to survive as a filmmaker. As Feng writes in his 1995 autobiography, when his film projects had to be aborted one after another due to negative feedback from the censorship board, he almost decided to make underground films.[61]

Conclusion

These works discussed in this chapter represent the formative years of Feng's career. In this period, he participated in the production of several very successful TV dramas and films, and his collaborations with renowned Chinese writers and filmmakers, such as Wang Shuo and Zheng Xiaolong, laid a foundation for his later films. In works that Feng produced independently during this period, he started to explore his own style, a style characterized by a concern for current social and cultural problems conveyed through the stories of little characters, and implicit and explicit cynicism similar to that found in Wang Shuo's writing. In his TV dramas from this period, Feng touches upon sensitive social issues, some of which were so controversial that they finally led to a ban on the work. Nonetheless, this foreshadows his obsession with making films that are not only entertaining, but also express a "social conscience." The failure of these works in the face of censorship resulted in a more cautious attitude towards critiques of China's society and politics.

This period was also important in forcing Feng to respond creatively to a dynamic political and economic situation. When state sponsorship mostly went to productions of main melody films, Feng have to act as a businessman to find funding for his own films. During the period, he made use of different modes of production ranging from co-production with state film studios, production with televisions companies, and independent production. In the process of working for the Good Dream company, he experienced the hardships of running a private entertainment enterprise in contemporary China. His company had to deal with difficulties arising from unstable financial support, competition with state-supported film or TV projects, and a lack of artistic freedom due to heightened ideological control.

Overall, in this period, his pursuit of a popular cinema that would be both welcomed by audiences and profitable, his attention to the living conditions of ordinary people, and his exploration of ways to express his social and political critiques without offending the censors, were all influenced by the socio-political context and his personal experiences in the early 1990s. Important themes and subjects in his early works, such as his concerns for the fate of little characters and implicit criticism of social issues, recur, with some variations, in his later works.

4

New Year Films and Chinese Cinema at the End of the 1990s

Introduction

The emergence of New Year films in 1996 was accompanied by the growing importance of private film production companies. This can be explained by transformations in the Chinese film industry brought about by industry reform, and changes in official film policy linked to the government's ambivalent attitude toward the function of the cinema—cinema was viewed as both a profitable business that should develop according to market demand, and a pedagogical tool that should be controlled by the Party in order to propagate official ideology and a positive Party image. The formation and increasing popularity of this genre can be seen as a result of Feng Xiaogang's creative struggle for survival under pressure from censorship, profit-imperatives, as well as from challenges from newly imported Hollywood blockbuster films.

This chapter begins with an introduction of the general situation of Chinese cinema in the second half of the 1990s. This period was heavily influenced by two significant events—the importation of Hollywood films in 1995, which cast enormous challenges for Chinese domestic productions, and the Changsha Conference in March 1996, in which ideological rectitude was reasserted as the basis for the further development of domestic films. This will be followed by an examination of the impact of these events on Chinese domestic films, including a decline in domestic film production, the "entertainmentization" of main melody films, and the emergence of a popular cinema. The largest part of this chapter focuses on the emergence and stylistic/thematic characteristics of Feng Xiaogang's New Year films. These films were products of industry reform, but were also keenly responsive to contemporary urban culture and the need for strategic compromises in the economically liberal, but ideologically restricted world of cinema.

The Situation of Domestic Film Production in the Second Half of the 1990s

The year 1995, before Feng's first New Year film, is noteworthy in bringing out the sort of paradox common in Chinese film history—scholars and critics referred to this year pessimistically as the "Chinese Filmmaker's Last Revelry,"[1] or optimistically as "an exceptional peak"[2] or, more simply, "a year of hope and danger."[3] Having experienced a continuous decline in attendance and box-office revenue since 1989, Chinese cinema for the first time in six years showed promising signs of revival. Box-office revenues in 1995 witnessed an increase of 15 percent over revenues in 1994.[4] Although part of the increase can be attributed to the entrance of Hollywood imports into China in 1995, many domestic productions also had excellent performances at the box office. For example, Jiang Wen's directorial debut, *In the Heat of the Sun* (Yangguang canlan de rizi; 姜文, 1995) had revenues as high as RMB 4 million in Beijing and Shanghai. Only a couple of months later, Ye Daying's *Red Cherry* (Hong yingtao; dir. Ye Daying, 1995) broke the record by earning RMB 10 million in Shanghai and Beijing. Even an art film, *King of Lanling* (Lanling wang; dir. Hu Xuehua 胡雪桦, 1995) a mythical story with little dialogue and a very lyrical style, made RMB 1.6 million during its first week of screening in only six movie theaters in Shanghai.[5] Other films such as *Red Flush* (Hong fen; dir. Li Shaohong, 1995), *Shanghai Triad* (Yao a yao, yao dao wai po qiao; dir. Zhang Yimou, 1995), and *July Seventh Incident* (Qi qi shibian; dir. Li Qiankuan 李前宽 and Xiao Guiyun 肖桂云, 1995) also performed very well at the box office.

Several internal and external factors contributed to the seemingly promising prosperity of Chinese cinema in 1995. First of all, economic reforms that had begun in the 1980s by targeting the distribution-exhibition sectors were beginning, in the early 1990s, to focus more fundamentally on pushing the state-owned studios to the forefront of commercialization. With limited state sponsorship, and an enormous burden from overstaffing, many studios had to rely for their earnings on the sale of licenses to private productions companies or the collection of "management fees" from co-productions with foreign studios.[6] Therefore, in the mid-1990s, even though the ownership of film production studios was still in the hands of the state, films produced by private or semi-private production companies demonstrated a great potential for success in the film market. Most of the successful films mentioned above were produced by non-state film production companies. For example, *Red Cherry* was made by the director's own production company Shishi (时事公司), while *In the Heat of the Sun* was a co-production of China Film

Corporation and Ganglong Film Production Company. Only *July Seventh Incident* was produced solely under state sponsorship. If the non-government productions in the early 1990s were a strong undercurrent largely ignored by film officials and critics, by the mid-1990s they began to move to the center of national attention.

An important external force also began to show its influence in 1995. In 1994, the Chinese Film Import and Export Corporation signed a contract with major Hollywood studios to import ten Hollywood films each year with a promise to raise the quota gradually until China's entry into the World Trade Organization, after which Hollywood would be allowed to export films to China without any restrictions or quotas. In 1995, ten Hollywood blockbusters, including *True Lies* and *The Fugitive*, entered Chinese movie theaters, bringing with them both "hope and danger" for Chinese cinema. Hollywood blockbusters attracted audiences back to movie theaters, and thus functioned as a driving force in the rejuvenation of a weak film market. Attendance had waned since the early 1990s and had shown a significant decline of 60% in 1993, but the impressive box-office revenue of the Hollywood films showed a resurgence of audience interest.[7] *True Lies* had revenues of RMB 8 million in Beijing and 13 million in Shanghai; Jackie Chan's film *Rumble in the Bronx* (Hong fan qu; dir. Stanley Tong, 1995) broke a record with revenues of RMB 3 million in Guangzhou.

In spite of the promise offered by these two forces, the prosperity of the film industry did not last long. After 1996, annual production of domestic films declined significantly from 110 films in 1996 to only about 80 films at the end of the 1990s. In the first six months of 1996, none of the films that were exhibited in movie theaters in Beijing gained box-office revenues of more than RMB 1 million. The major underlying reasons for this new decline in domestic filmmaking were the art officials' stress on ideological control of film content as evidenced at the Changsha Conference, and the ever-growing impact of Hollywood imports on domestic productions.

Industry Reform and the Changsha Conference

After the issuing of "Document No. Three" in 1993, initiating reforms in distribution and ticket pricing, several important official documents regarding film production followed. In 1995, MRFT issued a "Policy and Regulation on Reforming Production and Administration of Feature Films," which dismantled the sixteen state-owned film studios' monopoly over film production and allowed licensed state-owned local or film institutions from thirteen provinces to produce films.[8] In 1997, another MRFT document,

"Announcement of Issuing License for Single Feature Film Production," further opened the sector of film production to all state film production institutions. Although these reform measures ended monopolies over film production by allowing the participation of all qualified state film production institutions, none of the reform measures included private film companies. The autonomy that private film companies enjoyed was still extremely limited, because they still had no right to produce a film independently. In order to obtain a license for film production, private film companies had to co-produce their own films with state film companies by buying a license and paying management fees. Furthermore, although the economic potential of private film companies had been recognized in the film market of 1995, their filmmaking was still not legitimated by the authorities and remained under close surveillance through film censorship. Film officials continued to show their strong support for main melody films by requesting that China Film Company give these films priority in distribution and exhibition; no similar attention was paid to the development of private film companies.[9] The reinforcement of a conservative film policy was advocated at a conference of Chinese filmmakers held in March 1996 in Changsha, the capital of Hunan Province. This conference was attended not only by directors from major film studios, but also the Minister of Propaganda, Ding Guangen, the Minister of Culture, Liu Zhongde, and the Minister of Radio, Film and Television, Sun Jiazheng.

The so-called "Changsha Conference" was intended to rejuvenate domestic film production in the face of the Hollywood invasion by enhancing the quality of films. For this purpose, a project labeled "9550" was initiated. The goal was to produce fifty "excellent films" (*jingpin*) within the five years of the "Ninth Five-Year-Plan," an average of 10 films "excellent films" a year, a number that coincides with the number of films imported from Hollywood starting 1995. However, when it came to the question of which films should be considered "excellent", film officials promoted ideological rectitude as the criteria of foremost importance. Ding Guangen of the Ministry of Propaganda stressed in his talk that "films should have the function of making audiences love the Party and their socialist country, rather than arousing their concern and dissatisfaction; films should advocate justice prevailing over evil rather than pessimistic sentiments, and should bring happiness and beauty to the audiences, rather than wasting their time on absurdity and fabricated plots."[10] This conservative guidance of Chinese cinema, stressing the pedagogical and moralizing functions of cinema, neglected cinema's other roles as a form of entertainment, social criticism, personal/artistic expression and etc. Because of the reinforcement of this policy, some films that did not fit into Ding's standard of "excellent films," such as Wang Shuo's *I Am Your Dad* and Feng Xiaogang's *Living A Miserable Life*, were banned. According to Feng's recollection, among the twenty films made by Beijing Film Studio in 1996, eight did not pass the censors.[11] From the MRFT's list of the "important" (*zhongdian*) films of 1996, four subject matters appear to have been particularly supported by the MRFT: history, children, peasants, and the army. For example, *Zheng Chenggong* (Zheng chenggong; dir. Lu Weiguo 鲁卫国) is a film about the Ming Dynasty general who liberated Taiwan from Dutch colonists; *Liu Hulan* (Liu Hulan; dir. Shen Yaoting 沈耀庭, 1997) is a biographical film about a communist peasant girl who was killed by a warlord during the civil war; *Crane Kids* (He tong; dir. Ge Xiaoying, 葛晓英) tells the story of how three country boys protected several cranes in their village.[12] All of these films accentuated certain heightened emotions, such as patriotism, loyalty to the Party and love for nature; none exposed issues or problems or rendered any criticism, and only a few dealt with urban subjects. The annual film production of 1996 declined from more than 145 films in 1995 to only 110 films, the lowest point since 1990. Except for a couple of films whose tickets were purchased by state departments with the intention of implementing "political education," most of these films flopped in the market. On a list of the most successful films at market compiled by managers of major Chinese movie theaters, only three were the "important films" supported by the MRFT.[13]

Hollywood Imports

As for the impact of Hollywood imports, although they lured audiences back to the movie theaters, most domestic films, with meager production budgets averaging only about RMB 400,000 per film, had little hope of competing successfully with the multi-million dollar American productions. As a result, although several domestic films met with success in 1995, most domestic films became increasingly unappealing to audiences who gradually became accustomed to the high production quality of Hollywood blockbusters. The annual domestic film production of 1995 and 1996 was around 100 films per year; however, these films received only 30 percent of box office revenues, while the other 70 percent went to Hollywood imports. During the 45 days that *Titanic* was screened in Beijing, it earned about US$ 4 million US dollars at the box office, equivalent to 30 percent of Beijing's film market revenue that year.[14] In the late 1990s, an underground market of cheap pirated versions of Hollywood films at an average price of RMB 7 or 8 per film resulted in the flooding of Hollywood cinema throughout China. Given all this, the

Hollywood invasion generated both enthusiasm and alarm in Chinese cinema; its attractions seemed at once irresistible and disturbing.

Facing continued ideological control and the Hollywood invasion, 1997 marked the beginning of important transformations in Chinese cinema. For one thing, the inefficient promotion of main melody films and the rise of non-political entertainment films made the problem of how to control the Party's image an increasingly challenging task for Party cultural leaders. Therefore, stylistically, in the late 1990s main melody films began to break with the socialist realist style and assimilate features of the popular entertainment cinema. At the same time, transformations were also taking place in entertainment films. Because of these filmmakers' concurrent considerations of profit and unpleasant encounters with censorship, entertainment films began to show an increasingly supportive stance toward Party rhetoric. Thus, Chinese popular cinema at the end of the 1990s, exemplified by Feng's New Year films, show a kind of "doubleness"—its messages were often imposed or tightly controlled by the hegemony of state-sponsored filmmaking, but it still more-or-less served as a "voice" of the people.

"Entertainmentization" of main melody film

Revived after 1989 and reaching a peak of production in the early 1990s, main melody films began to undergo a transformation in the middle of the 1990s. Although the basic doctrine of these films continued unchanged through the 1990s, several changes can be witnessed in character, subject matter, and style. First, the "typage" in characters and events of the previous main melody films was replaced by more humanistic and naturalistic depictions of the protagonists. For example, *Choice Between Life and Death* (Shengsi jueze; dir. Yu Benzheng 孙本正 and Zhang Ping 张平, 2000) features a city mayor who is not only a loyal and virtuous Party cadre, but also a "family man"— a loving husband and father. The movie tells the story of his decisive struggle in a case of official corruption that involved his wife. In these "softer" main melody films, although the protagonists are still surrogates of official ideology, most of them are of a rather humble social status rather than members of the top leadership of the country. Furthermore, even though the messages that are being conveyed in these films are intended to be politically pedagogical, most of them are rendered under the cover of a seemingly totally apolitical story. Starting in the middle of the 1990s, the long list of winners of the Huabiao Award for Best Films, an official film award sponsored by MRFT and reflecting the criteria of film officials, began to include films which were not typical of the main melody stories directly related to real historical figures and events. For example, *Live in Peace* (An jü; dir. Hu Bingliu 胡柄榴, 1997) is a story of an elderly lady who offers all her life savings to help her maid, a young peasant girl, open a small restaurant. *Dark Eyes* (Hei yanjing; dir. Chen Guoxing 陈国星, 1997) is a story about a blind athlete whose life is dedicated to her career. While still consistent with Party propaganda, these films do not directly glorify the Party and its leaders, but promote more broadly humanistic virtues such as patriotism, self-sacrifice, and loyalty in ordinary Chinese people. For example, *Country Teacher* (Fenghuang qin; dir. He Qun 何群, 1994) portrays the sacrifices made by several country teachers as they teach poor peasant children in remote, impoverished villages and their perseverance in bringing not only knowledge, but also patriotism to their students. A 1995 film, *The Accused Uncle Shan Gang* (Beigao Shangang ye; dir. Fan Yuan 范元, 1995), concerns a case of whether an old Party secretary in the village should be held responsible for the death of a woman who committed suicide after being ordered by the secretary to submit to public viewing as punishment for her mistreatment of her mother-in-law. Both films were highly praised by film officials as good examples of main melody films of the middle of the 1990s.[15] In style, main melody films abandoned their emphasis on dialogue and theatrical qualities such as frontality, stationary camera work, and long takes, high-key lighting, and began to borrow such methods as fast-pace editing, last-minute rescue, realism in mise-en-scene, and multi-line narrative. In the meantime, cinematic novelties, such as three-dimensional animation and special effects were also being incorporated into main melody films. The 2003 film, *Stormy Sea* (Jingtao hailing; dir. Zhai Junjie 翟俊杰), a story depicting the heroic rescue of people from a severe flood by soldiers of the People's Liberation Army in June 1998, makes extensive use of computer graphics and 3-D animation in scenes depicting enormous waves, and villages and people being swept away by the flood. With the help of Tsinghua University technicians, seven-and-a-half minutes of special effects were added to thirty-five scenes. The film was awarded the Golden Rooster for Best Special Effects in 2003.[16] However, despite these transformations in subject matter and style, main melody films continued to receive substantial government support for distribution and promotion and recognition at domestic film festivals. From the list below, it is clear that almost every year, the winner of the Golden Rooster for Best Film was a main melody film.

- 1990, *Founding of the Nation*
- 1991, *Jiao Yulu*
- 1992, *Decisive Engagement*
- 1993, *Story of Qiuju*
- 1994, *Country Teachers*

- 1995, *The Accused Uncle Shan Gang*
- 1996, *Red Cherry*
- 1997, *Opium War*
- 1998, *Live in Peace*
- 1999, *Postman in the Mountain*
- 2000, *Choice Between Life and Death*
- 2001, *Mao Zedong in 1925*
- 2002, *Beautiful Big Feet; Rushing out of Amazon*
- 2003, *Warm; A Stormy Sea*

For example, *Choice Between Life and Death*, a film about the government's anti-corruption campaign, attained record profits of RMB 50 million at the box office,[17] the highest among all Chinese films in 2000. However, some film leaders realized that this "success" at the box office was only nominal. One film official even admitted that the high box-office income of *Choice Between Life and Death* could actually be attributed to the fact that the majority of the tickets were purchased by government work units, schools, and universities and distributed to their employees or students as a form of political education.[18] Although still functioning as mouthpieces of the government and propagating the government's new policies and heroic models, or simply legitimating the status quo, the changing face of main melody films suggests a concurrent transformation in the Party art policy, specifically, a switch from the glorification of Party and state leaders and heroic representations of major events in the history of the CCP and PRC to broader themes stressing humanistic virtues such as patriotism, hard-work, self-sacrifice, and loyalty. While main melody films began to retreat from their politically dogmatic position and compromise with some of the trends in entertainment films, non-political films, such as art films of Fifth Generation directors and entertainment films, began to move toward state positions. Their earlier attitudes of criticism and cynicism towards social issues were less pronounced, while the messages conveyed in these films became more supportive of official policy.

Assimilation to the Mainstream: Popular Cinema in the Late 1990s

In the second half of the 1990s, filmmakers who were not financially supported by the state still sought alternative modes of production. However, the fact that their funding came from various non-governmental sources did not prevent these films from becoming more entertaining and less politically critical. This trend can be seen clearly in the films of the Fifth Generation directors, whose film productions relied first primarily on foreign capital, then on domestic production companies.

As Hollywood began to export its films to the domestic Chinese market, it also began to be involved in Chinese film productions. Their first bankable stars in China were the already internationally famous Fifth Generation directors. Zhang Yimou's *Hero* (Yingxiong, 2002) was produced by Miramax, Chen Kaige's *Temptress of Moon* (Feng yue, 1996) was financed by a Hong Kong company, and *Together* (He ni zai yiqi, 2003) received investment from Sony. Although these films had adequate financial support and advanced filmmaking equipment, the demands for maximization of profit meant that they were inevitably designed as profit-generating tools. As a result, the center of the filmmaking process became the producer, rather than the director. The producer, representing investors and foreign studios, supervised every aspect of filmmaking from shooting to editing, and retained authority over the final cut. Under the impact of this mode of production, films of the Fifth Generation began to become less political and more commercialized. Priority was placed on pleasing audiences and meeting market demands, while the filmmakers' own intentions had to be compromised if they might impair box-office revenue. Chen Kaige had to re-edit *The Emperor and the Assassin* (Ci qing, 1999) after the initial viewing by critics and the press because many felt that the structure and narrative of the film were incomprehensible. When promoting the film *Hero* (2003) in an interview with CCTV (China Central Television), Zhang Yimou commented that the version of his final cut of the film was around 120 minutes, but because of the demands of the producer from Miramax, who pointed out that an American audience's interest in foreign language subtitled films usually lasted no more than 90 minutes, Zhang had to cut 30 minutes from the original version. In addition to changes in structure and length, many of these filmmakers abandoned the politically critical stance that had characterized their earlier films. The adoption of a critical political stance was very likely to cause troubles with the censors and thus posed the risk that the films might not reach the market. As a result, films by Fifth Generation directors in the second half of the 1990s began to share with other films a similar ambition to achieve good market performance and avoidance of controversial subjects. For example, after making *Farewell My Concubine* in 1993, whose retrospective of the Chinese people's painful experiences during the previous decades of social flux and political campaigns had caused censorship delays, Chen Kaige's next four films—*The Emperor and The Assassin, Temptress Moon* (Feng yue, 1996), *Killing Me Softly* (2002), and *Together* (He ni zai yiqi, 2002)—steered clear of overt criticism and retrospection. Rather, they featured thrilling suspense (*Killing Me Softly*), a story of a father's self sacrifice for his talented son (*Together*), and themes of love and betrayal (*Temptress Moon*). As the Fifth Generation's films became less political, they became increasingly commercialized throughout the early 2000s; this shift will be discussed further in Chapter 5.

The semi-independent or co-dependent cinema, which consisted primarily of films produced by private film production companies and distributed by state-owned sectors, also began to explore ways of making films that were attractive to film audiences and inoffensive to film authorities. Though privately produced, these films were still required to gain approval for exhibition from the censors, and to obtain a license from a state-owned studio in order to enter distribution channels. Therefore, nominally, these films were co-productions with the state film studios. Unlike state-sponsored films, these films had a diversity in their subject matters. However, because they relied on state film studios for distribution and remained under the surveillance of film censorship, any explicit criticism on sensitive issues could cause troubles with censorship and thus a loss at the box office. This issue was of considerably more importance for these private filmmakers than it was for Fifth Generation filmmakers who enjoyed adequate financial support from foreign investors and access to overseas markets. Films by private companies had to rely on a relatively restricted budget during production and a limited domestic film market. As a result, their survival demanded that they both make profits and cooperate with officialdom.

Although these films were mostly in the genres of comedy, romance, and urban melodrama, it was inevitable that they merge with the genres once identified most strongly with main melody films. Ye Daying's films, *Red Cherry* (Hong yingtao, 1995) and *Once Upon a Time in China* (Hongse lianren, 1998), made by his own production company and relatively successful at the box office, are good examples of this merger. The winner of Golden Rooster Film Award of Best Film of 1996, *Red Cherry*, a story of two orphans' experiences during World War II, appears to just take a humanistic approach to the question of individual suffering during the war. But these children's unusual backgrounds—both had parents who were high-ranking Chinese communist officials who had died during the civil war—and their constant recounting of their parents' heroic acts serve to emphasize the dedication of elite Chinese communists to the Chinese revolution, a hallmark of many main melody films. In *Once Upon a Time in China*, a young college student, the daughter of an officer in the Shanghai secret police, falls in love with an underground Communist and helps him to escape from her father's persecution. With the popular Hong Kong movie star, Leslie Cheung, playing the role of the underground Communist, this story of doomed love also draws attention to the trials and sacrifices endured by lovers for the sake of revolution. A similar mode of setting sentimental melodramatic stories against the background of China's revolution, and combining ordinary people's personal experiences with large themes such as patriotism, self-sacrifice, and collectivism can also be found in such films as *Days Without Lei Feng* (Likai leifeng de rizi; dir. Lei Xianhe 雷献禾, 1997), *Red River Valley* (Hong hegu; dir. Feng Xiaoning 冯小宁, 1997) and *Love Story by the Yellow River* (Huanghe juelian; dir. Feng Xiaoning, 1999). Because of the specific socio-political context, most of the films have a cooperative, rather than challenging, attitude to the official rhetoric about China's current situation, revolution, history, and the Party. Feng Xiaogang's New Year Films are also good examples of this kind of film and will be examined in detail below.

An Invisible Landscape—Underground Cinema

The third category of filmmaking, underground cinema, sometimes labeled Sixth Generation, was nearly invisible for ordinary Chinese audiences in the late 1990s. Because this group of film academy graduates lacked either the opportunity or desire to make films within the official film production system, most of them made films that did not rely on any official filmmaking entities and were usually funded by their own or their friends' savings. They did not bother to obtain distribution and exhibition licenses from state film studios; as a result, these films were inaccessible to ordinary Chinese audiences. However, in the early 2000s, these works began to attract the attention of foreign film critics and international film festivals. Lou Ye's *Suzhou River* won the Tiger Award at the 2000 Rotterdam International Film Festival and Wang Xiaoshuai's *Beijing Bicycle* won the Silver Bear at the Berlin International Film Festival in 2003. Also in the early 2000s, when a more democratic atmosphere revived in the Chinese cinema, these filmmakers surfaced from the underground, joined mainstream filmmaking, and began to be noticed by domestic audiences. Although the influence of these filmmakers on Chinese cinema of the 1990s was relatively insignificant, they demonstrate the promising potential for Chinese film in the 2000s.

This group of filmmakers' cinematic styles took form in the 1990s. In *Xiaoshan Returns Home* (Xiaoshan huijia, ca. 1996) and *Xiaowu* (Xiaowu, 1997), Jia Zhangke developed his own cinematic style characterized by the use of non-professional actors and hand-held camera and stories of people living in urbanized rural areas and marginalized by a rapidly transforming society. Wang Xiaoshuai's films, such as *The Days* (Dongchun de gushi, 1993) and *Frozen* (Jidu hanleng, 1996), although following more conventional filmmaking technique—steady camera, well-framed composition, and, sometimes, professional acting—express his concerns for a reality that provides marginalized people with more illusory than real benefits. Although the production value of these films could not compete with that of the state production companies, they willingly did what mainstream filmmakers were unable or refused to do, especially in terms of addressing controversial subjects such as poverty and class discrepancy and drawing attention to people from the lower levels of society. However, starting at the end of the 1990s, more and more independent filmmakers have been able to move out of the peripheries toward the center and enter the official filmmaking system. In some cases, making a successful independent film has become a passport for entry into the mainstream. Beginning the early 2000s, some Sixth Generation filmmakers, such as Luo Ye, Zhang Yuan, Jia Zhangke, and Wang Xiaoshuai, began to collaborate with state film studios or commercial film production companies and make films that gained access to domestic audiences. A discussion of the Sixth Generation's role in Chinese cinema will be developed in Chapter 5.

Emergence of New Year Celebration Films

Decline of Good Dream — Culmination of Conflict with Censorship

The 1996 collapse of Feng Xiaogang and Wang Shuo's company, Good Dream TV and Film Production and Consulting, demonstrated the devastating consequences of attempts to challenge the state's ideological control and resulted in Feng's exploration of a new type of film that did not overtly rebel against Party ideology, yet still allowed for certain degree of personal expression.

As already recounted in Chapter 3, during the five years of its existence, Good Dream produced three TV dramas and three films. Although these works dealt with different subjects—love (*Gone Forever with My Love*), corruption (*Behind the Moon*), the generation gap (*I Am Your Dad*), and disillusionment (*Living a Miserable Life*)—they all more or less focused on dark subjects such as social problems, the depravity of human beings, and inequality between classes. They reflected Feng's social conscience, and served as his commentary on issues in contemporary Chinese society. These films however, did not fare well with the censors.

The culmination of Feng's encounter with censorship came in 1996 after the Changsha Conference's reaffirmation of the pedagogical function of cinema. As we saw earlier in this chapter, this renewed orthodoxy resulted in a conservative backlash against non-political films; more than one third of the films produced and co-produced by Beijing Film Studio failed to pass the censors. Feng's film project, *Living a Miserable Life* (Guo zhe liangbei bu kan de shenghuo), was one of these that failed. Written and directed by Feng, the film tells a story of the devastating consequences of an extramarital affair. Liang Yazhou has been married to his highschool sweetheart, Song Xiaoying, for more than ten years. But their marriage enters a state of crisis when Liang falls in love with his personal assistant, Li Xiaodan, a young, attractive and energetic woman. This love triangle brings everything but happiness and harmony to the three, especially after the wife discovers her husband's infidelity. After much fighting, crying, regret, and finally confession, the husband leaves his mistress and returns to the family. As a film co-produced by Good Dream and Beijing Film Studio, the film script had to gain approval from the studio before shooting. After gaining approval, shooting of the film began in the spring of 1996. Unfortunately, two weeks later, Beijing Film Studio received an official letter from the Film Censorship Board of the Chinese Film Bureau, suggesting that the film studio "choose another subject" or "make substantial changes" to the script. According to the letter, without these changes the film would not be approved for release by the bureau. In this document, the censors state that:

> Cinema, as a medium that enjoys particular popularity among a mass audience, has the important function of guiding society's moral and ethical values. The script takes delight in depicting flirting with, chasing, and raping women and emphasizes sex and inappropriate feelings. Exposing sin without criticizing it is against well-accepted moral and ethical values and will be misleading to a mass audience. The script depicts a love triangle involving extramarital affairs, a "third person's" interference in a normal husband–wife relationship, adultery, and other inappropriate sexual relationships. All of these are despised by society. Without essential and substantial revisions, the script will not be approved for release.[19]

Although bewildered by unsubstantiated accusations such as the film's depiction of rape, Feng still wanted to revise the script in accordance with the censors' demands, knowing that the film had already been in production for half a month and over RMB 1 million had been spent. However, the director of Beijing Film Studio, Han Sanping, discouraged him from going ahead with the project. According to his experience, once the censorship board deemed the subject of a film "unhealthy" and "inappropriate" to Chinese audiences, it usually meant that the project had to be aborted, regardless of any revisions.

The failure of this project and another work produced by Good Dream, Wang Shuo's film *I Am Your Dad* (Wo shi ni baba; dir. Wang Shuo), which was also denied approval for distribution and exhibition by the censors, finally caused the company to lose its reputation among investors. Facing a total loss in these projects, Feng had only two choices—either keep making similar films as an underground director or abandon this style and explore other options. As Feng writes in his autobiography, when his film projects had to be aborted one after another due to negative feedback from the censorship board, he nearly decided to begin making underground films, choosing the darkest and most cynical subjects and exposing the ugliest side of everything.[20] He also writes that after the banning of these works, he was labeled "poisonous" by the film world, and no one dared to invest in his works.[21] Giving up the idea of being an independent filmmaker, he writes, "I decided to make films that wouldn't get shut down by the censors."[22] The downfall of Good Dream proved to be a turning point in Feng's career. Learning a lesson from his aborted and banned projects, but not wanting to directly confront the censors, he designed a brand new genre, the New Year Celebration Film, which was intended to appeal to general audiences and not overtly challenge the status quo.

The Hong Kong prototype

The genre of New Year celebration film (*hesui pian*) was borrowed from Hong Kong and possibly had its origin in Hollywood, where blockbuster hits are specifically released on major holidays. Originally, Hong Kong New Year films were mostly farcical comedies. These films became particularly popular in the mid-1980s. Sammo Hung Kam-bo's series of comedies, including *My Lucky Stars* (Fu xing gao zhao, 1985) and *Millionaire's Express* (Fu gui lie che, 1986), Johnnie To's *Eighth Happiness* (Baxing baoxi, 1988) and *The Fun, the Luck and the Tycoon* (1989), and Stephen Chow's films of the 1990s, were such examples of providing an amusing diversion at the end of the year. With an all-star cast, exquisite urban setting, frequent burlesque and hilarious elements in dialogues and action, and the inevitable happy ending, these slapstick films were meant to attract and please as large an audience as possible during a holiday season. In *Eighth Happiness*, for example, as many as eight top stars of Hong Kong cinema, such as Chow Yun-fat, Jacky Cheung (Zhang Xueyou), Cherie Chung (Zhong Chuhong), and Carol "Do Do" Cheng (Zheng Yuling), were in the film. The story is about how the three brothers of the Fang family, each with his own character and personality, find their "better half" after a series of funny incidents. With Chow Yun-fat playing a effeminate and flamboyant acting school student and Jacky Cheung in the role of a simpleminded young man without even a basic understanding of love, the film is filled with farcical and hilarious scenes from beginning to end.

Feng Xiaogang's New Year Films

In 1996, facing a bad reputation among censors and investors, Feng changed his style from "social conscience" to a safer alternative—comedy, a genre that was not only more easily accepted by the censors, but also more attractive to audiences. Inspired by the suggestion of Han Sanping, the director of Beijing Film Studio, Feng made Wang Shuo's short story *You Are Not a Common Person* (Ni bu shi ge su ren) into his first New Year Film *Party A, Party B* and made two other films in the following two years. In 1998, *Be There or Be Square* (Bujian busan), and in 1999, *Sorry Baby!* (Meiwan meiliao, 1999). Due to further changes in Chinese politics, economy, and cultural policies, Feng returned to the genre of "social conscience" in 2000. A discussion of this dimension of Feng's career and the transmigration of his style can be found in Chapter 5.

Plots

Party A, Party B

Party A, Party B tells the story of four friends, unemployed former staff-members of a state–film studio, who start a company called One-Day Dream Trip to help people to fulfill their dreams. In the process, they encounter a whole spectrum of people from Chinese society. Their clients include a bookstore keeper who wants to be General George S. Patton for a day; a gossipy Sichuanese cook who desperately wants to act like a revolutionary hero and keep a secret for one day regardless of any temptations or trials he might face; a robust husband who hopes to be abused in order to experience the life of his wife whom he bullies in real life; a rich man who is sick of having luxurious banquets and wishes to experience poverty and have nothing but plain food to eat; and a celebrity, who is longing for a private life and wants to live like a normal person. While making limited profits from the services they offer, they also help people who can't afford their services to get what they desperately need. When they discover a suicidal young man who has been refused by many girls because of his unattractive appearance, they arrange him a "date" with a "princess" from a foreign country (actually one of the four friends), who pretends to fall in love with him and persuades him not to take his own life. Liu Yuan, another founder of the company, lends his new apartment to a man who is unable to spend time with his wife after she is diagnosed with cancer because they do not have a home together. The film ends with the four friends eating dinner together on the eve of Chinese New Year; the viewer learns that they have had to close the company because they offered too many services for free.

Movie poster of *Party A, Party B*.

Like Feng's directorial debut, *Gone Forever with My Love*, this film is loosely based on Wang's short story *You Are Not a Common Person* (Ni bu shi ge suren). This story depicts a protagonist, named Feng Xiaogang, who runs a company that provides its clients with the service of praising people. While the use of sarcastic black humor rendered with Beijing local dialect and the image of humble and miserable little characters can be seen as traces of Wang's short story, the unrelenting mockery that, in Wang's story, is directed at college professors, high-ranking govenment officials, and loyal Party members, is shifted to famous movie stars, newly rich millionaires, and abusive, macho husbands. This change reflects the Feng's concern with materialism and commercialization in Chinese society.

The film easily passed the censors and soon achieved box-office earnings of RMB 15 million (around US$2 million) in Beijing, the highest of any film that year. In this film, Feng seemed to have found a model for success in the face of censorship and the demands of profit-making.

Be There or Be Square

Be There or Be Square, written and directed by Feng Xiaogang, was shot on location in Los Angeles in 1998, and is said to be the first Chinese domestic feature film shot entirely in America. With a cast and crew of only about thirty people, all flown in from China, and a tight shooting schedule of forty days, *Be There or Be Square*, released at the end of 1998, still managed to achieve remarkable success at the box office, breaking Feng's own record established with *Party A, Party B*.[23]

Be There or Be Square deals with the lives of two Chinese immigrants in the United States. The male protagonist, Liu Yuan, played by the popular star Ge You, has lived in the US for years. With neither a permanent job

Movie poster of *Be There or Be Square*.

nor a permanent place to live (he lives in an RV in a trailer park), he has to engage in various, sometimes strange businesses such as graveyard salesman, travel agent, extra for movies, and Chinese teacher. While helping a film crew find a luxurious mansion for location shooting, he meets the female protagonist, Li Qing, who had just arrived from China and was house-sitting a mansion for her friend. Persuaded by Liu Yuan, Li Qing agrees to let the film crew use the house for shooting. Unfortunately, the shooting not only damages the house, but also attracts the attention of thieves. On the night the shooting is finished, Li Qing is robbed at gunpoint and loses all her immigration documents. After this incident, Li Qing and Liu Yuan meet several more times, but each time some unfortunate incident occurs. For instance, when they meet for the second time, Li quits her job to join Liu's newly established travel agency, but soon discovers that her "clients" from China are actually a group of Chinese illegal immigrants who are quickly deported by the US government. Because of its involvement in the incident, the travel agency is forced out of business and Li Qing loses her job. For their next meeting they plan what is supposed to be a romantic dinner. But when they enter the restaurant, they find themselves in the midst of a robbery and are forced to give away all their belongings.

Along with the storyline of their delayed romance, the film also concentrates on the different lifestyles of the two characters. Unlike Liu Yuan's life philosophy of "I do whatever makes money," as he puts it at the beginning of the film, Li, after several unsuccessful attempts at establishing a career, finally opens her own flower shop and a school teaching Chinese. When the two finally fall in love with each other, Liu learns that his mother in China has been diagnosed with cancer. On their flight to China, their plane encounters major turbulence and appears likely to crash. As the couple is having their last kiss, the airplane manages to pull out of its descent, but Li Qing has found out that Liu has false teeth.

Sorry Baby!

In *Sorry Baby!* (1999), Ruan Dawei (played by Fu Biao, the same actor who played the violent husband in *Party A, Party B* and appeared frequently in Feng's next two films), the boss of a private travel agency in Beijing, has a rental contract with a bus driver Han Dong (played by Ge You) but refuses to pay him his salary of around RMB 100,000. To get his salary, Han follows Ruan everywhere, constantly reminding him of the debt, but without success. In desperation, Han kidnaps Ruan's girlfriend Liu Xiaoyun (Wu Qien-Lien or Wu Qianlian), a Chinese living in Singapore but currently hospitalized in

Beijing because of tuberculosis. Learning about his girlfriend's kidnapping, Ruan is not worried because he knows all too well that the kind-hearted Han can't be serious. He even invites Han to kill his girlfriend, if he dares. Ruan's response angers his girlfriend and she willingly cooperates with Han, who had already decided to abort the scheme by sending her back to the hospital and turning himself in to the police. Liu informs Han that she wants to use this opportunity to find out what is more important to her boyfriend, herself or the money. They send Ruan a videotape of a staged scene in which Han is beating Liu. Han also comes up with many unusual ideas that could "help" the stingy boss, who doesn't pay either his own employee's salary or his girlfriend's ransom, to spend a huge amount of money. Using Ruan's name, Han orders a luxurious banquet and first-class foot-massage service to be delivered to Ruan's house. Anticipating that Ruan would be angry after learning that the bills were all being charged to him, Han even sends a group of mental hospital nurses to "take care" of Ruan. Insulted and surprised by

Movie poster of *Sorry Baby!*

Han's audacity, Ruan becomes a bit worried and reports the case to the police. As the situation gets out of hand, Han Dong decides to surrender himself to the police. At this moment, Liu Xiaoyun speaks out and testifies that Han didn't kidnap her. Han Dong is subsequently set free. Disappointed by Ruan's selfishness, Liu breaks up with him and leaves for Singapore. When Liu returns to Beijing for New Year and reunites with Han, she finds out that Han's need for money is actually for his hospitalized sister.

Recurring Themes of New Year Films

Recurring themes, including the victory of little characters, mockery of the privileged, hidden social commentary, and an imagined America are part of a successful strategy that Feng has developed through his encounters with censorship and awareness of the preferences of a general audience. In the end, Feng succeeds in developing a kind of popular cinema characterized by what Jane M. Gaines describes as the place where "the forces of containment meet the forces that cannot be contained."[24] In Feng's films, there are no overt challenges to Party policy, but Feng's obsessions, concerns, and criticism are all elaborately disguised under the surface of entertaining light-comedy film.

Victory of Little Characters

In the first three New Year films, all the protagonists—the four friends in *Party A, Party B*, the tour bus driver in *Sorry Baby!*, and the self-employed immigrants in *Be There or Be Square*—can be considered "little characters" (*xiao renwu*), ordinary urban dwellers who struggle to make ends meet economically and are faced with various other challenges imposed by society. At the very beginning of *Party A, Party B*, a voice-over tells the audience that the four friends have lost their jobs in state–film studios and have had to open a small business to support themselves. At the end of the film, on the eve of Chinese New Year, the "leader" of their business, one of the four buddies, tells the others that all their efforts in the past months have turned out to be unprofitable and they will have to close the company the next year. The bus driver in *Sorry Baby!* not being paid for a year, lives in a dingy studio and needs to take care of his hospitalized sister. The two Chinese immigrants in *Be There* drift from one job to another and face frequent financial difficulties. In spite of their hardships, these characters share a sense of optimism and are kind and warm-hearted in their relationships with others. For example, in *Party A, Party B*, the four friends, although struggling to maintain the profitability of their business, find happiness in the process of helping ordinary people like themselves fulfill their dreams. One day they decide to make as many people happy as possible. So wherever they go, they offer compliments to people they meet. They tell a saleswoman in a furniture store that she is as beautiful as a flight stewardess and old ladies dancing *yangge* on the street that they are as youthful as they were in their thirties. In *Be There*, even though Liu Yuan is unable to hold a steady job, he offers generous help to Li Qing after she has been robbed by letting her stay in his small RV and buying her an air ticket back to China. Concentrating on the humble lives and careers of these ordinary people, and bringing out the admirable side of their personalities, Feng provides his little characters with dignity and pride. Although the difficulties these characters encounter seem enormous, at the end of the films, they receive what they most desire—the love of the woman to whom they have dedicated themselves, or the fulfillment of the tasks they have pursued with such effort. The love stories in all three films come to a happy ending as the male protagonists win over the female leads. In *Sorry Baby!* the two protagonists reunite and Han Dong gets his salary back. *Be There or Be Square* ends not only with Li Qing's opening of her own flower shop, but also the two protagonists' falling in love with each other. Feng's descriptions of the lives of these little characters demonstrate his acute understanding of the living conditions of ordinary people in contemporary China. However, more than this, by promoting the virtues and strengths in their humble lives, Feng reassures his audiences of the value of even insignificant people.

Although the "little character" role has been present throughout Chinese cinema, Feng's treatment of these people is quite different from that of his predecessors. During the Republican era (1911-1949), most of the little characters in cinema and literature are innocent, doomed, and defenseless people who are victimized by evil forces or massive social and political turmoil. The emergence of this kind of little character was tied to the iconoclasm initiated by the May Fourth Movement and the social criticism pervasive in Leftist cinema of the 1930s and 1940s. Most typical representatives are the female protagonists played by Ruan Lingyu in the movies such as *Little Toys*, *Goddess*, and *New Women*. These characters of fallen woman, virtuous mother, and exploited female writer are portrayed as victims of a conservative, feudal, patriarchal, and materialistic society. Similar characters can also be found in films such as *Spring River Flows East* and *Spring in a Small Town*. This kind of little character from the Republican period consists of people without hope of redemption or salvation from a desperate social context. The only solution to their problems is either their self-destruction (*Goddess*, *Spring River*) or the demise of the society in which they live (*Crows and Sparrows*). Victims of society, and failing in their attempts at redemption, the image of these little characters became an embodiment of the Chinese nation. They were, in fact, victims of a decayed and regressive culture and society that was the true target of the filmmakers' criticism.

Feng Xiaogang's "little characters" are similar in the sense that they are all far from perfect but they have admirable sides. They are people who pursue their simple dreams and strive for seemingly naïve but still admirable ideals. In *Party A, Party B*, the four protagonists' ambition is to help people fulfill their dreams no matter how humble or crazy these dreams are. They generously offer their help without asking anything in return. Like the virtuous prostitute-mother in *Goddess*, who sells her body only to finance her son's education; and Han Dong, the hard-working tour bus driver in *Sorry Baby!*, when unable to pay for his sick sister's treatment because of his boss's refusal to pay his salary, takes the desperate measure of kidnapping the boss's girlfriend. However, unlike the "little characters" of Republican cinema, whose ambitions turn into disillusion, disappointment, or perdition, the protagonists in Feng's early New Year films are rewarded with the realization of their dreams. In *Goddess*, not only does the villain steal the money that the mother has earned for her son's education, the mother ends up in jail after confronting and accidentally killing him. Unlike the misery of this character, the bus driver in *Sorry Baby!* not only gets his salary back, his sister rallies from a long-term coma, he reconciles with his boss, and also succeeds in winning the love of his girlfriend. Although the four protagonists in *Party A, Party B* ultimately fail in their business, they find joy in the process of helping people with their dreams. Furthermore, two of the friends fall in love and are happily married at the end of the film. Similarly, in *Be There*, the relationship between Liu Yuan and Li Qing finally comes to a happy ending, and Li's American dream is fulfilled as she opens her own business. In contrast to the mood of pessimism and desperation typical of little characters of Republican-era cinema, Feng's little characters, although frustrated by hardships, are finally rewarded with joy, delight, and success. Therefore, if Republican cinema's melodramatic depictions of the little characters' suffering conveys a subversive criticism of the evil reality, Feng's depictions of the optimistic and uplifting little characters, while not absolutely devoid of depictions of social injustice, do not meant to generate overt critiques of the status quo.

After 1949, another type of "little character" appeared on Chinese screens, as the edifice of socialist realist cinema was gradually erected. Mainly belonging to the proletariat class, i.e. peasants, workers and soldiers,[25] these little characters are either portrayed as suppressed proletarians, enlightened by communist thoughts, heroically struggling against and finally triumphing over the evil forces of warlords, landlords, and Japanese invaders (*White Haired Girl,*

Red Women's Detachment, Little Soldier Zhangga), or new citizens of a new society who wholeheartly dedicate themselves to socialist construction (*Li Shuangshuang, Young People from Our Village, Five Golden Flowers*). In Xie Jin's film *Red Women Detachment*, the intractable maidservant, Wu Qionghua, runs away from her wicked landlord-master and joins a Communist women's militia under the guidance of an underground Communist and then leads her troops to capture and defeat the evil landlord. Set against the background of the Great Leap Forward,[26] *Li Shuangshuang* depicts a young married woman's victory, with the support of a Party official, over her husband's "feudal" opposition to her participation in work for their village commune. In comparison to their counterparts of the Republican era, the victories and happiness of these little characters are all, unmistakably, attributed to the great leadership of the Party and Mao. In "Scar" cinema after the Cultural Revolution, the little characters, mostly educated intellectuals who were mentally or physically repressed and politically marginalized during the Cultural Revolution, serve as manifestations of the Chinese people's painful experiences from 1966 to 1976. Xie Jin's *Herdsman* (Mu maren), *Legend of Tianyun Mountain*, and *Hibiscus City* (Furong zhen) all feature little characters who, though virtuous Communists, were abused during the Cultural Revolution and other political movements because of their outspoken criticism of problems in the Party (Luo Qun in *Legend of Tianyun Mountain*) or indulgence in their work rather than politics (Qin Shutian in *Hibiscus Town*). These images do not merely direct the audience to commiserate with their individual experiences, they bear a more significant mission of representing the image of a nation that has endured political turbulence and great loss, but retains an enduring faith in the Party and communism. Depictions of these characters, similar to those during the first years of PRC cinema, emphasize that personal tragedies are in the past, while the present and future hold great promise. As such, they do not challenge the legitimacy of the Party. Rather, the tumultuous times are made the responsibility of evil groups with ulterior motives, such as "Lin Biao's Anti-Party Group" or the "Gang of Four." The latter group in many Scar films, for example, was accused of usurping the power of the Party during the Cultural Revolution and thus is held totally responsible for the "Ten Year Disaster."

Unlike their counterparts in the earlier PRC cinema, the little characters in Feng's first three New Year films do not serve as symbols of the greatness or failures of a nation. Rather, they represent the simple joy, sorrow, hardship, and success of people who are not the main focuses of the socialist realist cinema. Although the four unemployed film studio workers in *Party A, Party B*, the tour bus driver in *Sorry Baby!*, and the drifter in *Be There* can all be considered "proletariats" according to communist ideology (they lack their own means of production and hence sell their labor to live), they are also outside the systems of mainstream socialist society. They are not able to enjoy the socialist benefits such as free housing and medical service because they are self-employed city dwellers engaged in careers that are outside official or government-owned work units. This unusual social status becomes the basis of the narratives: the One-Day Dream Trip company could not have been established if the four friends had remained employees of the state film studios; it is also not very likely that Han Dong's salary payment would have been delayed for a year if he had worked for a state travel company. If their failures and hardships can be partly attributed to their status as social outcasts, then their successes are their own, having nothing to do with support from the state or Party. In films from the early years of the PRC, the little characters' triumphs over evil forces or overcoming of other barriers are a result of the arrival or assistance of a revolutionary figure. The slave servant, Wu Qionghua's conversion to Marxism in *Red Detachment of Women* would not have been possible without the enlightened guidance of the underground Communist, Hong Changqing. In *Li Shuangshuang,* the title character's struggle with her conservative husband is backed by the Party secretary of her village. In *Legend of Tianyun Mountain*, Luo Qun's rehabilitation is finally approved by certain important figures from above. Support from the Party or other official characters is, however, entirely absent in the little characters' accomplishments in Feng's New Year films. Therefore, instead of being portrayed as symbols of political conversion or indicators of the utopian life under Party leadership, the little characters in Feng's films are devoid of any explicit political agenda, and are not affiliated with mainstream Party rhetoric.

Feng's emphasis on the fate of little characters, outsiders to the social norm in contemporary China, reflect far-reaching social changes brought about by a decade of economic and social reforms. Starting early 1990s, entities once owned by the state, such as industrial factories, cultural institutes, and even administrative departments were either downsized or privatized, causing millions of employees to be laid off. Although the urban unemployment rate reached an unprecedented high, the lives of these unemployed people were ignored by the official press and media. Foregrounding the stories of these urban unemployed and neither caricaturing or idealizing them, Feng casts his little characters in a positive and realistic light. In doing so, Feng succeeds in not only helping the voices of the underprivileged to be heard, but also in striking a chord with Chinese audiences who were tired of the stock images of little characters in socialist cinema, characters who were simply spokespersons for the ideology of the privileged Party leadership. Through his characters, Feng also reaffirms for his audiences that although humble and victimized by uncontrollable social transformations, a virtuous and hard-working person with an optimistic attitude can still confront the menacing social milieu and be successful. At the same time, however, Feng's exposure of the living conditions of these underprivileged people was not meant to generate any criticism of the current situation of Chinese society. Rather, the happy endings in the three films, in which all the difficulties come to a positive resolution, reflect Feng's more measured attitude toward issues in contemporary China. As a filmmaker who had to abandon a cinema of "social conscience" for comedic films because of troubles with film censorship, Feng had to conceal his critique even while exposing social problems. Therefore, the representations of the little characters in these New Year films can be seen as a result of Feng's deliberate choices as a filmmaker caught between the urge to express his own concerns and the surveillance of film censors.

Mocking the Privileged

While casting the little characters as the main protagonists, people from the privileged stratums of society become the primary targets of his satire and cynicism. Whereas his little characters have a certain dignity, the "privileged"— rich people, celebrities, businessmen, police officers, and mental hospital doctors are often characterized by hypocrisy, pretension, incompetence, and dishonesty.

In *Party A, Party B*, three of the seven dreams that are fulfilled turn into nightmares; all three dreams belong to people who can be considered privileged in one way or another. For example, one such client, a rich businessman who drives a Mercedes-Benz and dresses in expensive suits, complains that he is sick of having a meticulously prepared feast every day and dreams of experiencing poverty and eating only plain food. After being sent to a remote village in the aftermath of a natural disaster, the rich man is at first very excited. But when Qian Kang, one of the four friends, comes to check on the man after a couple of months, the previously neat and sleek-looking businessman now has a beard and a pungent body odor, and desperately wants his luxurious life back. A dialogue between Qian and the businessman's host family provides a vivid caricature of the rich man's experience of poverty.

> *Qian*: Does he want to eat meat now?
> *The family*: Of course he does. You'd better bring him back now. He is almost like a yellow weasel and has eaten up all the chickens in the village. I feel that he could even eat a human now.

Sinking into the back seat of his luxury car and devouring a roast chicken brought to him by Qian, the man refuses to even step out of the car and bid farewell to the villagers, fearful that he might be stuck in the impoverished village forever. His dream of poverty not only becomes his nightmare, but also arouses his fear of the poor.

Another dream that turns into a nightmare is that of the singer and movie star, Tang Lijun, who is annoyed by the fans and the paparazzi flocking around her wherever she goes. Commissioning One-Day Dream Trip to issue a statement announcing that she will no longer participate in any performances and shows, Tang wants to retire from her public life and enjoy her privacy. As time passes by, she finds that the life of privacy, without invitations to parties, shows and concerts, is far from what she had expected and even becomes frightening. First her "loyal" agent and bodyguard leave her as her fame wanes, and then her attempt to resume her career fails to attract the interest of any of her former collaborators. Similar to the rich businessman's reaction to his realized dream, Tang regrets that she ever sought to realize her dream.

These two people's dreams are all about their yearning to escape from the present and return to a former life. Feng's satirical depiction reveals an awkward displacement in the current situations of these nouveau riche, as they are sandwiched between an irretrievable past and an unsatisfactory present. The dream-like past that they are longing for is lost forever when the dream really comes true, whereas their present is something that they seek to escape. Furthermore, these people's professed dreams of returning to a simple life are only lies; in the end, they find out that wealth and fame are the very things that they can't live without.

In addition to his mockery of the nouveau riche, Feng's early New Year films also use people representing authority, such as police officers and doctors of a mental hospital, as objects of amusement. In *Be There or Be Square*, Liu Yuan is shown teaching Chinese to a group of Los Angeles Police Department officers in Li Qing's flower shop. Ironically, the dialogues that Liu Yuan teaches are not commonly used in everyday life. Rather, they are only used in grand military parades, when high-ranking generals review the troops. During such parades, as part of the ceremony, the general, usually riding a convertible jeep, exchanges these set dialogues with the troops that are being reviewed:

> *General*: Hello Comrades! (*tongzhimen hao*)
> *Troop*: Hello General! (*shouzhang hao*)
> *General*: You must be working hard! (*tongzhi men xiku le*)
> *Troop*: Serve the people! (*wei renmin fuwu*)

This very typical dialogue of socialist China, unchanged for decades, is a very obvious indicator of the hierarchy dividing high-ranking military officials and subordinate troops. Appropriating this specific dialogue in the film, Feng reverses the hierarchy by placing his little character, Liu Yuan, in the position of the military official who is reviewing his army, while the LAPD, a symbol of America's political authority, are given the position of subordinate troops saluting their commander. Showing American police officers chanting their lines with a strong English accent, the film achieves a successful comic affect, and also enables Feng to create his own fantastic world where the authorities are subordinate, objects of ridicule, while the little character, Liu Yuan, is elevated to the prestigious status of commander.

Sometimes, Feng's mocking of the privileged is rendered through his uses of mental hospital as metaphor of an incompetent authority that fails to differentiate anger and madness, talent and stupidity, and truth and falsehood. In Feng's films, the mental hospital and its staff are either shutting normal people away in the hospital or treating the rightly angry as violently insane. In *Sorry Baby!* when Ruan Dawei, the boss of the travel agency, becomes infuriated about having to pay for all the extravagant services ordered by Han Dong, a group of doctors from a mental hospital, also ordered by Han, arrives at his doorstep, claiming that they have received an emergency call about a mental patient who needs to be hospitalized. Feeling that he has been made a fool by Han's ridicule, Ruan tries to push the male nurses and doctors out of his house. A doctor, without another word, quickly stuns Ruan with an electric baton and then explains to his assistant in an authoritative tone that Ruan is a patient with typical symptoms of paranoid schizophrenia. As soon as he learns that Ruan is not insane but only angry about Han's tricks, the doctor's tone suddenly changes from commanding to soliciting—as he still needs Ruan to pay his service fee. In this film, the image of the doctor is rude, unreasonable, and greedy. Such representation repeats in Feng's other films, as we will see in the next chapter, it became more cynical in his later works such *Big Shot's Funeral*. Through these caricatured depictions of the privileged, Feng finds an implicit way of making fun of an authority that is lacking integrity and questionable in probity.

Hidden Social Commentaries

Setting the New Year films against the background of contemporary China and centering the narrative around stories of little characters' hardships and happiness, Feng touches upon many issues prevalent in modern China, but these critiques are far less explicit and hard-hitting than those in his early works such as *Chicken Feathers on the Ground* and *Behind the Moon*. Instead, his criticisms are submerged beneath the surface of an optimistic and uplifting comical story. This change can be seen as a necessary strategy of survival for a filmmaker who had to obey the rules of the official moviemaking system, but couldn't abandon his previous style of "social conscience" entirely. From a broader perspective, this change can also be traced to the reinforcing of orthodox film policy at the Changsha Conference in 1996. This policy, as we saw earlier in this chapter, advocates that cinema should fulfill the function of educating audiences with uplifting sentiments such as patriotism and love for the Party, rather than exposing the dark side of society.[27] While promoting films that were pedagogical and politically correct, the film authority discouraged the production of films that "would arouse dissatisfaction with society and pessimism toward life."[28] In order to avoid trouble with the film officials, and thus enable a profitable return at the box office, commentaries on China's contemporary social and cultural problems in Feng's works have changed from explicit to implicit.

Feng's early works are very direct in their criticism of social and political problems in contemporary Chinese society. For example, *Chicken Feathers on the Ground* targets the inefficiency and bureaucracy of government work units in which administrative power is wielded for personal gain and where those at the bottom of the hierarchy are exploited in almost every aspect of life, from salary, housing, to even opportunities for a better education for their children. In this early work, the fate of such little characters offers little hope. For example, in *Chicken Feathers on the Ground*, no positive solution is provided for the protagonist, Little Lin. Instead, at the end of the series, he is shown aimlessly wandering the streets. When he looks up, he sees himself, standing on the other side of the street and gazing back with a desperate gaze. The strong sense of pessimism and hopelessness evident in little characters' failed attempts to change their social or financial status becomes even more prominent in *Behind the Moon*. Desirous of immediate personal wealth and inspired by the stories of overnight millionaires, products of the bubble economy of the early 1990s, the two protagonists spare no effort in getting money through legal and illegal means. However, in the process, they are constantly exploited and cheated by people such as bank managers and government officials who take advantage of their ambitions. At one point, the female protagonist even agrees to spend a night with an elder local official, who promises to help them with a bank mortgage. Their unrealistic fantasy finally costs one of their lives—the TV drama ends with a gunshot, the last sound Mu Ni, the male protagonist, hears as he is being executed. Although the work blames their self-destruction first on their own limitless greed, it also shows that the false promises of the economy, the pervasive corruption among government officials who trade their power for money, and the weakness in the financial system all precipitate their downfall. Because of their direct criticism of social problems, the release of these two works was delayed by censors.

Learning from this experience with censorship, Feng's later works avoid direct criticism of social and political problems. His New Year comedies, while touching upon many of the conundrums brought by economic reform, commercialization, and Westernization, are not meant to draw the audience's attention to these problems. Instead, whenever social or economic displacement is presented or implied in the film, a solution is also provided. Thus, the underlying effect of these films is to maintain rather than question the status quo.

In *Party A, Party B*, the rich man who dreams of living a simple life with only plain food to eat, is sent to live with a poor family in a remote village. The first part of the story seems to allude to the existence of differences between the poor and rich, but, in the final part of the story, social criticism is suppressed. After the rich man's two-month experience of poverty, he promises to help the village build a poultry farm. Thus the future of this poor village, and, indeed, all of China seems to be bright and prosperous. As one of the characters says at the end of this scene: "Everything is going to be fine! In a few years, if you still want to experience poverty, the only place we can send you to would be a remote desert." In *Sorry Baby!*, Han's inability to pay for his sister's medical service accurately portrays the dire situation of many people in the late 1990s, a period when blue-collar wages were extremely low and expenses for health care reached an unprecedented high. But at the end, all Han's problems are solved—he gets his salary back and his sister shows signs of improvement. Although the story of *Be There or Be Square* is set against an American social background, it still manages to expose problems of Chinese society. In the middle of the film, when Liu is working for a travel agency, the first tour he hosts consists of a large group of businessmen going from China to the US for a business trip. But their itinerary has nothing to do with business at all. Rather, they urge Liu to take them to strip clubs and shopping. The first part of this scene reminds Chinese audiences of "business trips" sponsored by government or state enterprises whose real purpose is more for leisure than official business. But the film later reveals that the group is actually a bunch of illegal immigrants who will be deported back to China by the US Department of Immigration. Thus, the film seems to touch on social problems, without challenging official rhetoric.

Another hidden commentary dealing with contemporary social issues addresses the Chinese audience's ambivalent attitude towards the Maoist era.

The audiences of his films are composed mostly of members of the generation born at the end of the 1960s and early 1970s, who experienced the Maoist era as children. As young children during the Cultural Revolution, they did not experience the strong sense of disillusionment of their elder brothers and sisters and did not remember the brutality of political persecution. Rather, the idealistic and revolutionary protagonists of socialist realist theater and cinema became their first heroes. However, as a result of the social and economic transformations that began to take place in the 1980s, Maoist values were thrown into question and so was the revolutionary heroism of Maoist culture. The resulting contradictory mixture of nostalgia and disillusionment is represented in Feng's films through his ironic appropriations of lines or plots from socialist cinema of the PRC and Soviet Union.

In *Party A, Party B,* one of the dreams the company helps to fulfill is that of being a hero. The Sichuanese cook, mentioned earlier, wants to be a revolutionary hero who does not give up his secret message, no matter what enticements are offered to him. The secret line given to him by the company is "I won't tell you, unless you kill me." Before his task begins, there is a dialogue between Liu Yuan and the cook that describes what will happen when the cook is about to be tortured for keeping the secret.

> *Cook:* Are there going to be any German shepherds and local villagers when I am being tortured?
>
> *Liu:* Yes, of course. Around 200 villagers will cry for you and say that you are an innocent and good man. Whoever cries really hard gets one more bag of chemical fertilizer.

To start the "dream" Liu also tells the cook that when he is being "arrested," he needs to throw a flowerpot out off the window to warn his fellow comrades.

The scenes they envision consist of many references to stereotypical images from socialist realist cinema—German shepherds barking in front of the enemy troops, villagers weeping over the death of a revolutionary martyr, and an underground revolutionary throwing flowerpots out of a window to warn other underground agents as he/she is about to be arrested. Similar scenes were the hallmarks of socialist films such as *Guerrilla on the Plain* (Pingyuan youjidui; dir. Su Li 苏里, Wu Zhaodi 武兆堤, 1955), *Zhang Ga, the Soldier Boy* (Xiaobing Zhangga; dir. Cui Wei 崔嵬 and Ouyang Hongying 欧阳红缨, 1963), and *Living Forever in Burning Flames* (Leihuo zhong yongsheng; dir. Shui Hua 水华, 1965), just to mention a few. However, soon after the depiction of these heroic scenes, the line from Liu Yuan, "Whoever cries really hard gets one more bag of chemical fertilizer," deconstructs the heroism he has just built up for the cook by indicating that all the "villagers" are hired extras, whose dramatic weeping are only to get more bags of chemical fertilizer, but not because they are moved by the heroic act. The audience's disillusionment with the Maoist era is represented by the irony of this simultaneous reconstruction and demystification of heroism.

The implicit rendering of commentaries on problems in China attests, first of all, to the compromises that Feng has to make in order to avoid direct conflict with the censors. By implying the existence of real problems, these films succeed in striking a chord with many Chinese people; at the same time, the positive solutions ensure the insecure and troubled mass audience that all social difficulties are just temporary and can be resolved within the existing system. Not only touching on contemporary social issues, Feng's New Year films also succeed in reflecting certain cultural phenomena that have obsessed Chinese people for decades. In doing so, his New Year films also resonate with his audience at a deeper cultural level.

Imagined America

A peculiar recurring image in Feng's New Year films is the image of the West, mostly America. This image addresses Chinese people's obsession with Western influence, an obsession that has manifested itself, in various social contexts, as both repulsion and attraction. A recurrent theme throughout the history of Chinese cinema, the image of America, in Feng's films continues this century-long investigation and reflects specific attitudes toward the West in the new era. In order to fully understand the significance of the image of the West in Feng's films, it is necessary to begin with a brief review of the origin and evolution of representations of the West in Chinese cinema in the past century.

Chinese national cinema evolved against a complex historical background from the late Qing Dynasty through the Republican and Communist periods. Much of this time has been filled with unpleasant encounters with the West. In the final few years of the Qing Dynasty, China was humiliated by military defeats and exploitative treaties, but also attracted by advanced Western technology and the democratic political system. As a result, two attitudes toward the West have frequently co-existed in Chinese culture. Both attitudes are reflected in Chinese popular cinema beginning in the early 20th century. Zhang Zhidong's dictum of *zhong xue wei ti, xi xue wei yong*—"Chinese learning for the essence, Western learning for practical use"—is a common formulation of this attitude. Scholars and intellectuals, aligning themselves with this conservative attitude toward the West, believe that "China" is the foundation of cultural and moral values. The purpose of learning from the West, according to this formulation, is only to serve China's material needs. However, this view came under increasing attack with the rise of calls for Westernization in the early 20th century. Beginning with the May Fourth Movement, cultural and ethical Westernization was a constant part of the agenda for Chinese intellectuals. They believed that China was far behind the West and should widely and openly adopt everything that is Western, not only its technology but also its ideology.

In a century characterized both by the inundation of Western-style urbanization and industrialization in China, often the result of China's inability to respond effectively to foreign powers and military interference, and by threats to China's own long-standing traditions and civilization from modernization and social transformation, Zhang Zhidong's position seemed increasingly untenable. However, China's radically different socio-political background and the deep entrenchment of traditional values meant that total Westernization was impossible. In other words, despite the calls for complete Westernization in the May Fourth period, Chinese culture in the 20th century retained an ambivalent attitude toward both Chinese tradition and Western modernity. In Chinese cinema, this ambivalence is reflected in a contradictory representation of the West as either idealized or demonized, or, sometimes, a mixture of both.

A representative work in this regard from the silent-film era is Sun Yu's film *Little Toys* (Xiao wanyi, 1933), which tells the tragic personal story of the female protagonist, Sister Ye, during the economic and political turbulence of the 1920s and 1930s. At the beginning of the story, Ye is an innovative toymaker living with her husband and children in a small village. But as the process of industrialization begins, and is followed by eruptions of civil war and Japanese invasion, her happy family faces one calamity after another. Her husband dies, her son is kidnapped, and her daughter is killed during the war, leaving only the bereaved Sister Ye. Her toy making career is also affected by the rapid development of urban industrialization. In the film, Western technology, represented by the foreign toy making industry, is portrayed both as a threat that needs to be resisted and as an attraction that needs to be emulated. The foreign toys in the film are not as sophisticated as those made by Sister Ye and consist mostly of war toys—model tanks, soldiers, and airplanes—which stand allegorically for foreign power and menace, figuring Western technology in its artificiality, ugliness, and inhumanity. This is further suggested through juxtapositions of children playing with these toys with real war scenes when war breaks out. The contradictory attitude towards Westernization is also evidenced in Sister Ye's attitude toward Western technology. When her fellow villagers get frustrated by the unpopularity of their toys, Sister Ye appeals for solidarity and says that if they stand together and fight against the foreign imports, sooner or later their hand-made toys will be able to compete with machine-made ones. However, her suggestion to Mr. Yuan, a rich young man from the city who is in love with her, seems to contradict her resentment for foreign imports: she encourages him to study toy-making technology abroad, in order to better contribute to the declining toy industry of China. The mixed message, indicating both the good and evil sides of Westernization, became a recurring theme in Chinese popular cinema and appealed to Chinese audiences who were frightened and confused by the modern transformation of society.

Given certain social and historical conditions, the image of the West can tend toward either the negative or positive, depending on the social-historical context. For example, in Chinese popular films of the early 1980s, when China had just gone trough the ten years of turmoil of the Cultural Revolution, the image of the West, exemplified by the United States and functioning as a symbol of modernization, was cast in a much more positive light than in the 1930s. In a popular film, *Love Story in Lu Mountain* (Lu shan lian; dir. Huang Zumou, 1980), the US is depicted as a virtual paradise of beautiful landscapes and leisurely bourgeois lifestyles. A love story between an American-born Chinese woman and a Chinese man, the film tells of how their love became impossible during the Cultural Revolution and how they were able to finally reunite only after it ended. In the middle of the film, there is a flashback sequence depicting the girl's life in America with her family. The sequence shows a location-shot of a beautiful lakeshore. The father, dressed in a jacket and jeans and smoking a cigar, is taking a break during a hunting trip with his daughter. Then, the mother, driving a car, enters the frame and shows them a newspaper containing news of the restoration of Sino-American relationships. In the mise-en-scene, the costume, landscape, hunting activity, and automobile, all bathed in a pure and bright sunshine, construct the image of a free, happy, and leisurely life in the United States. With the normalization of Sino-American relationship in the early 1980s, similarly positive images of America also appeared in films such as *Loyalty* (Hai wai chi zi; dir. Ou Fan 欧凡 and Xing Jitian 邢吉田, 1979), *Herdsman* (Mu ma ren; dir. Xie Jin 谢晋, 1982), and others.

In the 1990s, the representation of the West in Chinese popular cinema resumed the earlier mixture of attraction and repulsion. China's opening of its door to the West brought a new round of transformations to Chinese society, politics, economics, and culture. Also, for the first time in PRC history, ordinary people were allowed to go abroad and experience for themselves real life in the West.

The opening monologue of a popular TV show, *Beijinger in New York*, co-written and co-directed by Feng Xiaogang, encapsulates the essence of Chinese people's perceptions of the West in the early 1990s: "If you love him, bring him to New York—for him it's heaven. If you hate him, bring him to New York—for him it's hell." Based on a semi-biographical novel written by Cao Guilin, the story concerns a Chinese cellist's pursuit of the American dream. The cellist, Wang Qiming, not only gives up his career as a musician and becomes a savvy businessman, but also divorces his wife and parts ways with his adolescent daughter. At the end of the drama, Wang, now an unhappy millionaire, stands drunk and depressed in Times Square, making a rude and defiant gesture with his middle finger, that, none of the passersby pay any attention to. In the TV series, America is depicted as a place filled with enormous opportunities, but it is also a place where an innocent person can easily ruin him/herself.

In the second half of the 1990s, as the interaction between the US and China increased and American culture, symbolized by Hollywood cinema, McDonald's fast food, and Michael Jackson's pop music, inundated almost every corner of China, obsession over the US became a more prominent theme in popular cinema. In Feng Xiaogang's *Party A, Party B*, Hollywood cinema becomes the subject of both emulation and irony. In the film, in order to fulfill a bookseller's dream of being a general, the members of One-Day Dream Trip dress him up and help him "be" General Patton for a day. All this "general's" activities—riding a jeep on the battlefield, leading a military meeting, and visiting a hospital—are directly copied from the Hollywood blockbuster film, *Patton* (Franklin J. Schaffner, 1970), a winner of seven Academy awards (including Best Picture, Best Director, and Best Actor), which was imported into China in the 1980s. Although this Hollywood film functions as an indispensable factor in the realization of the bookseller's general dream, the director, by exposing and exaggerating the artificiality of the filmmaking process, also accentuates the playfulness and irony in his own remake of a Hollywood film. In the first sequence, the general rides in a jeep with his two assistants through an open field where a real military exercise is taking place, overtly revealing the artificiality of the war scene. On the jeep, a ragged American national flag hangs upside down. While pretending that they are in a battlefield in Germany, the three say nothing at all about the war; rather, they discuss the shortage of ice cream, American-made Coca Cola, Camel cigarettes, and chewing gum for American soldiers. In the following sequence, the general is visiting a hospital where he meets a black soldier, who turns out to be a herdsman paid to play the role. His black face and his character's name, Tom, are clear references to the stereotypical representation of race in Hollywood cinema. When the general asks his opinion of the war, Tom only looks confused and says repeatedly that no one is taking care of his sheep. By altering just several details in the mise-en-scene, Feng Xiaogang successfully turns a Hollywood epic film into a farcical comedy. Although functioning as a model on which the dream is based, the Hollywood film also serves as an object of mockery and derision.

The representation of America becomes a recurring theme in Feng's later films. His second New Year film, *Be There or Be Square* (Bu jian bu san, 1999) was shot on-location in Los Angeles. The film, which can be seen as a cinematic version of his 1990s TV show *Beijingers in New York*, focuses on two Chinese immigrants' experiences in the US. As mentioned above, the female protagonist succeeds through her hard work, in opening her own flower shop, while the male protagonist, though having stayed in the US much longer, drifts from one job to another and has never had a stable life. For the two protagonists, the US is a place filled with both opportunity and decadence. The lifestyles of the two are both Americanized, yet they contrast greatly with each other. Li Qing represents the uplifting mode of the American dream— she achieves upward mobility through hard work. Despite being robbed of everything during her first week in the US and hardly speaking a word of English, she manages to start a successful career. As the narrative proceeds, the audience sees Li become legitimately middle-class. Her path to success is clearly marked by improvements in her material surroundings. Each time she reunites with Liu, something has changed for the better in her life. Her occupation changes from a cleaning lady at a BMW dealership to the owner of a flower shop. Her dwelling changes from one room in a shared multi-bedroom apartment to a nicely decorated apartment all her own. The car that she drives also changes from an old coupe to a stylish convertible.

The image of Li Qing, in other words, is that of the model Chinese immigrant to the US. She starts with only meager resources, but succeeds in creating an impressive life and career. Such images became widespread in the early 1990s through popular works such as *Beijingers in New York*, and the 1992 bestseller, *A Chinese Woman in Manhattan* (Manhadun de Zhongguo nuren) by Zhou Li. The book, which Zhou claims to be her autobiography, focuses on the transformation of a poor Chinese woman into a wealthy American businesswoman. After experiencing a heartbreaking love affair during the Cultural Revolution, she leaves for the US in 1985 and, in less than four years, has become a wealthy and well-connected businesswoman involved in international trade.[29] Although accused by acquaintances of fabricating and exaggerating her success, *A Chinese Woman in Manhattan* was reprinted four times and sold at least 500,000 copies nationwide within five mouths of its release.[30]

Although Li Qing's story is somewhat similar to "Zhou's fantasy of easy access of the American dream"[31] as she opens her flower shop only two years after her arrival in the US, Feng's version of the successful American dream is much more realistic, because he also reveals the hardships and disillusionment of the American fantasy through his leading man, Liu Yuan. Throughout the film, Liu fails to show any improvement in his career or lifestyle. He never moves out of his RV in the trailer park and continues to drive a dilapidated Ford van. Although he seems already assimilated into American culture—he can, for example exchange elaborate jive handshakes with his African-American friend—he still feels great sense of displacement. In the beginning of the film, when Li loses everything and asks Liu for his advice on her future plans, Liu discourages her from even staying in the States by saying that it is even difficult to be a stripper. He asks, "You think it is just a question of putting aside one's dignity? The strippers have to be able to do the splits and lift their legs up as high as someone's head." America, for Liu, is a place, where a person can barely earn a living even if he/she willingly gives up everything. Other details in his life show the difficulties of surviving in the US. One example is his philosophy, "I do anything that makes money." The variety of jobs in which he has been or hopes to be engaged include roles as a Chinese film extra, selling life insurance to Chinese immigrants, selling cemetery plots, serving as vice-president of a Chinese travel agency, and acting as a *feng shui* master. Unlike the fantastic image of the American dream in Zhou Li's book, which includes life in a luxurious apartment near Central Park, doing business with mainstream American businesses, and even marrying a blond-haired American man, Feng's portrayal of Li and Liu's experiences creates an America that is both attractive and intimidating.

The ambivalent perception of the US is also reflected in the film's mise-en-scene, consisting of images of a world that is both advanced and decadent. Shot on location in Southern California, the film is filled with "exotic details" that are very appealing to ordinary Chinese who have never left China. These scenes include depictions of luxurious mansions, the self-contained RV where Liu lives, Li's VW Beetle with a trunk under the front hood, self-service gas stations, answering machines, and even parking meters. On the other hand, America also has its dark side, usually a reflection of the stereotypical image of the US portrayed by China's media. For example, the frequent random robberies in the film—twice within the first thirty minutes of the film and both at gun point—makes use of American's image as a country filled with violence.

Feng's first two New Year films, *Party A, Party B* and *Be There or Be Square*, both feature an imagined US presented as a subject of both attraction and repulsion. Both views of the US have obsessed Chinese people for decades. Several periods in recent Chinese history have been marked by widespread anti-American sentiment, usually linked to hostile encounters between China and the US. For example, from the establishment of the PRC in 1949 through to the restoration of Sino-US relationships in 1979, a nationwide anti-American sentiment was prevalent. According to Mao Zedong, the US was a "paper tiger," which like Hitler, the Russian Czars, and the Japanese Imperialists, was seemingly powerful, but actually weak politically, because it was divorced from its people. As Mao put it, "If the US monopoly capitalist groups persist in pushing their policies of aggression and war, the day is bound to come when they will be hanged by the people of the whole world. The same fate awaits the accomplices of the United States."[32] As a result, Americans in socialist realist films are usually pictured as opponents of the communist revolutionary forces. In war films such as *Scouting Across the Yangzi River* (Du jiang zhencha ji; dir. Tang Xiaodan 汤晓丹, 1954) and *Heroic Sons and Daughters* (Yingxiong ernu; dir. Wu Zhaodi, 武兆堤, 1964), American military consultants and soldiers are depicted in the same way as Japanese invaders and corrupt Nationalist troops.

In the 1980s and 1990s, despite political friction between the US and China, anti-American sentiment never became very prominent until the US bombing of the Chinese Embassy in Yugoslavia in 1999. After the incident, a series of demonstrations in front of the US embassy in Beijing and its consulates in other cities ended with extreme acts such as burning American flags and throwing inkbottles at the wall of the embassy. The US president Bill Clinton apologized to China and ordered the embassy to fly its flag at half-mast to express the US's sorrow at the event. In Feng's New Year film for 1999, *Sorry Baby!*, a dialogue makes implicit reference to this issue. Toward the end of the film, Xiao Yun comes to Ruan's house to persuade him not to take revenge on Han Dong for the kidnapping. Ruan says that it would not be a big deal if he beat Han Dong up, because he could claim that it was just a mistake and apologize to Han. Then Han could throw inkbottles to break his window glass and he would fly a flag at half-mast for Han. This is a repetition of the embassy-bombing event, only without any of the keywords such as bombing, embassy, Yugoslavia, China or US. In this way, a seemingly non-political scene is actually loaded with political connotations. This short dialogue itself also reflects an attitude of suspicion toward the American political and diplomatic rhetoric about the event. Ruan's initial proposal to beat Han up, then shirk responsibility for the act by saying that it was just a mistake and apologizing to Han, alludes to the US explanation that the bombing was a mistake caused by out-of-date maps used by CIA. However,

Feng's very implicit way of dealing with this event shows his unwillingness to align his film with China's official condemnation of the US. Feng chooses a middle path, neither identifying absolutely with official rhetoric, nor supporting the American interpretation. Instead, he offers an implicit reference to the event that would be understood by sophisticated audiences.

The implicit reference to the embassy bombing in *Sorry Baby!* and other images of the US in Feng's New Year films indicate the ambivalent attitude toward the West that is embedded in Chinese culture. Further, these images also reveal the fact that Feng is concerned about the cultural, rather than political aspect, of these issues. For example, the imagined US in *Be There* is rendered from the perspectives of confrontation, assimilation, and interaction between American and Chinese culture. In *Sorry Baby!*, when politics could potentially play an important role in the events his film is dealing with, he chooses to evade direct associations with any political agenda. This apolitical attitude toward China's contemporary situation can, perhaps, be attributed to his awareness of the power of film censorship. Whenever he targets specific social problems and issues, he has to carefully mask them with light-hearted romantic comedy. In doing so, his audience will not be disturbed by the dark sides of reality and, more importantly, he will be able to circumvent film censorship.

Conclusion

Because of the huge success of Feng's New Year trilogy (*Party A, Party B, Be There or Be Square*, and *Sorry Baby!*) at the box office from 1997 to 1999, by 2000 this genre had come to be considered a lucrative business model and a way of making quick money. At the end of 2000, Chinese movie theaters were suddenly filled with posters promoting a number of different New Year films including *Defense and Counterattack* (Fangshou fanji, 2000, dir. Liang Tian; 梁天, 2000), *Beautiful House* (Meili de jia; dir. An Zhanjun 安这军, 2000), and *Family Tie* (Kaoshi yi jia qin; dir. Liu Xiaoguang 刘晓光, 2000). All were comedic in form and emphasized contemporary subjects that were popular in Chinese society, such as criticisms of the Chinese soccer team (*Defense and Counterattack*), housing problems for people with low incomes (*Beautiful House*), and a family's experience with the annual college entry examinations (*Family Tie*). Even the prestigious Fifth Generation director, Zhang Yimou, followed this vogue and made *Happy Times* (Xingfu shiguang).

In the face of exquisitely produced Hollywood imports, Feng's New Year films also proved to be successful explorations of a genre of film that could strengthen China's national film industry. His depiction of the life of little characters and their simple joys, frustrations, desires, and successes in contemporary China, and his revelation of certain important issues in Chinese society show his intention to make films for ordinary Chinese rather than international film festivals or elite film critics. As he said in an interview, "I'd rather make fun movies for one billion people than serious ones for a small group of cultural critics."[33] Through the theme of the victory of the little characters, who, though insignificant and unimportant are good-natured, and can finally achieve seemingly unreachable goals, Feng reassures his audiences of the value of these grassroots people in a society in constant flux. On the other hand, the images of the "big shots," who are portrayed as the forces that challenge and undermine the little characters' already miserable situation, are the subjects of mockery and satire. In the meantime, by accentuating issues and problems inherent in contemporary Chinese society, Feng also implies that the social context is another major driving force that shapes the distinction and inequality between the life of little characters and "big shots." Emphasizing the virtue and values of little characters and exposing the depravity and illegitimacy of the privileged stratum in a society with many issues and problems, Feng succeeds in creating a genre that establishes "a sort of tacit 'contract' between filmmakers and audience" through these shared thematic significances.[34]

The emergence of Chinese New Year films in the mid-1990s can be seen as the result of interactions between the internal forces of industry reform, regulations imposed by censorship, and the filmmaker's own attempts at self-expression. In the mid-1990s, withering support from the government for anything other than main melody films forced state-owned studios to seek out collaborations with non-state film production enterprises. As a result, works such as the New Year films, though produced privately, had access to the official sectors of filmmaking. Also because this collaboration was entirely profit-motivated, the films favored on both sides were those that could generate a good box-office return. Thus, this overall situation of the film industry led to the popularity of entertaining films such as romantic comedies and Feng's New Year films. In the meantime, the rise of comedic films was also associated with persistent official endeavors to control the ideology of Chinese cinema. After the Changsha Conference in 1996, it becomes very obvious that in addition to such content as ethics, morality, violence, sex, and religion, Chinese film authorities were also particularly concerned about ideological correctness of the film content. In this regard, apolitical light-hearted comedy was attractive as a genre that would not cause troubles with censorship. Sandwiched between profit imperatives resulting from the collaboration between state-owned and private production companies, and the careful surveillance of film content by censors, Feng changed his style from social conscience film, which had the potential to disturb audiences with its scathing portrayal and indictment of social problems, to lighthearted romantic comedy in which audiences could be comforted by the fact that all problems and difficulties were only transient. In the New Year films, Feng's vacillation between explicit social commentary and support for mainstream communist rhetoric reflects the "doubleness of the dream product [which] is often formulated as the way the ideological coexists with utopian," and explains why his films are so popular as "this is the utopian sensibility or strain that offsets the ideological in those popular, crowd-pleasing works that do so well at the box office."[35]

5

The "Corporate Era" of Chinese Cinema in the New Millennium and Feng's Post-New Year Production

Introduction

The new millennium has been a promising yet challenging time for Chinese cinema. The two forces that drove Chinese filmmaking in the 1990s—the ubiquitous ideological surveillance of ideology and the invasion of Hollywood cinema—have been, in many ways, transformed. The arbitrary decisions of the former were replaced by a more systematic film legislation while Hollywood cinema has gradually lost its predominance due to the pervasiveness of cheap pirated versions and the emergence of domestic blockbusters. Yet, despite these seemingly positive changes, the film industry has been under increasing pressure to maximize profits due to the rapid development of commercialization in almost every industry in China. Furthermore, after China's entrance into the World Trade Organization in 2002, and in light of its preparations for the 2008 Olympic Games, its desire to be recognized as an important member of the global market and economy has become increasingly urgent. Under these circumstances, forces of commercialization and Westernization have expanded pell-mell, first into the physical environment of China, and then into areas including art, cinema, and popular culture. In the process, popular films have been increasingly faced with the pressures of commodification rather than politics, and have sometimes had to answer the needs of both a domestic audience and potential foreign film distributors.

Though already an established filmmaker known for his popular films, Feng Xiaogang has inevitably been impacted by these tendencies. When the ideological control gradually loosened, his films began to touch upon more sensitive subjects and his social commentaries were rendered more directly.

Because of a loosening of official control over film ideology and more diversified demand in the film market, Feng has succeeded in gradually resurrecting subjects that used to be sensitive and returning to the classical romanticism of his early works such as *Behind the Moon* and *Chicken Feathers on the Ground*. However, with the film industry's growing demand for profitability and Chinese cinema's ambition to be recognized by the West, he has had to vacillate between expressing his own agenda and satisfying the expectations of his investors and audience. Given these pressures, in the first years of the new millennium, Feng's cinema has shown a different kind of "doubleness." At this time, the restrictions to his self-expression are more a result of capitalism and commercialism than politics. As a result, his films have combined direct social commentary or his personal artistic agenda with distracting elements intended to appeal to the mass audience or investors. We see, for example, more tie-ins for the products of investors in his films and farcical scenes at odds with the serious drama of his films. In his New Year films, what Feng was striving for was typical of a popular film director in a post-socialist society—a middle path between an artist's free expression on social issues and the film authorities' attempt to maintain the status quo. But since the beginning of the new millennium, new forces have emerged within Chinese cinema. The dilemma that Feng faced changed from a uniquely Chinese one to a more universal one, shared by many third world film directors working in a world of industrialized film production.

In Chinese cinema, the transformations have been taking place at different levels. The first years of the new millennium witnessed the emergence of a "corporative era" within the Chinese film industry as many major state-owned studios began to merge or rebuild themselves as large media or entertainment corporations. And then, around 2002, when the notion of an "industrializing Chinese cinema" became a central government initiative, highly commercialized modes of film production, advanced technologies, and high production-value blockbuster films burst onto the scene of Chinese cinema.

The mergers and integrations took place both vertically and horizontally in state film studios and many other kinds of state-owned enterprises. By combining production, distribution, and exhibition channels into one corporation, the newly established corporations are able to include all the vertical sectors of the movie industry. At the same time, by expanding their business into theme parks, travel resorts, and even real estate, these corporations became networks of media and entertainment groups. Unfortunately, the formal resemblance of these newly established media conglomerates to their Western counterparts did not lead to the same level of success enjoyed by the Western media groups. Most of the media groups in China performed poorly because of obstacles such as a lack of government support, huge financial and staff burdens and old bureaucratic system of managements. The industrialization of the cinema world can be seen as a measure initiated by the state film administration to supplement the unsatisfactory results of the reform of the state-owned film studios. In 2003, for the first time in Chinese film history, cinema was recognized as an "industry" in an official film administrative document.[1] Several other such documents followed. This signaled the opening of film production and exhibition to private and foreign investors and encouraged a greater diversity of genres and subjects. The film authorities' intention to maximize profits from the movie industry could not be more obvious.

Under pressing profit imperatives, entertainment films, advocated in the 1990s by only a handful of directors including Feng Xiaogang, finally triumphed over other genres of cinema and began to have a magnetic appeal to filmmakers from different backgrounds. Films featuring popular subject matter and high production quality comprised the majority of Chinese films produced in the early 2000s. Some filmmakers, represented by the prestigious Fifth Generation directors, Zhang Yimou and Chen Kaige, began to take advantage of the vogue of materialism and consumerism in Chinese society to promote a "cinema of attractions." By de-emphasizing narrative, but providing beautiful and astonishing visual effects, all-star casts, and lavish special effects, the two directors recent films, *Hero* (Ying xiong; dir. Zhang Yimou, 2002), *House of Flying Daggers* (Shi mian mai fu; dir. Zhang Yimou, 2004) and *Promise* (Wu ji; dir. Chen Kaige, 2005) provide the audience with a visual feast. In order to attract the widest possible audience, they not only used transnational Asian stars from the Mainland, Hong Kong, Taiwan, Korea and Japan, but also utilized a broad range of advertising methods ranging from extravagant premiers to exaggerated tabloid news stories. Although successful in attracting large audiences to the movie theaters, these films failed to gain either good reviews from film critics or positive "word-of-mouth" responses from general audiences. A young audience member was so disappointed by *The Promise* that he made a short DV film, re-editing and adding a new soundtrack to footage from the original film, with the intention of mocking Chen Kaige's blockbuster. The short film, titled *A Bloody Case Caused by a Mantou* (Yige mantou yinfa de xuean; dir. Hu Ge), was widely circulated on the Internet and seems to have gained popularity at least equal to *The Promise*.

Feng's films from the early 2000s represented the other tendency of entertainment films. Although paying equally unapologetic attention to visuality and box-office revenue, he took a different approach to lure audiences. Not content to merely satisfy ordinary Chinese with an escapist view of reality, these films touch upon either current social problems or universal and humanistic themes and thus echoed their audience's concerns and obsessions. From *Sigh* (Yisheng tanxi, 2001), *Big Shot's Funeral* (Da wan, 2002), and *Cell Phone* (Shou ji, 2003), to *A World Without Thieves* (Tianxia wuzei, 2004) and *The Banquet* (Ye yan, 2006), light-hearted comedy was replaced with bittersweet drama or even historical epic tragedy, but a sense of humor and cynicism remained. Feng's films from this period foreground the irredeemable dark side of human beings with the effects of rapid commercial expansion, and articulate his concerns over the impact and dangers brought on by wealth and power—decaying morality in the face of the temptation of fame (*Sigh, Cell Phone, The Banquet*), the intrusion of commercialism into ordinary people's lives (*Big Shot's Funeral*), and the doomed destiny of people marginalized by a materialistic society (*A World Without Thieves*). However, Feng should not be seen as an absolute rebel against the trends of commercialization. Although dealing with more sensitive subjects, his films have adopted numerous commercial elements in their production and promotion. Previously casting only Ge You as his regular male lead, his recent films have begun to feature all-star casts from different regions of China; and instead of telling stories of urban people in a contemporary society using only prosaic film techniques, he has begun to depict conspiracies and power struggles in the imperial household relying on lavish special effects and extravagant mise-en-scenes. His latest film, *The Banquet*, expresses his ambition to handle high-budget blockbuster films instead of only urban cinema; he even ventured into making a historical-costume drama film, an entirely new genre of film for him. In these films, the compromises have been more with commercial demands than political ideology.

This chapter begins by providing a general picture of Chinese cinema, with a special emphasis on the mergers and mega-mergers taking place in state-owned studios in the early 2000s and the series of official documents that attempted to industrialized Chinese cinema. Against this background, I will examine the increasing enthusiasm of local and foreign production companies for Chinese domestic films and local Chinese markets. Through this examination, I will argue for the emergence of a highly commercialized and profit-driven mainstream cinema in the new millennium, which attracted filmmakers from different background. Many Fifth Generation directors, such as Zhang Yimou and Chen Kaige, for example, shifted their attention from art cinema to popular cinema and began to be absorbed into the mainstream. If Chinese cinema in the second half of the 1990s was economically liberal, but ideologically restricted, in the early 2000s the barriers of censorship began to be lifted. As a result, there was an increase in both film productions and the diversity of film subject matter. In particular, popular cinema, revived by Feng in the mid-1990s, became the major force in the Chinese film market from 2000 to 2006. The largest part of the chapter introduces Feng Xiaogang's five most recent films, made from 2000 to 2006. As mentioned earlier, these films show a shift from light-hearted romantic comedy to serious dramas and tragedies, and a new kind of "doubleness," in which the site of the filmmaker's resistance and cooperation changed from political ideology to commercialization. After testing the waters of censorship with *Sigh*, a film featuring a devastatingly tragic story of an extramarital love affair without any comedic elements, Feng's films grew increasingly cynical and critical. In *Big Shot's Funeral* and *A World Without Thieves* Feng replaced the little characters' victories with big shots' frustration, thus exposing poignant problems brought about by commercialization, materialism, and the development of high-technology. In these films, Feng's criticisms of social problems were no longer implicit, as in his earlier films, but had become explicit. In *The Banquet*, a Shakespearean court drama, he went a step further by dealing with the devastation and crudity brought by struggles over power, fame and love among people in the highest levels of society. In spite of these changes, however, Feng could not escape the box-office mania and the expansion of commercialization that characterized the film industry during this period. Even as his films grew more and more cynical, they also began to cooperate with his investors' needs and the demand of maximizing profits. Feng's filmmaking in the early 2000s signifies the double-edged consequences of commercialization, which is characterized by a more unapologetic pursuit for profit-maximization and a demand for a less ideologically determined industry.

"Corporate Era" of Chinese Film Industry

On December 11, 2001, following long-term negotiations beginning in 1986, China officially became the 143rd member of the World Trade Organization (WTO). China's long delayed entrance into the WTO was due to debates regarding the effect this entry would have on the global economy.[2] On the one hand, as the most populous country in the world, China is the world's largest market. Its market of over 1.3 billion people provides corporations with opportunities for rapid growth in product sales. On the other hand, the cheap labor, inexpensive industrial land, and educated workforce that make China an ideal manufacturing center also threaten other established centers. Not only would developing countries that had historically offered cheap labor suffer from Chinese competition, developed countries, such as the US, were also threatened with the loss of thousands of manufacturing jobs. But attitudes toward China's entry into the WTO varied in different industries, depending on the expected benefits or losses that would result. Businessmen who favored China's accession to the WTO included Hollywood moguls, who envisioned great potential benefits for Hollywood. According to Jack Valenti, the chairman and Chief Executive Officer of the Motion Picture Association of America, China promised the Hollywood film industry that the following benefits would be given to Hollywood upon China's entry into the WTO:[3]

- China will double the quota of "revenue sharing" films from 10 to 20. (Revenue sharing means that China splits the box-office receipts on a 50-50 basis). China will also allow an additional 20 foreign films per year on flat fee licensing terms. By the third year, the combined film quota will be increased from 40 to 50 films.
- China will, for the first time, permit foreign investment in joint ventures engaged in the distribution of videos.
- China will lift its investment ban on cinema ownership. US investors will be allowed to own up to 49% of companies that build, own, and operate cinemas.
- China will reduce tariffs on films from the current level of 9% of the value of the film to 5%. Tariffs on home videos will drop from 15% to 10%.
- China will also assume full obligations to protect intellectual property, as required by the WTO's Agreement on Trade Related Intellectual Property.

All these measures, which seemed to offer few reciprocal benefits for China, if fully implemented, would lift almost all the major barriers to the entrance of US films into the Chinese market. The potential benefits for Hollywood were tremendous. Valenti estimated in a talk delivered in 1999 that "if the barriers to film distribution were lifted, and if a legitimate video sales and rentals market captured the market now lost to piracy, an increase in US revenues in China in excess of $200 million is achievable."[4]

In contrast to the rosy picture of Hollywood cinema's potential in China, if Valenti's dream came true, domestic Chinese cinema would be faced with nothing more than an expansion of the menace that had been hanging over the Chinese market even before Valenti's optimistic talk. As we saw in Chapter 4, for example, when Hollywood films were officially imported into China in the mid-1990s, 70 percent of total box-office revenue went to Hollywood imports. The most popular film in box-office returns was the juggernaut *Titanic* in 1997, which collected about US$4 million from Beijing's movie theaters alone, and 173 million dollars nationwide.[5] Starting in 2003, as part of its obligations as a member of the WTO, China had to raise the quota of imported films to twenty pictures per year. Although the box-office revenues of these films did not return to the impressive amounts recorded by Hollywood imports in the 1990s (mainly because of pervasive cheap pirated versions and inadequate show times due to a limited number of screens and first-class movie theaters), their potential still should not be underestimated. In 2003, the total box-office revenue of the top ten among the twenty imported films, all from Hollywood, was US$299 million, which is much more than the 200 million estimated by Valenti.[6] It was not until 2004 that the total box-office revenue of domestic films exceeded that of the imports, with 10% more income than imported films.[7] In 2005, the total box-office income reached a historical high of RMB 2 billion, of which the total revenue generated by domestic films greatly exceeded that of the imported films— approximately 60% of the total revenue came from domestic films.[8] But a closer examination of this figure shows that the apparent success may be somewhat misleading. In 2005, among the 260 films that passed the censors and gained exhibition licenses, only 150 found their way into movie theaters, while more than 100 films were never screened for an audience.[9] With more than one-third of domestic productions losing money, the remaining 150 films took 60% of the total box-office revenue, whereas the approximately 20 imported films took 40%. In the near future, when the number of imported films doubles or triples, domestic films will struggle to maintain such a record.

Besides the threats posed by imported foreign films, an internal force emerging in the early 2000s also precipitated the dramatic reconstruction of the state-owned film industry. At the end of the 1990s, the central government began issuing documents to initiate reform within Chinese culture. These documents were intended to encourage both the generation of profits from the rich resources of Chinese culture and promote the value of Chinese culture in the world as China gradually became one of its important members. In 2000, the document "Notice on Economic Policies Supporting Development of Cultural Institutions" (Guanyu zhichi wenhua shiye fazhan ruogan jingji zhengce de tongzhi) was issued by the State Council of the PRC. This document reinforced the policy of taxation of profitable cultural sectors such as TV ads, nightclubs, golf courses, commercial publications and the box-office income of imported films. It also increased government support for non-profit cultural institutions and projects such as the State Symphony Orchestra, National Library and main melody films.[10] This document, along with several others issued in the early 2000s, tended to reduce the state's burden of full sponsorship of non-profit cultural institutions and looked for ways to finance these institutions and non-profit projects through alternative sources. In 2003, even more specific measures for re-constructing previously state-owned cultural institutions were implemented after a meeting on the problem of reforming "cultural institutions" held by the Central Government in June. At the meeting, nine cities and provinces, including Beijing, Shanghai, Guangdong and Zhejiang, and 35 cultural institutions were chosen as the places where these reforms would be implemented. During this experimental period, the main industries targeted for reform were sectors of the so-called mass culture—publishing, media, performance and film, while the main purpose of the reforms were to bring an end to the decade-long full state-sponsorship in most of these sectors and to push them to the forefront of a market economy by refashioning them from state-owned institutions to modern enterprises with various source of investments. Consequently, several large-scale mergers took place in industries such as publishing, television and broadcasting and cinema, and between previously state-owned cultural institutions, private companies and joint ventures with foreign companies. Against this background of a government-promoted industrialization of Chinese culture, a new and even more dramatic round of industry reforms in Chinese cinema was implemented in the early 2000s.

Beginning in 1999, some state-owned studios began to be either reconstructed as joint-venture companies with private investments or incorporated into large entertainment-related enterprises. Next, as the three sectors of production, distribution, and exhibition were opened to private companies, many local and international investors got involved in the moviemaking industry. Gradually, films made by these local, non-state production companies became a vital force in Chinese cinema.

The beginning of these reforms in the state-owned filmmaking business was signaled by a document co-issued by The Ministry of Culture and The State Administration of Radio, Film, and Television (SARFT, formerly MRFT): "Guanyu jiakuai dianying chanye fazhan de ruogan yijian" (Opinions on Speeding the Development of the Film Industry).[11] This document outlined ways "to enhance the capacity of production and operation." Among these ways, the foremost was the reconstruction of state filmmaking businesses into enterprise groups by means of either the integration of the previously separated sectors of production, distribution, exhibition, printing, VCD/DVD production, and sales into one enterprise/corporation, or the merging of state-owned film studios with other state-owned entertainment enterprises.

This officially endorsed method for strengthening state filmmaking institutions was soon brought into effect in the reforms of major film studios. Beijing Film Studio, the most prolific filmmaking center in the 1990s, and other state-owned filmmaking-related institutions in Beijing, including Beijing Film Printing and Recording Factory, China Film Equipment Company, China Film Co-Production Corporation, and the Movie Channel of China Central TV station, were merged into a large enterprise called China Film Group (CFG).[12] This merger in 1999, before the issuing of "Opinions on Deepening the Reform of Film Industry," represented the first stage of reform—the transformation of state-owned studios into media empires consisting of all vertical sections of the film industry. In 2004, another major move regarding the ownership of the supposedly state-owned enterprises was taken by CFG. After several international media companies became shareholders in some of CFG's subsidiary companies, the group was changed from a property of the state to a Chinese-foreign joint-venture enterprise. In November 2004, Sony Picture Television Group and China Film Group co-organized a company, Huasuo TV and Film Digital Production, which was to focus on digital TV and film production, with CFG holding 51% of the company shares and Sony, 49%.[13] At around the same time, another of CFG's subsidiary production companies, a company specializing in co-productions with foreign companies, Zhongying Hua'an Hengdian Film and TV Corporation Ltd., was founded through investments from CFG, the Hengdian Group (a private enterprise whose business encompasses electronics, pharmaceutical and chemical production, film and entertainment, and property investment), and Time Warner Inc.[14] The previously independent Beijing Film Studio, after merging all its assets with the CFG, not only became one of the subsidiary branches of the parent company, but was also physically removed from its site in a busy area in the northwestern part of the city and relocated to the northeastern outskirts of the city where a huge complex consisting of 20 shooting stages, a public square, and movie theaters will be constructed.[15] Although in some ways echoing Thomas Ince's groundbreaking endeavor in establishing his own studio, "Inceville," in a remote part of the Santa Ynez Canyon near Hollywood in 1914, laying the foundation for the money machine of Hollywood some ten years later, the new location of the Beijing Film Studio was a cause for both hope and concern among its employees. The director of BFS, Han Sanping, though optimistic about the capacity for filmmaking at the new site and the possibility of meeting BFS's target of producing 10 films annually after its merger with the CGF, remained concerned that BFS would become merely a production unit of one of CFG's subsidiary companies. As a result, the previously preeminent and self-contained Beijing Film Studio could very possibly be relegated to history.[16]

In 2001, BFS's model for reform was borrowed by the Shanghai Film Studio (SFS), which merged with ten other moviemaking-related institutions, including Shanghai Animated Film Studio, Shanghai Scientific and Educational Film Studio, Shanghai Dubbing Film Studio, Shanghai Film Technology, and Shanghai Union Theater Chain to form a new entity called Shanghai Film Group Corporation (SFGC).[17] Similar to the way in which CFG was constructed, the SFGC not only embraced all sectors of film industry, but also resorted to foreign capital to strengthen its financial power. In June 2001, the US-based industrial giant, Kodak Company, invested US$4 million in SFGC's opening of a new movie theater, Kodak Cinema World, in a busy commercial area of Shanghai.[18] In 2003, Warner Brother International signed contracts with the SFGC for an ambitious plan to open ten first-class movie theaters in China.[19] In April 2004, the Japanese media and advertising company, Dentsu Group joined SFGC in co-founding Shanghai SFGC-Dentsu Culture and Communication Corp. Ltd., a corporation which will import Japanese animated films for a cartoon channel of Shanghai TV station.[20] These mergers, which first established a comprehensive corporation encompassing all the major sectors of the film industry and then attracted investments from domestic and international media groups, represent one of the modes of industry reform—mergers between film studios and other entertainment-related businesses.

Another mode of reform, the acquisition of state-owned film studios by private-owned groups or enterprises whose own businesses were not related to film production, is represented by the reconstruction of the Changchun Film Studio (CFS), one of the earliest Communist filmmaking centers. In 2000, Changchun Film Studio announced its intent to reorganize the studio into a joint-stock company with Guoxin Investment Group. Guoxin, a provincial investment enterprise engaging in real estate construction and management, was to invest RMB 13.5 million in the project.[21] If the reorganization of the Beijing Film Studio provided certain possibilities for the strengthening of the studio, the deal between CFS and Guoxin was more of an exploitation of the assets and properties of the state-owned studio. Since the end of the 1990s, in the name of co-development, Guoxin's newly constructed apartment buildings have occupied the majority of the land where CFS's production studios were once located. Accused of selling out state-properties, the director of the CFS, Zhao Guoguang (also a major shareholder in Guoxin), promised to use RMB 3 billion earned from selling CFS's land to Guoxin plus bank loans to build a theme-park/movie theater equivalent to Universal Studios in Los Angeles. This project, consisting of technologically advanced movie theaters and other film-related adventure projects, would be located in the outskirts of the city of Changchun.

A similar direction has also been taken by Xi'an Film Studio (XFS), which, in May 2000, was reorganized into Xiying Company Limited (XCL) along with eight other companies, none of which were film-related. Also selling part of its land to the College of Film, TV, and Communication of the Xi'an Foreign Language Institute, XCL planned to use the earnings to build an extravagant complex functioning as a TV and film production center, travel resort, and theme park in the suburbs of the city of Xi'an.

In both cases, after the selling of the studios' physical facilities, new production centers remained only in the planning stages and the film production of both studios declined dramatically. Most "productions" of these two state-owned studios in recent years have been only nominally linked to the studios. The studios have merely outsourced their equipment or staff and casts to film projects undertaken by private or foreign companies, rather than truly participating in the whole process of moviemaking. In 2004, CFS produced 13 films, but none were made independently by the studio.[22] In 2005, one of the major feature films on the production list of CFS was a Sino-American co-production, *Smile* (Weixiao; dir. Jeffery Kramer, 2005). In this film, investment from CFS was only 10% of the total production budget, and none of the scriptwriters, directors, or cast members came from CFS.[23]

The "corporate era" of Chinese cinema brought some significant changes that were unthinkable in the decades when the cinema was fully controlled by the Party as a propaganda tool. Most importantly, the involvement of foreign capital in all sectors of the film industry undermined the very ideological foundations of Chinese cinema. Previously regarded as a pedagogical tool helping to support Party policy, Chinese cinema increasingly had to answer to the demands of domestic and foreign investors for profits. As a result, Party film policy had to change in order to both legitimate the Party-approved industry reforms and to lift barriers that had served as impediments to the progress of reform. The striving for profit and commercialization in every possible way became a major preoccupation of the Chinese filmmaking industry in the early 2000s.

Softer Censorship and Loosening Control

On April 19, 2005, a seminar on American film and TV censorship and rating systems, organized by an American educational institute, was held in Beijing. The seminar was attended by not only many Chinese directors, such as Chen Kaige and Feng Xiaogang, but also government officials and film administration authorities.[24] Indeed, starting in the early 2000s Chinese film officials showed their interest in foreign rating systems on many such occasions. This signaled their willingness to consider the adoption of a rating system that would fit the special needs of China's culture, society, and politics. During the same period, some specific regulations for the system were also discussed. For example, some officials believed that the age of sixteen should serve as a major line of demarcation in ratings.[25] The director of SARFT, Tong Gang, also said that China would not simply copy the rating systems used in other countries; instead, China's rating system would have its own characteristics.[26] Whatever the case, a transformation from hard censorship, which decides what is permitted on the screen, to the soft censorship of a rating system, which does not proscribe the content of films but rather classifies them as appropriate for certain segments of the public, appeared very likely to take place in Chinese cinema.

The first signs of this transformation can be found in a document regarding film censorship issued by SARFT in September 2003. Based on the *Film Censorship Regulation*, SARFT issued *Regulations of Film Script Approval and Film Censorship (Tentative)*, which required all licensed filmmaking institutions to first submit a draft script of 1,000 words in order to get approval for shooting. According to this new regulation, after the film was completed, as long as the content is not related to certain sensitive subjects, for example, Cultural Revolution and June Fourth Movement, the film could be submitted to local film censorship boards, rather than the film censorship committee of the SARFT. In calling for a brief preview of a film project before shooting started and by disseminating power from a central censorship committee to other local or provincial censorship committees, these measures not only reduced the possibility of censoring a completed film and thus causing a total waste of resources and money, but also provided space for different approaches and opinions in film censorship. Out of 214 films that were produced and submitted to film censors in 2004, only one film, a Hong Kong production, *Jianghu* (Jianghu; dir. Huang Jingfu 黄精甫, 2004), was denied approval for exhibition in Mainland China because of its depiction of violence.[27] In comparison to 1997, when 88 films were produced, but only 44 obtained approval for release from the censorship board, the year of 2004 demonstrated the significant changes brought about by the new film censorship legislation.[28]

In August 2004, the Film Censorship Center of the Zhejiang Provincial Administration of Radio, Film, and TV became the first local censorship committee authorized by the SARFT to censor films produced by provincially licensed production companies.[29] Later in the same year, Guangdong province was also granted the authority to censor locally produced films.[30] On many occasions in 2005, Tong Gang of SARFT has indicated that a rating system that fits the situation of Chinese cinema will soon be implemented to reflect ongoing changes in censorship policies.[31] Consequently, the year 2005 witnessed as many as 261 films passing censorship, the largest number of films to gain approval for exhibition in the history Chinese cinema.

Not only was the control of film content loosened, other aspects of film administration became less strict with the passing of new legislation. In September 2003, SARFT issued *Regulations on the Administration of Sino-Overseas Co-Production Films*, which, in comparison with similar legislation issued in 1994, provided foreign investors with greater freedom in producing films in China. For example, according to the 1994 legislation, feature films written and directed by Chinese filmmakers were not allowed to be solely sponsored by foreign investors. But, in the 2003 legislation, this limitation was eliminated. Another document further opened up the sectors of distribution and exhibition to foreign and private investors. The *Provisional Rules for Operational Qualification Access of Film Production, Distribution and Exhibition Enterprises*, issued by SARFT in early 2003, allowed non-state film production companies to apply for production licenses, a privilege that had formerly been the exclusive prerogative of state-owned studios. In addition, the sectors of distribution and exhibition were all opened to non-state film companies. According to the document, any company with registered capital of more than RMB 5 million, after certain application procedures, could participate in distributing domestic films. In terms of the exhibition sector, the regulation encouraged private companies to invest in the operation of theater chains. After the issuing of these documents, not only were domestic private companies finally granted access to the previously state-monopolized film industry, foreign capital's involvement in the operation of Chinese moviemaking was also no longer a taboo. Also in 2003, SARFT issued *Regulations of Foreign Investment Movie Theaters (Tentative)*, which allowed foreign investors to open movie theaters in China. The underlining purpose of this new legislation was to legitimate and encourage foreign investment in the sector of film exhibition and thereby to import the Western form of film exhibition, consisting of multi-screen theaters with high-tech video and audio effects, into China.

Because of these pieces of legislation, previously centralized film censorship was replaced by local censorship centers and will possibly be replaced by a film rating system, and the previous state monopolies over film production, distribution, and exhibition gave way to the legitimate involvement of private and foreign capital in these sectors. Although the fate of state-owned studios is still not clear after these dramatic industry reforms, it is certain that private film companies benefited greatly from these new policies. Among all sectors in the film industry, only the distribution of imported films was still monopolized by state companies, all other sectors were opened to non-state investors. Since 2001, all domestically produced box-office hits have been made by private film companies. In 2001, Feng Xiaogang's *Big Shot's Funeral*, a film co-produced by Huayi Brothers and Taihe Film and TV Investment Company, a private film company, and Warner Brothers (Asia), took first place at the box office with revenues of RMB 30 million. In 2002, the first place was Zhang Yimou's *Hero*, made by a private company, Beijing New Picture Company (Beijing xin huamian yingye youxian gongsi). In 2003, the top film was Feng's *Cell Phone*, a production of Huayi Brothers and Taihe. In 2004 Zhang Yimou's juggernaut *House of Flying Daggers*, another New Picture production, was the box-office hit. In 2005, the champion at the box office was Chen Kaige's *The Promise*, a co-production of Chen Kaige's own production company, Beijing 21st century Shengkai Culture and Communication Company, and China Film Group.

The impact of the changing film policy on Chinese cinema has not only been seen in the burgeoning production of private film companies, but also in an increased number of annual film productions. Chinese domestic film production in 2004 reached a record of 212 films, which almost doubled the annual average of film production after 1990.[32] Investment in these films has been mainly from non-state companies, which indisputably have become the main force in Chinese film industry. For example, among the RMB 4.8 billion used in production of CFG's films, only 60 million came from either CFG or the government, with the remainder coming from either private or foreign film companies.[33]

Another influence of the loosened ideological control of Chinese cinema has been the surfacing of the previously banned underground Sixth Generation filmmakers. As we saw in Chapter 4, important films of the Sixth Generation, including Jia Zhangke's four films made before 2003, *Xiaoshan Returns Home* (1995), *Xiaowu* (1997), *Platform* (Zhantai, 2000), and *Unknown Pleasure* (Ren xiaoyao, 2002), were denied approval for exhibition by the censorship committee. But Jia's film, *World* (Shijie, 2005), made after the changes in censorship regulations in 2003, encountered no significant difficulties with the censorship board. In an interview, Jia mentioned that his reason for attempting to resurface from the underground was not related to a desire to change his style. Rather, it was the relaxed environment of censorship that made him want to participate. "Originally...the censorship apparatus was to a large degree restricting our freedom of choice. But now it looks like we'll have the chance to express ourselves freely, and that's why I'm willing to give it a try."[34] After *World* was submitted for review, although Jia was prepared for requests for revisions from the censors, he was surprised that, with the exception of a few lines of vulgar language, the majority of the film was allowed to remain intact.[35] Not coincidentally, another underground filmmaker, Wang Xiaoshuai, also emerged in mainstream cinema in 2005. The ban over his previously highly acclaimed film *Beijing Bicycle* was lifted and his new film *Shanghai Dream* (Qinghong, 2005) was also approved by the film censors and submitted to the Cannes Film Festival as China's official submission.[36] Similar cases can be found in the work of other Sixth Generation directors, such as Lou Ye, Zhang Yuan, Zhang Yang and Jiang Wen.

Commercialization and the Domestic Turn of Chinese Cinema

If the second half of the 1990s featured four different modes of production, the early years of the new millennium have witnessed a ubiquitous compliance with a mainstream tendency toward commercialization, as filmmakers from all backgrounds—Fifth or Sixth Generation filmmakers, specialists in main melody or commercial films—were driven by the pervasive profit imperatives.

This tendency toward commercialization could not have taken place in Chinese cinema without the government's implementation of several policies promoting the full-scale industrialization of Chinese culture. In the early 2000s, after many decades of indecision over how to view the function of cinema, the film administration officials finally took the audacious step of acknowledging cinema as an industry that should operate primarily under market demand and aim at profit-making, rather than a propaganda tool under full control of the Party. Previously, official documents had always referred to cinema as "a cause" or *shiye*, indicating that cinema was an undertaking that bore mostly political and pedagogical functions. However, in the early 2000s, many documents issued by the SARFT began to refer to cinema as an "industry" or *chanye*. Furthermore, in many documents issued by SARFT, the Ministries of Culture and Propaganda, and in talks given by film officials, it became increasingly clear that one of the foremost tasks for all film officials was to industrialize Chinese cinema so that it could perform well in both domestic and international markets.

In early 2003, Zhao Shi, Vice Director of the Film Bureau at SARFT, gave a talk at the National Conference of Film Production in which she reviewed Chinese cinema in 2002 and proposed guidelines for its further development in 2003. In the talk, entitled *To Fully Implement the Essence of the Sixteen National Congress and to Foster and Promote the Film Industry's Reform, Development and Innovation* (Quanmian guanche shiliu da jingsheng jiakuai tuijin dianying shengchanye de gaige fazhan chuangxin), Zhao admitted the Chinese cinema's industrialization was still primitive and immature; thus, she suggested that the major task of 2003 would be to consider how to propel this process of industrialization. She commented,

It is clearly indicated in the report of the Sixteenth National Congress that, "Developing culture industry is a major way of letting the socialist advantaged culture[37] prosper and satisfying people's spiritual and cultural needs. Comrade Li Changchun[38] also specifically indicated at the meeting of directors of all-China propaganda departments that "Film and TV productions and art-related work-units should accelerate their paces toward marketization. Facing the needs of market, industrialization and enterprise are the basic paths of developing culture. Film industry is the most promising pillar-industry among culture industries, as it is a special industry, a knowledge-intensive industry characterized by visual-audio art, high-technology, high-investment and high-risk, and also a culture and entertainment industry extremely popular among the people.[39]

This very explicit emphasis on developing Chinese cinema into an industry was later reinforced by many other official documents issued by SARFT, the most important of which was "Several Suggestions on Fostering the Development of the Film Industry" (Quanyu jiakuai dianying chanye fazhan de ruogan yijian), issued by SARFT in February, 2004. This document argued for the establishment of a more market-oriented film industry with diversity in many aspects, such as sources of investment, film genres and subjects, modes of productions and channels of distribution. In the section on "Objectives and Mission of the Film Industry," it specifies,

The first two decades of the new millennium are the most strategically crucial period for the development of the Chinese film industry. We need to reform film institutions and systems and establish a mode of industry operated by market demands, the independent operation of film enterprises and government legal supervision. We need to build a film production and operation system with multiple investment sources, diversified modes of management and production, multiple channels of distribution and multiple levels of product development…[40]

Sanctioned by the central administrative agency, the trend toward commercialization expanded into almost every aspect of Chinese cinema. Not only were state-owned studios re-organized into media groups, private and foreign film production companies also became more aggressive in joining this trend. The highly commercialized and profit-driven model of Hollywood productions proved especially tantalizing to Chinese state and private film productions. Furthermore, the success of Feng's films at the domestic box-office in the late 1990s drove the attention of Chinese and foreign filmmakers to the potential of domestic filmmakers and films with localized subject matter. As a result, the feverish commercialization of cinema has been accompanied by a domestic turn: the targeting of domestic audiences with the unmistakable goal of making profits. Not only have prestigious Fifth Generation directors, such as Zhang Yimou and Chen Kaige, abandoned their elitist *auteur* pretensions and begun to make films meant to appeal to the general domestic audience, the previously subversive Sixth Generation directors, including Zhang Yuan, Jia Zhangke, and Lou Ye, have given up their position as dissidents and begun to be absorbed into commercial film production.

Starting in 2000, Fifth Generation directors have shown an unapologetic attitude toward the making of pure entertainment films. Zhang Yimou's collaboration with the savvy businessman Zhang Weiping, the founder of Beijing New Picture Company, in 1996, signaled a turning point in his film career. Zhang Yimou's seven films made after 1996, *Be Cool* (You hua haohao shuo, 1997), *The Road Home* (Wo de fuqin muqin, 1999), *Not One Less* (Yige dou bu neng shao, 1999), *Happy Times* (Xingfu shiguang, 2000), *Hero* (Yingxiong, 2002), *House of Flying Daggers* (Shimian maifu, 2004), *Riding Alone for Thousands of Miles* (Qianli zou dan qi, 2005) and *Curse of the Golden Flower* (Mancheng jindai huangjinjia, 2006) were all sponsored by the New Picture Company.

In comparison with the films Zhang made before 1996, such as *To Live* (Huozhe, 1994), *Raise the Red Lantern* (Da hong denglong gaogao gua, 1991), and *Judou* (Ju dou, 1990), there are both similarities and differences with his more recent films. While Zhang has totally given up iconoclastic targeting of decadence and depravity in the Chinese political system (*To Live*), Chinese culture and history (*Raise the Red Lantern*), and humanity (*Judou*), he has continued to strive to produce films that are appreciated by foreign film critics. But at the same time, he also paid close attention to the domestic audience's response to his films. For instance, in 2000, encouraged by the success of New Year films, he followed suit with the film *Happy Times*, targeting the New Year audience. The film tells the story of an aging bachelor, Zhao, an unemployed factory worker, who woos an obese woman by claiming that he is a manager of a hotel. Taking advantage of his love and "wealth," his new girlfriend shirks her responsibility for raising her blind stepdaughter and lets the man take care of her. Zhao and his former colleagues, all unemployed workers, devise one ploy after another to fool the girl into believing his lies. In the process, a tender friendship develops. In an interview, Zhang explains that *Happy Times* is a tragi-comedy (*beixiju*), through which he wants to provide a touching story about honest human relationships in a materialistic world.[41] However, this intention appears not to have reached his audiences.

The film was first released in January 2001 in Dalian, the northeast port-city where the film was shot. According to an article published in *Yangcheng wanbao* (Yangcheng evening news) on March 15, 2001, the film's open ending, which does not provide any clear resolutions for the blind girl's fate nor of Zhao's plot to cover up his lies, disappointed not only audiences in Dalian and Beijing but also potential foreign distributors. In order to save the film from a box-office Waterloo, Zhang recalled the whole cast and crew and re-shot the entire ending.[42] Re-released in Shanghai and Guangzhou in March, the new version, which is now circulated in the overseas market, ends with the girl knowing all Zhao's plots and leaving him to find her father in the south; Zhao is killed in a car accident while looking for her. This ending still did not manage to rescue the film at the box office. The tragic ending was totally out-of-place in the traditionally happy atmosphere of Chinese New Year. In the first Saturday of the film's initial release in Shanghai, one of the first-run theaters sold only sixteen tickets. In Huanyi Theater, another first-run movie theater, the total income of the first week of exhibition was only RMB 16,000, while another lesser known domestic film, *Gua Sha Treatment* (Gua sha; dir. Zheng Xiaolong 郑晓龙, 2001) earned RMB 60,000.[43] The box-office failure of *Happy Times* was not offset by positive film reviews. Harsh reviews criticizing flaws in the plot and narrative, the altered ending, Zhang's inability to deal with contemporary subjects, and the methods used in casting the film (Zhang used a national call to recruit the leading characters), appeared in almost all major newspapers in China.[44] Zhang's attempt to cater to the tastes of a popular audience by altering the ending after the film was already released resulted in miserable total box-office revenues of only around RMB 8 million nationwide, almost four times less than the income of Feng's New Year film, *Big Shot's Funeral*, released at the end of same year.[45]

Apparently having learnt his lesson from his failed attempt at New Year films, Zhang's next two films, *Hero* and *House of Flying Daggers*, both set in ancient China, began to follow another trend that seemed more promising not only domestically, but also internationally. In 2000, Asian-American film director Ang Lee's *Crouching Tiger, Hidden Dragon* (Wohu canglong), collected four awards at the 73rd Annual Academy Awards. Whereas Chinese fans of martial art films, who are accustomed to the astonishing high-flying fights common in Hong Kong cinema, giggled with disdain over the artificial special effects and naïve plots of *Crouching Tiger*, American audiences found it poetic and attractive. A *New York Times* review writes that in the fight and actions scenes, "Mr. Lee has found a way to make even the action feel poetic and spiritual, while sparked by a high adrenaline content."[46] In China, the unexpected awards and acclaim the film received from the West inspired many Chinese filmmakers to explore the potential of this genre. He Ping made *Warriors of Heaven and Earth* (Tiandi yingxiong, 2003), a Tang Dynasty (7th to 10th century) story of two warriors' endeavor to protect a princess on an adventure trip, while Chen Kaige's blockbuster film *Promise* (Wu ji), a mixture of action, mystery, fantasy, and romance, was started in 2004 and released in 2005.

Three of the four films Zhang Yimou has made after 2000 were martial art films. *Hero* provides a new take on the millennia-old tale of the assassination of the King of Qin. Extremely similar to the narrative structure of Akiro Kurosawa's film *Rashomon* (1950), in which four witnesses to a murder have strikingly contradictory accounts of the event, *Hero* tells the story of the assassination from different characters' perspectives. However, dwarfed by its exquisitely and artificially constructed visual effects, the contradictory accounts of stories and counter-stories in *Hero* do not succeed in creating an equally exquisite sense of narrative complexity. Instead, audiences were frequently distracted by the beautiful but excessively poetic rendition of fights and war scenes, and the constantly shifting perspective created more confusion than suspense. Besides, intrusions of many contemporary vernacular words, such as "one-night stand" (*yi ye qing* 一夜情) and "peace" (*heping* 和平), in the dialogue between swordsmen and kings from the third century BC caused much spontaneous laughter and giggling at the theater.[47] Like *Hero*, *House of Flying Daggers* features beautifully crafted visual effects, but still has fatal flaws in plots and narrative. Set in the Tang Dynasty, the film is an action/suspense/ love story between a local captain and a member of an anti-government organization. In addition to several less than compelling plots, the most prominent flaw surrounds the apparent stabbing death of the female protagonist in the second half of the film. Following her "death," she is brought back to life on as many as four occasions to save her lover.

These two films distinguished themselves from Zhang's films in the early 1990s by their clear profitmaking intention. Not only did they feature an international cast of bankable Asian stars from Mainland China, Hong Kong, Japan, and Taiwan and extensive deployments of Zhang's hallmarks of visuality meant to attract as large audiences as possible in Asia and the world, the ways these films were promoted also showed the unmistakable concern for maximizing profits. *Hero* became the first non-main-melody film to be advertised in official Party organs. Its trailer was shown on stations of China Central TV as well as other local stations; even the most influential primetime news show on CCTV, *Xinwen lianbo*, a hard-line promoter of the Party's domestic and international policies, devoted two minutes to cover its grand opening in China.[48] The Ministry of Culture even issued an official document requesting local film authorities to prevent and confiscate pirated versions of *Hero* to ensure a high box-office income.[49] Although pirated DVDs and VCDs have been extremely pervasive in China for almost a decade, the Ministry of Culture has only issued two official documents urging its local departments to take measures against piracy. The administrative document regarding *Hero* is the only one specifically related to a domestic Chinese film.

When promoting *House of Flying Daggers*, the premiere ceremony was an extravagant three-hour gala, costing RMB 20 million and showing only trailers and previews of the film. Not only were many popular celebrities from China, Hong Kong and Taiwan invited to the ceremony, government officials, such as the Party Secretary of Beijing, Liu Qi, and Vice Secretary, Long Xinmin, were also in attendance. After the film was released on June 15, SARFT postponed the releases of Hollywood films, such as *Lord of the Rings: The Return of the King*, and many other domestic films, such as Johnnie To's *Breaking News* (Da shijian), to the middle of August, thus granting the entire summer season exclusively to *Flying Daggers*.[50] Many methods that the government had previously used to promote state-sponsored main melody films in the early 1990s were borrowed to promote this private-company-made blockbuster. Thanks to this effective marketing, the mediocre films *Hero* and *House of Flying Daggers* became the most profitable films of the year, collecting RMB 2.5 billion and RMB 1.5 billion, respectively. These two cases of Zhang Yimou's films reveal two tendencies resulting from the commercialization of the film industry. On the one hand, the participation of the state propaganda department in the commercial moviemaking business reveals the film authorities' supportive attitude towards the maximization of profit through any means. On the other hand, the previously elitist and subversive filmmakers' unholy alliance with government propaganda organs in film promotion and distribution also indicates the filmmakers' compromised integrity in the face of a fervent drive for profit-making.

Feng Xiaogang's Cinema in the New Millienium

The early 2000s was a time of transition in Feng's career and a time with new challenges and predicaments. As a hunger for money became the most persistent trend in Chinese cinema and many filmmakers showed their unapologetic embrace of commercial films, Feng Xiaogang's relation to the new trends was complicated. Although his highly entertaining popular films are thought to blatantly serve the needs of profit-maximization, they are not entirely compromised. While inevitably impacted by the pressures for profit-making and becoming more and more commercialized, his films also expose the dark side of society and humanity to warn the audiences of the dangers of expanding commercialization and materialism.

The work that signals the beginning of a new transformation of Feng's career is *Sigh* (Yisheng tanxi, 2000). With this film, he abandoned the lighthearted comedy featuring a little character's victory over the privileged stratums, and moved instead toward a tragic drama of privileged people's physical and moral downfall and their failed attempts at redeeming themselves.

Sigh: Testing the Water of Censorship

Sigh tells the story of a middle-aged and well-established writer, Liang Yazhou, who has been invited to live in a beach resort to write a script. At the resort he is assigned a personal assistant, a charming young woman named Li Xiaodan. Despite being happily married, Liang finds himself falling for the young and attractive assistant. After two months, Liang returns to Beijing, where both his family and Li live. In Beijing, Liang begins to live a double life in which he constantly alternates between the roles of good husband and romantic lover. Attempting to keep family intact, but at the same time attracted to Li, he is torn between breaking up with his lover and divorcing his wife, Song Xiaoying. When the two women finally confront each other, their conversation is surprisingly calm. Li sits quietly while Song talks about her own romance with Liang. As Song tells her love story, their daughter brings a glass of water to Li. Moved by her hospitality, Li takes a sip, only to find that the water is undrinkable—the daughter added salt to it in resentment at the "other woman" who has come between her parents. Swallowing the salty water, Li leaves Liang's house and never returns. The film ends with Liang and his family on a vacation. As he answers a call on his cell phone, he turns around and looks directly at the camera with a fearful gaze. In this film, the love affair is depicted as something without beauty or romance, and something that causes only pain and destruction. The final shot of Liang's fearful gaze reveals that even though he finally returns to his wife, the damage to their relationship and to his own perception of love is permanent. Making a film about infidelity in 2000 required Feng to have both business acumen and moral courage.

Incited by the success of New Year films at the box office in three consecutive years, the market for Chinese popular cinema in 2000 seemed to offer the potential for even greater profits from New Year films. Therefore, at least six New Year films were made with the hope of taking a share of the prize. Being the creator of this genre in Chinese cinema, Feng was well aware that a simple repetition of the light comedic mode of his earlier films would not necessarily result in good box-office returns. So, in 2000, he retreated from comedy and stepped into the very different territory of family drama.

This transition proved to be a successful business move: *Sigh*, released in the summer of 2000, had a total box-office revenue of 30 million RMB, better than all of that year's New Year films.

As discussed in Chapter 3, Feng's directing career began with films directly targeting social issues and problems. One of the major reasons for his decision to stop making "social conscience" films was the pressure of a tightened film policy in the mid-1990s. His last film project with Good Dream, *Living a Miserable Life*, had to be aborted, since the censors deemed the content to be "obscene and vulgar." Although producing mainly comedic films since this encounter with censorship, Feng was unwilling to bid a final farewell to the films of "social conscience" that had interested him in his early career. In 2000, a very unusual act signaled his return to his early style—he chose to resume the aborted film project, *Living a Miserable Life*, which was proclaimed "dead" by the censors. Although it is not clear whether Feng's risky choice to re-shoot this aborted film was intended as a courageous act of contempt for the indisputable authority of the censors, he at least succeeded in testing the waters to see whether a subject that was once considered inappropriate could be tolerated four years later. When the final version was submitted to the censors, only the ending was thought to be "inappropriate" and in need of changes. According to Feng, the end of the movie had originally contained a scene filmed beautifully on a tree-lined street in which the husband snuck out to see his lover many years after their breakup. Film censors advised that the scene be changed, because they thought that the affair ought to have ended after the husband's return home.[51] The current version ends with Liang gazing fearfully into the camera, implying that underneath the harmonious picture of a reunited family lies an incurable traumatic memory of the affair. Although the altered ending somewhat changed the director's original perception of how the story should end, in comparison to the lengthy letter in 1996 accusing the film of depicting material that was immoral, obscene, and inappropriate, the minor changes requested *Sigh* in 2000 did indicate a greater tolerance in regard to the subject of extramarital affairs. The passing of the film, therefore, already signaled a loosened control over film ideology.

The exposure of the dark side of modern life and explicit criticism of the problems in Chinese society also became dominant themes in Feng's next two films. The characteristic styles of *Sigh* and the other two films will be discussed together in the latter part of this chapter. However, before his style fully changed to tragic drama, he briefly returned to New Year comedic film in 2001, when a Hollywood studio showed an interest in his comedic work. The film produced in collaboration between Feng and the Columbia Asia

Company, *Big Shot's Funeral* (Da wanr, 2002), not only encapsulates all the hallmarks of his New Year film, but also raises a question about the translatability of the indigenous New Year comedy into a different cultural context in the age of globalization.

Big Shot's Funeral: A Hollywood Production and a Summary of New Year Comedy

Plot

A famous American director, Don Taylor, comes to Beijing to make his version of *Last Emperor*. While shooting a large scene inside the Forbidden City he senses that he is experiencing a crisis of creativity and has no idea how to continue the film. In the meantime, an unemployed cameraman, You You, has been hired by the director's assistant, an American-born Chinese woman, Lucy, to follow Taylor around for a documentary about the making of the film. Through Lucy's interpretation, the two become friends and exchange many ideas on Chinese history, the life of the Emperor, and the film. While visiting a Buddhist temple for inspiration, Taylor starts a conversation with You You about how death is viewed by different cultures. You You tells him that in Chinese culture, if a person dies above the age of seventy, his/her death will not be considered a tragedy. Rather, at the funeral, people will have a banquet and happily celebrate his/her life. As You You could not find a word to describe the notion of *xisang* (literally, happy funeral, 喜丧), Taylor, as if understanding what You You has just described in his mixture of poor English and Beijing-accented Mandarin, coins the term "comedy funeral." As the shooting is not making any progress, and the film is already over budget, Taylor's American producer, Tony, flies to Beijing to inform him that a young Japanese MTV director will take over the shooting, but that Taylor's name can still stay in the credits. Fired and feeling that all his ingenuity and talent in filmmaking are spent, Taylor has a severe heart attack. Before collapsing into a coma he tells You You, who happens to be filming him, that he wants You You to give him a "comedy funeral." One of You You's friends, Wang Xiaozhu, who seems very experienced in organizing parties and galas, is called to help. Assuming that the funeral will be sponsored by either Taylor's own money or the film company, they start to plan a very grand and solemn funeral. But later, they are told that no one will provide them with any financial support for the funeral and they have to fund it themselves. After several failed attempts to find sponsors for the funeral, You You arrives at the unusual idea of raising money for the funeral by auctioning and selling off advertisement spots. At the auction, after ferocious competition, companies such as *Cozy Cola, Outpack Steakhouse* and *666 Cigarettes*, receive the right to put their ads in the funeral in one way or another. As a result, not only is the site of the funeral filled with giant blow-up ads and posters for beers, cigarettes, and breast firming cream, space on Taylor's body itself is also sold for ads for household consumer products, such as contact lenses, shampoo, shoes, and sunglasses. As the preparations become increasingly absurd, Taylor miraculously recovers and all You You's efforts turn out to be in vain. Now facing great debts, the poor You You pretends to lose his mind and hides in a mental hospital, where he meets genuinely crazy people who have crazy ideas about how to make profits from speculating on Internet companies, real-estate projects, etc. Taylor resumes his position as the director of the film and gets You You out of the hospital. The film ends with a scene in a make-up room, where You You and Lucy are about to kiss. Then it turns out that the couple is being filmed by Taylor, who looks directly at the camera and urges the couple, "Come on guys, I'm not going to say 'cut' until you kiss . . . Cut!"

Big Shot's Funeral was the box-office champion for 2001, collecting RMB 30 million in total, twice as much as the total income of Zhang Yimou's sentimental love story *Road Home* (Wode fuqin muqin, 2001), released in the same year. Financed by Sony Picture Entertainment's Hong Kong based subsidiary, Columbia Pictures Film Production Asia, and including a cast from China (Ge You as You You and Ying Da as Wang Xiaozhu), Hong Kong (Rosamund Kwan as Lucy), and the US (Canadian Donald Sutherland as Taylor), *Big Shot* is Feng's first collaboration with a Hollywood film company. However, when the news of the collaboration was released, it caused more concern than excitement among Chinese film critics. In a lecture delivered on an educational program on Channel 10 of China Central TV, Dai Jinhua commented that she had once supported Feng's films unconditionally, since she believed that only Feng's mode of cinema could strengthen the Chinese national film industry. However, she felt frustrated as she watched *Big Shot* because Feng, a filmmaker who used to dedicate his filmmaking to domestic film audiences and the domestic market, now aligned himself with foreign capital. And, the profits generated from this film would not be re-invested into future domestic film productions, but would be slipped into the pockets of Hollywood producers. In other words, this was completely contrary to Feng's original commitment to domestic cinema.[52] In a live chat room interview, Feng defended himself with typically humorous language, saying that he was *shen zai Cao ying, xin zai Han* (身在曹营心在汉, an ancient idiom from the Chinese classic *Romance of the Three Kingdoms*, meaning that one works for a new boss, but remains loyal to the old one) and *chili pawai* (吃里扒外, a derogative idiom, meaning that one is supported by someone while secretly helping others).[53]

Indeed, Feng's return to New Year film in 2001 was more an attempt to expand his influence to the West, than an indication that he was affiliating himself with foreign investors—the two films he directed after *Big Shot* were sponsored by domestic film companies. And, as will be made clear in the following discussion, the film itself demonstrates that the light comedy of Feng's New Year films had finally developed into a unique genre with fundamental narrative components, plot, settings, and characters.[54]

Victory of the Little Characters

As in Feng's previous New Year films, the leading character in *Big Shot*, You You, is again a socially insignificant person who seems to have little talent or ingenuity. Before working for Taylor, You You is an unemployed cameraman. Divorced and living in a messy studio, he makes his living by shooting commercial ads. His duties as the cameraman for Taylor's documentary were limited. As Lucy tells him during the interview, "You can't take days off. Except for Taylor's sleeping, you have to follow him everywhere. You are only an eye. You have no right to edit the film, no right of authorship. You cannot have your own attitude, because we don't need your attitude." In the early part of the film, You You was indeed only an eye, quietly following Taylor's every move, completely unnoticed. Even after being granted authorization to plan Taylor's funeral, he still seems lost. He starts his preparations by watching tapes of famous funerals, and then has to resort to asking his friend for assistance.

However, like all the protagonists in Feng's New Year films, You You, a seeming nobody, is able to achieve his goals because of his admirable qualities—these are the forces that imbue his ordinary life with meaning and dynamism. Throughout the love relationship between You You and Lucy, You You demonstrates tenderness, care, generosity, and humor that help him to finally win her over. After Lucy is fired by the new director, You You provides her with comfort and shelter. When the money he raises is more than enough to cover the funeral expenses, he decides to give most of the surplus money to Taylor's bereaved family and the recently unemployed Lucy, and then donates the rest to charity projects. He does not take advantage of this opportunity to become wealthy himself. As the organizer of Taylor's funeral, You You is dutiful and faithful. He refuses the proposition of a media mogul to cover the costs of the funeral if You You agrees to let his new star attend the funeral as Taylor's mistress. His decision to sell space in the funeral to advertisers, although absurd, is a necessary expedient given that he has failed to find anyone willing to offer unconditional financial support, and he refuses to compromise with those whose assistance comes with degrading demands. Furthermore, this idea not only proves successful in raising money for the funeral, but also fulfils Taylor's wish for a "comedy funeral."

You You is another addition to Feng's constellation of little characters, characters who, though being insignificant and unimportant nobodies, finally succeed in achieving seemingly unattainable goals thanks to their good nature, humor, and wisdom. Regardless of their professions or background, they represent the values and attitudes of grassroots society in an age of constant social flux.

Mocking the Privileged Stratum

Contrary to the humble You You's success in winning Lucy's love and arranging for Taylor's comedy funeral, the big shots in the film, including the famous Hollywood director, the boss of the media company who wants to trade his new star for the funeral, and the specialists at the mental hospital who have the authority to determine another person's sanity, are forces that threaten to undermine You You's already miserable situation. Taylor's last wish, unaccompanied by financial support, pushes the unemployed freelance cameraman into the uncomfortable position of a funeral organizer for an internationally acclaimed film director. As You You figures out his own way of raising money to fulfill his friend's last wish, Taylor recovers and conceals the news of his recovery from You You, allowing the situation to develop into an absurd crisis. The Hollywood studio producer's first response after learning of You You's plan is to ask Lucy to give You You his bank account number, so that the money will not go into You You's pocket. The two inconsiderate, greedy, and exploitative big shots, although privileged because of their fame and power, seem to lack the humble You You's generosity and kindness.

At the end of the film, there is a very meaningful scene in which Feng casts the image of the authorities in a satirical light. After Taylor's recovery, You You pretends to be insane and hides in a mental hospital. Taylor pays his debts and wants to have him released from the hospital. In order to gain his release, You You has to pass a test proving his sanity in front of a committee consisting of a doctor and specialists from the hospital. As part of the test, You You is required to tell a story; You You takes advantage of this opportunity to make fun of the doctors by joking that they too are patients in a hospital:

You You: In a mental hospital, the doctors want to let the patients take care of themselves. So they decide to select the patients who are mentally healthier to supervise the others. So a doctor comes to the first floor holding a banana and asks, "What is this?" "A banana," a patient answers. "You are the supervisor of the first floor," the doctor says. Then he comes to the second floor, holding an apple and asks, "What is this?" "An apple," a patient answers. "You are the supervisor of the second floor," he says. And he comes to the third floor and holds a machine, with a handle and a trumpet-like loudspeaker, which is a...

A doctor: Gramophone.

You You (to the doctor): You are the supervisor of the third floor.

This joke, tricking the doctor who is testing his sanity into an admission that he himself is one of the patients in the hospital, is a typical example of Feng's satirical reversal of authority. This satire is carefully hidden beneath the surface of the scene. After You You tells the joke, the camera pulls back and reveals Taylor and other crews members on the site—You You's test is merely an artificially staged scene, not real life. For a film that has to guarantee a profitable return, a little character's rebellion against authority is best left fictional.

Interestingly, in an independent film written by Feng and directed by Wang Shuo, *I Am Your Dad* (Wo shi ni baba; 1996), the same metaphor of the mental hospital succeeds in overtly and directly questioning the sanity of the authorities. Telling the story of a divorced father's unsuccessful attempt at true friendship with his adolescent son, the film is adapted from Wang Shuo's novel of the same title, but Feng, as the scriptwriter, adds many new plots and scenes. One of these depicts the father's adventure in a mental hospital. In the middle of the film, one of their neighbors, a professional actor who has never played anything but an extra, suddenly goes crazy. The father, played by Feng himself, takes him to a mental asylum located in an intimidating mansion that looks like a haunted house from the outside and a prison from the inside. Ironically, after being asked several simple questions by a small figure in the shadows, the father is diagnosed as insane, while his neighbor walks out of the asylum freely. Threatened by a couple of robust, baton-waving nurses, the father's attempt to plead his sanity proves to be in vain, and he finally admits that he is mentally ill. The mental hospital here clearly functions as a metaphor for an official institution that fails to distinguish the normal from the insane and even forces a sane person to deny his sanity. *Dad* did not pass the censors and is still banned in China. So it is understandable why a similarly satirical take on authority in *Big Shot's Funeral* is less critical than in *Dad*: under the burden of profit-making, Feng had to make the satire subtle and not overtly subversive.

Hidden Social Commentary

Similar to other New Year films, *Big Shot's Funeral* emphasizes the virtue and values of little characters and exposes the depravity and immorality of the privileged stratum. In the process of portraying the interaction, conflicts, and compromises between the two groups, Feng also succeeds in accentuating issues and problems inherent in contemporary Chinese society and implying that the social context is the driving force behind the inequalities that exist between the lives of little characters and "big shots."

You You's comedy funeral, filled with ridiculous ideas such as dressing Taylor's body with sponsored goods (for example, a Puma shoe on the left foot, an Italian leather shoe on the right), and playing the *largo* of a traditional funeral hymn at a jauntier *allegro*, as one sponsor wants to use it as the background music for his mineral water, depicts the absurd extent of commercialization in China. The most direct target of his satire is the saturation of commercial advertisement into almost every corner of society. In China today, the brand names of both domestic and imported products appear not only in prime time TV commercials, but in almost every possible space. For example, the most popular show during the traditional Spring Festival, the Spring Festival Gala of China Central TV Station, has the names of sponsoring wines, sport beverages, and DVD players added to its title every year; Kentucky Fried Chicken has opened a franchise in Beihai Park, the ancient Chinese royal garden. Reflecting another feature of advertising in China, You You's funeral planning is centered on how to maximize profits from very limited resources. One of the more extreme examples of absurdity caused by the intrusion of commercial advertisement was the division of Taylor's hair into two parts for the comparison of a certain brand of shampoo. As we have seen earlier in this chapter, the major goal of the reconstruction and merging of the state-owned studios into large corporations and enterprises is the maximization of profits that can be generated from each unit.

As in his other comedy films, Feng also stresses the contemporaneity of the story through a cynical exposure of many newly emerged social, economic, and political phenomena. In the mental hospital scene, the patients fantasize about luxurious real estate projects and speculating in the dot-com industry. These fantasies reflect common easy-money illusions in the real estate and dot-com industries created by the bubble economy in the late 1990s and early 2000s. These poor characters are victims of an irrationality linked to the widespread commercialization of a so-called money-hungry society. In this scene, a patient who used to be a real estate developer is mumbling to himself his secret of "success," which can be summarized as "not aiming for the best, but aiming for the most expensive (*buqiu zuihao, danqiu zuigui*)." His monologue, depicting a real estate project with all conceivable extravagances, such as a 24/7 British butler, an upper-class private school and a hospital outfitted like a five-star hotel, but making no mention of the quality of the project itself, reveals the crazy extent of materialism stimulated by rapid economic growth and savvy businessmen's lack of integrity in their pursuit for profits. Another scene, in which Lucy and You You's friend Louie Wang, a pretentious event planner, are having their first meeting, shares a close resemblance with Chinese TV news' depiction of Chinese Party leaders holding diplomatic meetings with their foreign guests, and is rendered with a sense of mockery toward China's monotonous TV news broadcasts and the superficiality of all these diplomatic events. Appropriating the techniques of TV news, the scene opens with a dolly shot pushing from a long shot to a

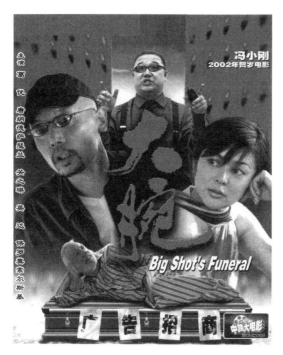

Movie poster of *Big Shot's Funeral*

medium and features a symmetrical composition with Lucy and Louie sitting in the middle of a spacious room, flanked by their associates and with a translator sitting behind. At the supposedly casual meeting to discuss funeral arrangements, Louie Wang maintains such an annoyingly boring tone as he spouts off about his company's foreign policy that Lucy has to interrupt him by saying, "Please cut the crap and get down to the business." With a mise-en-scene similar to that of China's TV news' treatment of political events and Louie Wang's useless reiteration of politics, Feng is making fun of a constrained media spreading news that is totally unrelated to China's reality and of interest to only a very few viewers.

Like the social commentary in his first three New Year films, in this Hollywood commercial production, issues are carefully buried under humorous and absurd plots that prevent them from becoming overt criticisms. This ambiguity allows a sophisticated audience to detect poignancy and cynicism while addressing an ordinary audience's concern for humor and hilarity. At the same time, it raises no objections from the film authorities.

Translatability of Chinese Popular Cinema in an Age of Globalization

Big Shot is Feng's first attempt to extend the audience for his films into the West. In doing so, he struggles to preserve the humor elements that are the hallmark of his cinema, while making them also appealing to non-Chinese audiences. As he commented on this film, "I am really hoping to expand my audience with this one. The Chinese people have a great sense of humor. And if that can translate into other languages, it will be even more significant than the success of an action film."[55] However, Feng's ambition to refresh the Western audiences' perception of Chinese cinema seems to have been frustrated by inadequate show times and harsh reviews complaining of the incomprehensibility of the film's humor. Although completed in 2002, the film has been shelved by Columbia and not released in either art house theaters or major movie chains in English-speaking countries. The critiques of people who have seen the film have not been favorable. An Australian scholar of China studies, Stephanie Donald, writes in her review, "*Big Shot's Funeral* is a comedy for a local audience, or anyone who has experienced the shift to commercialization in the People's Republic. It doesn't pamper the international audience, rather it confuses and teases them with the English scenes that illuminate nothing except the cultural irrelevance of the big shot himself."[56] Other similar reviews can be found in some American newspapers, such as *Deseret News* from Utah, which reads, "Few of the twists and turns of the film are as clever as director Feng Xiaogang and his co-screenwriters seem to think they are... though there are a few laughs here, but they come from moments the filmmakers probably didn't intend to be funny."[57]

One of the reasons for the failure of Feng's style of humor among Western audiences is its linguistic-based rather than slapstick humor. Some humorous lines, spoken by his characters with Beijing dialects, do not even appeal to audiences from Shanghai and Guangzhou. It seems Feng took this issue into account in making *Big Shot*, as many of the dialogues in the film are in English and spoken by native speakers. Nonetheless, Western audiences' lack of understanding of the cultural and social context of contemporary China becomes another barrier to appreciating the humor in the film. For example, in one of the most hilarious scenes, the CEO of a website company, *Sogou,* quotes a famous classical poem to describe his vision for the company's future. Chinese audiences find this scene extremely funny for a variety of reasons. First, the name of the company, *Sogou,* literally meaning "searching dog," is an appropriation of the name of a real website company, *Sohu,* meaning "searching fox," run by a CEO who promoted himself as an MIT graduate and cultivated an image of a Bill Gates-like, young, smart, and savvy businessman. When the character introduces himself as the CEO of *Sogou,* most audience members know exactly who is being made fun of. Secondly, the quote, "In life we should be heroes among the living/After death let us be heroes among the ghosts," is a very famous line from a poem written by Li Qiangzhao (1184-1151), a renowned female poet, and dedicated to the brave general Xiang Yu. But in the film, the poem is used ironically to suggest that, while the CEOs in the high-tech industry may seem heroic, their way of running their businesses is actually irrational and impetuous. The rosy picture they paint of a prosperous future is, in reality, just a grand illusion. To fully understand the humor in this scene, one has to be familiar with contemporary Chinese society and have a knowledge of classical Chinese literature. Therefore, the lack of an understanding of Chinese culture and literature serves as a major barrier to foreign audiences' full comprehension of Feng's humor.

However, comparing Feng's films with other Chinese films that have enjoyed popularity in the West—the action films starring kungfu movie stars such as Bruce Lee, Jackie Chan, and Jet Li, and the Fifth Generation films such as *Yellow Earth, Judou,* and *Raise the Red Lantern*—one might arrive at the paradoxical fact that the subject of esoteric Chinese kungfu and the self-ethnographic representation of rural China are more appealing to Western audiences than Feng's story of mad commercialization in a modern society. The untranslatability of Feng's humor relating to China's present reality reveals the poignant fact that even though the world has entered an age of globalization, the interaction of culture between the modern East and West is often only unidirectional. This one-way communication, on the one hand, is due to the perpetuation of cultural imperialism, taking the form of the penetration of a hegemonic culture into the Third World, an example being the dominance of Hollywood film and television in almost every corner of the world—"a violence of American cultural imperialism."[58] On the other hand, it also reflects an Orientalist perception of the East in Western media and culture. Because of the penetration of Western technology, political systems, and culture into Third World countries, global capitalism has resulted in a hegemony of Anglo-American culture that constitutes a barrier for dialogue between the East and West. Although increasing interaction and communication between the East and West has meant that images of China are no longer limited to characters in Pearl Buck's novels, American popular culture still prefers exotic stories of ancient Chinese swordsmen and oppressed women in a patriarchal family. The list of Chinese films that have met with success in American movie theaters or been nominated for Academy Awards illustrates this fact. The most popular Chinese films in the US include *Crouching Tiger, Hidden Dragon*, *Rush Hour*, and *Hero*, all martial-art/action/kungfu films; Academy Award nominations have gone to films such as *Raise the Red Lantern* and *Farewell My Concubine*. Apart from the subversive films of the Sixth Generation directors, films of contemporary urban China have aroused hardly any interest among either film audiences or film critics. As Jonathan Rosenbaum writes in *Movie Wars: How Hollywood and the Media Limit What Movies We Can See*, the American audience, because of the dominance of Eurocentric/American-centered Hollywood cinema, has developed an isolationism that causes them to "think of foreigners in stereotypical terms…and similarly, think of non-Americans as wannabe Americans….and think about much of the rest of world in shorthand: Communists are nonreligious, the French worship Jerry Lewis, Iranians are subject to heavy censorship in the arts, the Chinese produce fortune cookies."[59] Because of this isolationism and the stereotypical thinking resulting from cultural imperialism, Chinese urban cinema—including not only the films of Feng Xiaogang, but also films of other talented Chinese film directors who mainly focus on contemporary urban subjects, such as the Fifth Generation director, Huang Jianxin and some Sixth Generation director, such as Lu Chuan—stand little chance of success in the West.

    Big Shot's Funeral, produced within the Hollywood moviemaking system, can be seen as a work that reinforces Feng's New Year genre. Like many works in this genre, it features conflicts and confrontations between ordinary people and the privileged stratum of society, people advantaged because of their wealth or social status in a society undergoing cultural and economic transformation. At the same time, as a work produced in the new millennium, a time of dramatic transformations in almost every aspect of China, the film also began to inject cynicism into the comedy of earlier New Year films. While the theme of little characters' triumph over the privileged has been preserved, added to this are cynical critiques targeting issues brought about by social change, such as the pervasive hunger for wealth and the unprecedented expansion of commercialization. The emergence of this more overt criticism can be seen as a result of a loosening of official control over ideology, and the implementation of new policies intended to regulate films more systematically. This new approach has been successful in providing more space for the development of non-state film productions. The mixture of fanciful comedy and cynical drama in *Big Shot* also suggests a turning point in Feng's own filmmaking career, the beginnings of a departure from melodramatic, romantic comedy toward a cinema of "social conscience." In this cinema, the character of his early works—the exposure of social and individual depravity in an age of materialism and consumerism—has replaced the sentimental celebration of the values of little characters in a state of social flux.

Sigh (2000), Cell Phone (2003), and a World Without Thieves (2004): Social Criticism in a Commercialized World

Plot

Cell Phone (2003) starts in a small town where the town's first telephone has just been installed. In a small village near the town, a peasant woman is asking a young man, Yan Shouyi, to take her to the town to make a phone call to her husband. Many years later, Yan Shouyi, already middle-aged, has become a popular TV talk show host in a big city. He has it all, maybe too much— a wife, a nice job, a BMW, and a mistress. His life and work would not have taken this path if he had not been equipped with the latest wireless communication technology—the cell phone. But the *cell phone* is also the cause of the end of his marriage: his wife accidentally answers a phone call from his mistress complaining about his missing date. After getting a divorce, Yan starts a new relationship with a college teacher, Shen Xue, while still occasionally dating his old mistress, Wu Yue. On the several occasions when his double life is about to be discovered by Shen, Yan deftly covers the truth with lies. Almost every such moment has something to do with cell phones— a new red cell phone he bought for Wu Yue arouses Shen's suspicion; while making a secret phone call to Wu Yue in his restroom, he bumps into Shen; his awkward reaction to an instant message sent by Wu Yue to his cell phone prompts questions from his girlfriend. The cell phone, step by step, brings him deeper and deeper into a world of deception and infidelity. His close friend, a university professor and writer for his television show, Fei Mou, is involved in a similar love affair, which is soon discovered by his wife. Yan's infidelity is also finally discovered by Shen who sees a digital picture of Yan and Wu making love, a picture taken by the digital camera built into Wu's new cell phone. Not only are Yan's relationships destroyed, his career also ends as Wu threatens to expose their relationship and takes over his position as talk show host. At the end of the film, throwing it into fire, Yan swears that he will never again own a cell phone.

Cell Phone, earning RMB 53 million at the box office, was the most successful film of 2003.[60] In fact, it even beat the most popular imported film of 2003, *Harry Potter and the Chamber of Secrets* (dir. Chris Columbus, 2002), which had a box office revenue of RMB 52 million.[61] Based on Liu Zhenyun's novel of the same title, *Cell Phone* continues the theme of male infidelity that Feng began dealing with in *Sigh*, but incorporates an even more overt critique. Compared to the "seven-year-itch" type of marriage crisis experienced by Liang Yazhou in *Sigh*, Yan in *Cell Phone* is a philanderer who has never been faithful to any of the women he has had relationships with. Besides, Yan is not the only cheating husband in the film. His seemingly conservative university-professor friend is also having an affair with a student. Instead of presenting the subject of infidelity in the form of a marital drama, as in *Sigh*, *Cell Phone* addresses the subject through the director's satirical take on consumerism and his exposure of the moral crises and ethical issues brought by expansion of high technology into our everyday lives.

A World Without Thieves (2004) tells the story of an innocent hard-working peasant, Sha Gen, and two veteran thieves, Wang Li and Wang Bo. The couple meets the boy in rural western China, having just sold a car that they gained through blackmailing a rich person in Beijing. Wang Li, the wife, believing that she is pregnant, wants to quit being a thief and raise her child properly, while the husband, Wang Bo, holds the belief: once a thief, forever a thief. He persuades his wife to try their luck one last time on the train back to the city. Sha Gen, an orphan who earns his living by building Buddhist temples in remote areas and is going home to get married with all his savings from years of hard work, is a passenger on the same train. Naively believing that there are no thieves in the world, Sha Gen boards on the train with all his money in cash and soon becomes the target of many different groups of thieves, among them, Wang Bo and Wang Li and a gang of thieves led by master Uncle Li. Most of the film takes place on the train, where Sha Gen makes friends with the couple without knowing their true identity. Wang Li develops a fondness for the young man and wants to protect his innocence and naïve illusion of a world without thieves. The train becomes a battleground on which the couple has to confront the ruthless, cunning, and cynical Uncle Li, who wants to use this opportunity as a training exercise for his apprentices. As the drama unfolds with the couple's efforts to guard Sha Gen's money and the other thieves' attempts to steal it, plainclothes police officers also begin to play a game of cat-and-mouse with the thieves in the hope of catching all of them at once. Finally, in a brutal fight between Wang Bo and Uncle Li, Wang is killed. Before his death, he succeeds in his final effort to return Sha Gen's cash, and Sha Gen's fantasy of a world without thieves remains intact.

Based on Zhao Benfu's short story, starring Hong Kong actor Andy Lau, Taiwanese actress Rene Liu, and Mainland Chinese actor Ge You, *A World Without Thieves* was one of the most highly anticipated films of the year. Although losing out to Zhang Yimou's martial arts blockbuster film, *House of Flying Daggers*, at the box office, *Thieves* still managed impressive box-office revenues of RMB 100 million during the first two weeks of its exhibition, maintaining Feng's long time record of success at the box office.[62]

Movie poster of *A World Without Thieves*

Since the release of Feng's first New Year film in 1996, audiences had come to expect to be entertained by one of Feng's comedies at the end of almost every year. But starting in 2000, audiences were surprised by the change in Feng's film from lighthearted comedy to serious dramas or even tragedy. In the film, *Thieves*, the mood of pessimism and tragedy could not be more obvious. Although several episodes of comic relief with Feng's typical humor provide the audience with expected entertainment, the majority of the film is clouded by the couple's doomed destiny and their useless redemption. Shocked by the pessimistic cynicism and the tragic subject matter, both unprecedented in Feng's New Year films, the press and some film critics observed that *Thieves* signaled a turning point in Feng's filmmaking career, suggesting that Feng was attempting to earn himself a spot in the ranks of art film directors.[63] This opinion, I would suggest, is a misunderstanding of Feng's cinema. Comparing the three films Feng made in the new millennium with his earlier works, it is very clear that from *Sigh* to *Cell Phone* and *Thieves*, Feng actually re-visited the subjects that had interested him in his early career. This change not only demonstrates Feng's obsession with the fate of Chinese people and problems in the society under the impact of social transformation, but also indicates the arrival of a more relaxed era of Chinese cinema, in which the number of films was rapidly increasing and becoming more and more diverse.

Vanishing Little Characters and Big Shots' Frustration

One of the significant distinctions between Feng's New Year cinema and his recent works is that none of the protagonists in his last three films have been ordinary people. All the characters in the three films, *Sigh*, *Cell Phone*, and *Thieves*, are either successful or wealthy. However, their accomplishments and money have not brought them a happy life. Switching from a celebration of the values of the little characters and their hard-earned successes, Feng shifted his attention to "big shots" who are rich and successful, but morally and ethically bankrupt. In *Sigh*, Liang Yazhou is a not an ordinary scriptwriter. His producer willingly pays for two months rent at a luxurious resort hotel while Liang writes a new script. His new apartment, located in one of Beijing's most famous upscale neighborhoods, is exquisitely decorated and designed. In spite of this success, his wavering between his wife and his mistress brings the life of the three into a deeper crisis. Similar to Liang, in *Cell Phone*, Yan Shouyi is a famous TV talk show host whose success is marked by his luxury car, latest model of cell phone, and spacious apartments. Yet, this character is also marked by his unapologetic infidelity to the three women he has had serious relationships with. Furthermore, even his old-fashioned producer, Fei Mou, who used to believe that having a mistress would cause nothing but trouble, is also having an affair. Although the thief couple in *Thieves* does not have problems with infidelity, as "successful" thieves they are social outcasts. Yet, their virtuoso pick-pocketing reveals that they are experts in their circle. And, their success as thieves is also proven by trophies—a BMW car and a huge amount of savings in the bank. However, though not needing any more money, the greedy husband still wants to steal poor Sha Gen's lifetime savings. All these leading characters, although rich and prominent, are somehow immoral or corrupt. By contrasting their success with their immorality, Feng indicates that these big shots' wealth is totally out of proportion with their sincerity and honesty. Reminding his audiences that the wealth and social status of these big shots brought them only destruction, betrayal and depravity, Feng explicitly points out that fame and money are only grand illusions.

Furthermore, contrary to the little characters' final accomplishments either in relationships (*Party A, Party B, Be There or Be Square*) or in their pursuits (*Sorry Baby!*), the big shots in *Sigh, Cell Phone* and *Thieves* finally gain only frustrated romance, career decline, or total disillusionment. At the end of *Sigh*, Liang Yazhou's fearful stare directly at the camera after answering what is likely a call from his mistress negates the harmony that he had regained after the reunion with his wife. In *Cell Phone*, the retributions that Yan endures include not only falling-outs with all his lovers, but also the forced resignation from his talk show due to his mistress's blackmail. At the end of the film, a voice-over says with a great sense of melancholy that Fei Mou, the renowned university professor, has quit his job and has been seen in an Eastern European country teaching Chinese. In *Thieves,* although the two thieves' mission of protecting Sha Gen's money from being stolen is accomplished, the couple's dream of living happily ever after collapses in the last scene of the film when the pregnant wife learns from a police officer that her husband has been killed. In these films, tragedies and irresolvable depression replace the endings of the earlier New Year films in which delayed romances ended with a wedding and joyful reunion (*Party A* and *Sorry Baby!*) or the resolutions of all troubles (*Be There* and *Sorry Baby!*).

In these three films, the "big shots," although having directly or indirectly benefited from the social flux, are also depicted as victims who are "suffering" from their success. For example, the extramarital affairs in *Sigh* and *Cell Phone* reflect the newly emergent social phenomenon of successful men taking mistresses as symbols of, or accessories to, success. The big shots' suffering in Feng's films functions as a warning of the declining morality among the nouveau-riche, and remind ordinary audiences that wealth and fame will not necessarily bring a happy life. To reinforce these messages, through a theme of futile redemption, Feng also stresses in the three films that once the damage has been done and sins have been committed, any attempts at redemption are in vain.

Futile Redemption

In Feng's New Year films, although his protagonists occasionally made mistakes, they are all given the opportunity to correct them. The cause of their mistakes is either something outside of their control, or something that does depend on their willing assent. In addition, the process of redemption serves as an indicator of perseverance and reveals an admirable side of their character. For instance, in *Sorry Baby!*, Han Dong's kidnapping of Xiao Yun is an act into which he has been forced by his boss's refusal to pay his salary and his urgent need of money for his sick sister. As soon as he realizes the consequences of this mistake, he lets Xiao Yun go and decides to turn himself in. So the latter part of the kidnapping, in fact, has nothing to do with Han Dong. Rather, it is actually used by Xiao Yun to test the extent of the boss's love for her. But in Feng's recent films, the protagonists' mistakes touch directly upon their families and their own lives, and can hardly be easily corrected. These mistakes stem from immorality or unlawfulness, due to either weaknesses of character or moral depravity and decadence. Even after the dire results of their actions have been realized, the protagonists fail to see their deeds as wrong, nor are their attempts at redemption successful. In *Sigh* and *Cell Phone*, Liang, Yan, and Mo do not seem to want to end their unfaithful affairs—their affairs end only when their spouses or girlfriends find out the truth accidentally. In *Thieves*, the couple would not have chosen to quit stealing if the wife had not been expecting a child. In *Cell Phone*, having never been faithful to his wife, girlfriends, or lovers, Yan's only regret is for his little son, who was born after his wife divorced him, rather than for the three women he cheats. But his attempts to act as a good father are all rejected by his wife, who gives the son her surname, refuses all his help, and even does not allow him to see his son. In *Thieves*, although the two thieves gain moral redemption by protecting Sha Gen's money, this redemption comes at the cost of the husband's life, making their wish to start a brand new life impossible. Furthermore, although Sha Gen's illusion of a world without thieves remains intact on this trip thanks to the couple's help, it remains highly questionable whether this illusion could be protected in a world that has not only thieves, but also numerous other threats.

Although absent from Feng's New Year films, images of frustrated characters and themes of failed redemption appear in many of Feng's early works such as *Chicken Feathers on the Ground* and *Behind the Moon*. As discussed in Chapter 3, Feng's early works are permeated by pessimistic depictions of innocent people's suffering, inequalities brought about by social hierarchization and hopeless attempts at redemption from guilt. The depiction of frustrated redemption resulting in perdition and irreparable damage in Feng's latest films was also prominent in Feng's early works; this suggests that Feng's latest works actually complete a resurrection of the style that he had begun to develop in his early films.

One of the major factors contributing to this change in Feng's cinema was the changing environment of filmmaking in the early 2000s. Not only were private film companies granted more freedom in production and distribution, but limits on film content and subject matter imposed by film censorship were also reduced. This loosened ideological control provided filmmakers a greater possibility to make the types of films that attracted them most. For Feng himself, although profit making was still an imperative, he was able to move beyond mere repetition of the bankable style of light comedy, and explore alternative ways of commenting on issues of concern to him. Although the barrier of censorship had become less formidable, he had to face the challenge of pleasing investors, a challenge that sometimes brought him into another kind of predicament.

Feng's New Compromises in the Commercialized World

As we have seen in *Big Shot's Funeral*, Feng's criticism of the expansion of consumerism and commercialization was very cynical and pointed. Yet, with the sponsorship of brand name companies and the pressures of profit making, Feng's films have inevitably collaborated with the menacing power of consumerism.

In a talk delivered at China's Communication University after the release of *A World Without Thieves*, Feng admits that several plots of the films were deliberately designed to attract the audiences and thus to ensure good box-office revenue. According to him, the sentimental ending where the husband, played by the Hong Kong popular movie star, Andy Lau, is killed ruthlessly by Uncle Li, was specifically designed for its tear-jerking effect. "Commercial films are for the purpose of money."[64] He said that in order to appeal to the audience's expectation for funny dialogues and humorous lines, the hallmarks of his early films, he has had to sacrifice the stylistic consistency of his tragic films by adding some farcical scenes.[65] One of such scenes is a robbery that is rendered more like a hilarious and playful prank, than a frightening and dangerous act. The two robbers, a stutterer and his feminized assistant, wearing cartoonish masks and waving plastic toy guns, ask for IC cards, IP cards, and IQ cards, thinking that IQ must be also a kind of prepaid phone card. Feng admitted that this scene is totally at odds with the whole style of the film, but "as long as the audiences like it, the style has to be sacrificed."[66]

In addition to the pressure from profit making, Feng also has to deal with his investors' needs. Feng's production company and the sponsor of almost all his recent films, Huayi Brothers TV and Film Investment Company, runs its business in a way quite similar to that of You You in *Big Shot's Funeral*. Just as You You sold space in Taylor's funeral, Huayi uses the promise of certain slots or times of appearance for commercial logos and tie-ins to attracts investors. In this way, instead of relying solely on the production company's own money, the financial pressures of film production are shared by sponsors who are seeking to advertise their products in a popular film. However, this situation increases pressure on the film director, as he/she has to find appropriate ways to present the sponsors' products or logos in the film. Furthermore, the greater the investments a film attracts, the more ads a film has to bear. As a result, if a film is financed by many companies from different industries, the film has to function as a lengthy series of exquisite and sophisticated commercials by inserting as many tie-ins as possible. Often, these tie-ins are made too overt. For example, in *Sigh*, the story of an intimate family affair, signs of commercial ads, brand names, and commercial slogans are everywhere: Ikea furniture fills Liang's newly decorated apartment; his secret meetings with his lover take place in one of Beijing's Starbucks cafés; one of the subplots in the film concerns the scriptwriter's search for a new apartment in which his wife constantly mentions a real estate project, *Classic Europe* (Oulu jingdian), even giving specific directions to its location, price and quality. Not surprisingly, all these brand names can be found in the film's list of sponsors in the final credits.

At a press conference held by the Huayi Brothers investment company before the shooting of *Cell Phone*, the president and CEO of Huayi, Wang Zhongjun, announced that the company had already signed investment and advertisement contracts with four companies—Motorola, BMW, China Mobile, and Mtone Wireless—whose investments in the film comprised almost half of the total budget.[67] What the four companies got in return was numerous tie-ins of their products in the film. A film about cell phones certainly provided an ideal platform for advertisements of cell phones. From beginning to end, the audience is introduced to (or, bombarded with) the many special functions of the various models of Motorola cell phones used by every character in the film. The newest model of the year, MotoA70, was officially launched in the Chinese market through this film. Commercials for a wireless service provider, China Mobile, appear many times in the film; and other brand names or products, such as BMW and a text message company, also appear frequently. An upscale steakhouse owned by one of the sponsors of the film is not only mentioned by Yan Shouyi verbally, but also becomes the location for the crucial scene of the first confrontation between his wife and his lover.

While these tie-ins can be rendered appropriately in an urban film about modern technology, a film such as *Thieves*, taking place in a rural area and featuring groups of thieves and a young peasant, poses much greater challenges for a seamless insertion of commercial advertisements. However, having a budget RMB 10 million greater than that of the *Cell Phone* and featuring an all-star cast from three regions of China, meant that even more sponsors wanted their products to appear in the film. It is not surprising, then, that both the number and artificiality of tie-ins in this film have increased. The first six minutes of the film have three easily identifiable tie-ins: a Mini Cooper, a Canon digital camera, and a BMW. Because one of the sponsors is Nokia, all the cell phones that the husband steals are, not surprisingly, made by Nokia. In the middle of the film, a thief disguised as a tour guide holds a small banner with the logos of a website company and a Beijing local newspaper, both sponsors of the film. However, the most awkward is a scene featuring the latest HP tablet computer, carried by a plainclothes police officer on the train. When he needs help from the guards on the train to identify the thieves, he brings the HP laptop on which the photos of the suspects are saved. In a close up of the computer, the police officer goes out of his way to demonstrate how to use the computer to connect to wireless equipment and how to turn the LCD screen around and use it for handwriting. Tie-ins for Canon digital cameras, Visa cards, and various other bank cards are spread throughout the film, even in scenes that seem to have nothing to do with technology or urban life. When asked about his attitude toward the numerous tie-ins in the film, Feng sounds somewhat frustrated: "Inserting ads into a film would definitely harm the film, but it could relieve the producer's burdens…"[68] In another interview, he expresses his concern in a more obvious way, "If a film's budget was over 80 million, I just don't know what the film would look like, just imagine how many advertisements I would have to find a place for."[69] It seems that although the previous barriers of ideological control had been loosened in the new millennium, Feng had to face the dilemma of how to achieve a balance between his artistic pursuit and the interests of his sponsors.

Movie poster of *The Banquet*

The Banquet: The Paradox of Commercializing Shakespeare

Feng's recent film, *The Banquet* (Ye yan, 2006), is a loose adaptation of Shakespeare's *Hamlet*. Thematically, there is not much difference between this film and Feng's recent films. As a drama concentrating on courtly intrigues and conspiracies, the film explicitly foregrounds recurring themes of the frustration and failed redemption of the powerful. It also reminds the audience of the corruption and depravity that are inherent not only among privileged people, but among human beings in general. Visually, *The Banquet* contrasts dramatically with Feng's previous works. With an investment reaching nearly US$30 million, six times more than the budget of Feng's previous film, *The Banquet* is a visual feast featuring exquisitely made consumes, lavishly crafted palace settings and carefully choreographed martial art scenes. Ironically, as the most expensive film that Feng has ever made, *The Banquet* is also the film that Feng has had the least control of. Although generating more box-office revenue than Feng's previous productions, it has also received highly critical reviews from both film critics and general audiences.

Plot

Loosely based on the plot of Shakespeare's *Hamlet*, this historical costume drama depicts the tragedy of the young widowed Empress Wan Er as she struggles to deal with a series of conflicting emotions and situations: the need to avenge her husband's murder; her feelings for her new husband, the new Emperor, who is also the brother and murderer of her late husband; her lost love for the Crown Prince; and her ever-growing desire to usurp the throne. The first half of the film, dramatically different from that of *Hamlet*, elaborates the complicated power struggles and sophisticated conspiracies among almost all the characters. Heartbroken by his father's new marriage to Wan Er, who was his secret love, the Crown Prince retreats to a remote village fully devoting himself to the study of folk songs and dances. After his father's death, the assassins sent by the new Emperor to take his life and the messenger sent by the Empress to recall him to court appear at his doorstep at the same time, a situation that forces him to choose between keeping the tranquil life of a hermit or getting involved in a bloody political struggles. The new Emperor, although successful in usurping power, faces severe challenges from his court officials who question not only the legitimacy of his enthronement but also the morality of his marriage to his sister-in-law. All these struggles culminate in a scene in the second half of the film in which the Emperor hosts a banquet in honor of the Empress. The banquet becomes a battlefield for the different players to achieve their goals. At the banquet, the Empress intends to poison the Emperor by having him drink wine from her cup which is contaminated by deadly poison. But the cup of wine is given instead to Qing Nü, Minister Yin's daughter who is in love with the Crown Prince, by the Emperor to acknowledge her dance performance. Watching the dancer die in great agony, the Emperor is devastated and heartbroken; knowing that the wine offered by his wife is lethal, he still drains the cup and dies with the last words, "How could I refuse the toast you offered me?" Just when everything seems fully under the Empress's control—justice is being served and the Crown Prince is about to become the Emperor—many unexpected incidents occur that ruin her plans. First, the Prince has no intention of being an Emperor. For him, it is a sinful title that has been contaminated by the blood of many people. Then, blaming his sister's death on the Empress, Minister Yin's son aims his poisoned sword at her, but accidentally kills the Prince who is trying to protect her. The Empress, losing both her enemies and loved ones at the banquet, now faces no obstacles on her path to becoming queen. But, before her enthronement ceremony, she is suddenly stabbed in the back by someone she thought she knew well. The last scene of the film shows the Empress turning around in great agony and looking, with a gaze filled by surprise, disappointment and fear, at the murderer who appears off-screen.

Feng's version of Hamlet: Grand illusions of the grassroots

In adapting the classical *Hamlet* into a luxurious martial art pageant about usurpers and intrigues, a type of film totally different from all his previous works, Feng faced the dual challenge of proving his competency in making a new style of blockbuster film and preserving the essence of his personal imprint. Therefore, Feng downplayed the Prince's hesitation between an audacious revenge and timid acceptance of the status quo, but accentuated the Empress's ambition and desire for power, fame and love. Empress Wan, the most important character, encapsulated all Feng's efforts in the new project. Replacing the noble Prince's humanistic query "to be or not to be," she represents a savvy and ambitious woman's paradoxical actions in the face of conflicting desires and bids for power. The Empress's background is not specified in the film, but it is implied in a voice-over that she used to be a court maiden who developed tender affection for the Prince before her marriage to the Emperor. Although her strategy of survival was pragmatic, her desires were very unrealistic. After her husband's murder and the new Emperor's usurpation of the throne, she chose to survive by accepting his proposition of marriage even though despising his immoral intrigues. She gradually fell in love with her new husband, but when she saw that he intended to kill the Prince, she coerced some court officials into helping her overthrow the Emperor and return power to the Prince. Contrary to the little characters in Feng's New Year films, whose hard work and sacrifice was always rewarded, the Empress's unrealistic ambition only led her on a road to perdition. However, also different from the inherently corrupt and ruthless big shots in Feng's recent films, the Empress Wan appeared to be sincere and loyal in her relations to her loved ones.

In portraying the Empress's paradoxical personality and ultimate disillusionment, Feng reminded his audiences of the price someone from the grassroots has to pay in becoming a big shot. No matter how deliberate her plans were, she was still not as skillful as her experienced enemies in scheming conspiracies. Her sudden death at the end of the film, and especially her surprised and desperate gaze, indicated her total failure and incapacity. All her seemingly crafty and well-designed efforts and schemes were used against her by someone she knew and trusted. In this film, not only the character of the Empress is paradoxical, almost all the characters are propelled by unsatisfied aspirations, not matter whether high or low, moral or immoral. Pu, the governor of Yan province, attempted to restore order and prevent the new Emperor's enthronement; but, in the end, he was brutally punished and beaten to death by the Emperor. The ambition of Minister Yin and his son to take advantage of the Empress's assassination plan to get rid of both her and the Emperor and then make the son the new ruler ended in the son's death and his father's exile. Even the unconditional love of Minister Yin's daughter for the Prince failed to receive a sincere return—the Prince only had deep affection for the Empress. In a way, Feng is not just envisioning the hopelessness of a little character gaining power, he also emphasizes the insecurity and dissatisfaction that permeate the lives of the powerful and the unholy nature of political struggles.

Feng goes to Hollywood: Ambition, control and integrity

Not only did the text of the film signify the characters' desire and ambition, the making and marketing of the film also testified to the director's own desire and ambition to be recognized not merely as a comedy film director popular in the Chinese domestic film market, but as a director able to handle films with high production value and serious subject matter that would be attractive to international audiences. With a cast of many bankable stars, including Zhang Ziyi, Ge You and Zhou Xun, and an international crew, including Oscar Award winners Tim Yip (Ye Jintian) as art director and Tan Dun as composer, the film explicitly aimed at an international audience. At the Cannes Film Festival in May, several months before the film's release, the production company, Huayi Brothers Company, spent RMB 4 million (US$500 thousand) to promote the film among international film distributors. Some months later, *The Banquet* also got involved in a rivalry with Zhang Yimou's new film, *Curse of the Golden Flower*, over being chosen as the PRC representative in the competition for Best Foreign Film at the Oscars. In late September, although the SARFT announced that *Curse of the Golden Flower* would be submitted to Oscar committee, *The Banquet* succeeded in getting approval from the Federation of Motion Picture Producers of Hong Kong as the film representing Hong Kong in the Oscar race.

Feng's ambition to prove his ability as a maker of profitable blockbuster films that could compete with those of other Fifth Generation directors was explicit from the very beginning of the project. In an on-line interview, when asked about the reasons for choosing this subject, Feng answered with his typical cynicism. The major reason he offered was that he always thought making a blockbuster-tragedy film is much easier than making a comedy. In comedy films the director has to make careful calculation to ensure that the audience will laugh at the right moments, while it seems in Chinese blockbuster films the director need not pay such close attention to integrity of the narrative. Implying that the harsh criticisms of recent blockbuster films such as *Promise* (Wu ji; dir. Chen Kaige, 2006) and *House of Flying Daggers* (Shimian maifu; dir. Zhang Yimou, 2005) are due to the directors' inability to make the narratives and stories of the films attractive to their audiences, Feng declared that making blockbuster films is no longer a privilege of Fifth Generation directors. Feng claimed that with equally adequate financial resources and manpower, he could easily do a better job than those "paper tigers."[70]

The final product, to some extent, justified Feng's claims. He did create astonishingly exquisite visual effects and breathtaking fight scenes. As if consciously making a contrast to Zhang Yimou's use of bright colors, Feng chose black, white and subdued red in costumes and setting. Also different from mostly computer-graphic generated fairyland-like mise-en-scene in *Promise, The Banquet* featured a Rembrandtesque setting with overarching ceilings and towering pillars looming in the shadows and main characters lit in harsh light. In terms of the story, Feng did a better job in making a coherent narrative without any fatal flaws. In terms of commercial success, this film's box-office return, RMB 100 million, is the highest of all Feng's films. Ironically, despite these achievements, *The Banquet* was also the film that received the harshest criticism from general audiences and critics. Feng's fans, who used to be attracted by the cynical and humorous renditions of current social issues and problems in his previous films, found themselves somewhat lost in the courtly intrigues and conspiracies among Emperor, Empress, Prince and court officials in *The Banquet*. Particularly, they found some lines of supposed comic relief inappropriate and ridiculous and the open ending, which did not clearly specify the murderer, obscure and odd. While some critics appreciated Feng's bravery in exploring a new style and acknowledged certain accomplishments, others, contextualizing the film in an ever-growing trend of blockbuster commercial films, believed that Feng's attempt at "going international" would only bring him into a risky dead-end.[71]

A similar irony was reflected in the paradoxical relation between the high production value of the film and the extent of director's personal imprint. As the most expensive film that Feng ever made, *The Banquet* is also the film over which the director had the least control. This was the first film that Feng agreed to make in response to a producer's demand, and also a film that was unapologetic in its intention to appeal to foreign audiences. In a film with a multi-million dollar budget and an all-star cast and crew, Feng definitely had the best talent and abundant resources at his disposal, but, as his role was reduced to just one link in a Fordian chain of production, he had much less control over the final product. In his previous productions, he worked not only as a director, but also scriptwriter, and sometimes set-designer; this gave him confidence regarding what the final product would look like. In *The Banquet*, his collaborations with Tan Dun and Tim Yip did succeed in helping Feng to realize his ambition of surprising his audiences with breathtaking visual and audio effects. However, as a veteran script-writer, he did not feel comfortable with changing even a single word in the script, as the subject of the film and style of the language were alien to him. Therefore, totally out of Feng's expectation, the dialogs became the major source of criticism after the film was released. The script-writer, Sheng Heyu, recommended to Feng by Feng's cameraman Zhang Li, is an expert at writing historical dramas for TV, among which *Emperor Hanwu* (Hanwu di; dir. Hu Mei, 58 episodes) and *Moving Towards the Republic* (Zouxiang gonghe; dir. Zhang Li, 60 episodes) were the most popular. Although very apt at capturing the essence of classical Chinese and blending it with vernacular Chinese, Sheng lacked experience in commercial screenplay writing. The dialogues in the film sometimes appeared to be redundant and too lyric; they sounded awkward to contemporary audiences. For example, after the Prince revealed the truth of his father's murder in a short play, the Emperor, after a long silence, said "You are a great artist." The rather contemporary phrase "great artist", *weida de yishujia*, sounded very strange coming out of the mouth of an Emperor living hundreds of years ago.

If these problems were caused by Feng's lack of experience and resulting failure to anticipate potential issues in a collective working mode, then there were other problems that were inevitable no matter how insightful the director might be. During the making of the film, not only did the Chinese producer's demands need to be satisfied, foreign film distributors' preferences were also paramount. After the shooting was completed, Feng made a rough cut of the film and submitted it to his foreign distributors. But they thought it was too long and hired a Hollywood editor cut it into a 90-minute version, which not only had a faster pace but also was entirely missing some subplots such as the love between the Prince and Qing Nü. Never having had to argue with his producers and investors in previous projects, Feng could not accept this version. He pleaded that it would only turn the film, meant to be a bottle of old wine, into a cup of soda. Although some of the storylines were kept intact, other changes were not negotiable. For instance, before the shooting started, many film distributors expressed their expectations for martial art scenes with Zhang Ziyi, as they thought this could guarantee the interest of Western audiences who were impressed by Zhang's fighting in films such as

Crouching Tiger, Hidden Dragon and *Rush Hour*. Therefore, although there was no such scene in the original script and Feng was clearly aware of the awkwardness of a martial art scene for an apparently weak and sentimental Empress, Feng still had to add a duet-dance-like fighting scene in which the Empress and the Prince were remembering their youth when they were both learning martial arts from the late Emperor.[72] Explicitly targeting the international audiences and made under a highly commercialized mode of production, *The Banquet* is a film that realizes the director's ambition for sumptuous visuality and recognition in a broader market. Paradoxically, the realization of these desires came at the price of sacrificing a certain degree of artistic integrity and control over the final product. As Feng admitted, "In *The Banquet*, I tried to accomplish a total breakthrough, making it totally different from *Cell Phone* and *A World Without Thieves*, releasing a sentiment deeply hidden in my heart and experimenting with my ideas of visual effects. Probably my audiences would think such intentions are not sincere, as I am not making a film that really touches me, but to merely show off the techniques. But as director, I always want to pursue something that is truly mine, something that is not easily manipulated by others."[73] The reality Feng faced in the new millennium is quite different from that in the 1990s. In his New Year films, the problems that Feng had to deal with was typical of a popular comedy film director in a post-socialist society—a middle path between the artist's cynical and satirical commendations on social issues and the film authorities' attempt to maintain a positive image of the status quo. But since the beginning of the new millennium, for Chinese film administrations, the control of film content became less important than industrializing the film industry. As a result, many new forces, such as private production companies, foreign capitals and Hollywood film companies have became more and more preeminent in Chinese cinema. The dilemma that Feng faced changed from a uniquely Chinese one to a more universal one, shared by many film directors working in a highly commercialized motion picture industry, but still striving to achieve personal expression.

Conclusion

In Feng Xiaogang's filmmaking career, the new millennium brought about a new kind of popular cinema in which he was able to appropriate the subjects and styles of his early works while also being increasingly constrained by economic considerations. If the Hollywood-sponsored production of *Big Shot*, featuring all the hallmarks of the New Year genre, could be seen as a conclusion to the stage of light-comedic films in Feng's career, then his recent films, which concern themselves with such subjects as male infidelity, ethical corruption in the age of high-technology, compromised morality in an era of materialism, and other inequities in social institutions, signaled the coming of a relatively democratic atmosphere in Chinese contemporary cinema.

In comparison to the comic resolutions of Feng's New Year films, which reassured his audiences that all their challenges and hardships would be only temporary, his latest films provide no positive resolutions. Rather, by incorporating depictions of social and personal corruption, Feng shows directly or metaphorically the serious disorders plaguing contemporary China and the Chinese people. These films, therefore, were not comforting but heightened the audience's reactions of pity and fear. In his early films, little characters are victorious: they are able to escape their troubles, they are rewarded with the objects of their love and pursuits. These films oriented and guided his audience in a society filled with inequalities, and thus supported the status quo. But in his latest films, he has emphasized the "big shot's" frustration and suffering, casting them as targets of criticism and cynicism and leaving them in the midst of their troubles without providing any ready solutions. In doing so, he disturbs his audiences with a potentially subversive message warning of the danger of moral decline in a money-hungry society.

Another significant distinction between his New Year films and his latest works is the degree to which commercialization has intruded into the films. This challenge rose unexpectedly as China's cinema entered a "corporate era," featuring a blatant drive for profit. Feng's production company has attracted financial investments for films by selling advertisement slots within the films and relying on box-office income to finance later films. As a result, ensuring good box-office revenue and satisfying the demands of investors have become new challenges for Feng. The change in political context and the emergence of these challenges result in a new kind of popular cinema that is both an authentic work of the filmmaker's self-expression, and a product imposed by the capitalistic industry.

These transformations reflected ongoing changes in Chinese cinema of the 2000s. The two major challenges of the 1990s, film censorship and Hollywood intrusion, had a reduced impact. After issuing legislation and reform measures targeting the monopolistic and arbitrary nature of the old censorship system, a thematically diverse range of films was granted a place in the official film market. The change of Feng's filmmaking to the subjects he dealt with in his early career would not have been possible without the loosened climate of censorship in the early 2000s. Hollywood dominance was also diminished by the runaway success of several domestic films in the early 2000s. Domestic films occupied the top box-office positions from 2003 to 2005. In spite of these changes, these two forces did not entirely disappear. The censors' power to ban films touching upon certain sensitive subjects remains unchallenged. For example, Feng's film project, *Remembering 1942* (Wengu 1942), a film concerning the history of one of the greatest famines in China's history, is still awaiting official approval to begin shooting.[74]

A new challenge in the 2000s emerged from within the film industry itself. As the most significant force in shaping the corporate era of Chinese cinema, private companies in all sectors of the film industry have had a dramatic influence on Chinese cinema. The perpetuation of the success of Feng's films in the late 1990s and early 2000s signaled the rising influence of private film productions. However, this success has come at a price, as a more blatant pursuit of profits has forced filmmakers working for these companies to bear the burden of ensuring their films' profitability. Therefore, in the new era, the question of how a filmmaker can balance his artistic pursuits and the interests of his sponsors has become a new dilemma. In Feng's case, the loosened control of censorship opened up the possibility of exposing social problems that had once been forbidden to filmmakers; but more urgent imperatives of profit making replaced one shackle with another. His films in the new era, therefore, have become a contradictory mix of both commercial and authentic.

6

Conclusion

Due to the constant social, economic, and political transformations still underway in contemporary China, as well as my own close association with the era, the difficulty of concluding a study of contemporary cinema and of one of its most active filmmakers is obvious. The rapid changes preclude any easy predictions of the future, and my own involvement makes it almost impossible to adopt a transcendent, historicizing perspective. Feng's filmmaking activities in the new millennium have shown such great diversity that it is impossible to accurately predict the future of his cinema. Though clearly proud of his contributions to a national cinema, he has, nonetheless, worked for a foreign film studio; though best-known as a director of comedies, he has switched to serious drama and tragedy, and plans to make a historical film about a great famine during the Republican era.[1] These changes, and others—for example, his shift to comedy director in the second half of the 1990s, and the change in his style in the early 2000s—are actually a result of attempts to articulate his obsession with Chinese society and culture, and the fate of Chinese people during a period of immense social upheaval. Through the recurring themes of the victory of little characters, the depravity of "big shots," and cynical and humorous criticism of social problems, Feng has used his popular cinema as a unique way to express his concern for the happiness and sorrow in ordinary Chinese people's lives, his belief in the value of seemingly insignificant characters, and his criticism of the depravity and decadence of the privileged social stratum. His film succeeded in capturing various contradictions caused by social and political transformations: the prosperity and insecurity, confidence and fear, the audacity and timidity. The achievement of his films lies in his ability of highlighting the deeper meanings of this confusion resulting from a thousands-year-old culture's encounter with commercialization and Westernization.

The ups and downs of Feng's filmmaking career have corresponded to the trajectory of private Chinese film productions since the late 1980s, a trajectory which can be seen as a direct result of film officials' indecision regarding the function of cinema, i.e. whether it should be treated as an industry and thus guided by market forces, or function as part of a government propaganda apparatus and be under full state control. As we have seen in this study, from the 1989 Tian'anmen Incident to the mid-1990s, an emphasis on cinema's pedagogical and political functions meant that the productions of non-state owned film companies encountered more difficulties in gaining access to official channels of distribution and exhibition. Feng's early works of social criticism were discouraged by film censorship, but when he began making light-hearted romantic comedies that did not challenge official Party rhetoric, such interference ceased. In these New Year films, his social commentary had to be carefully submerged beneath seemingly non-political scenes and plots, and addressed only to sophisticated audiences. At the turn of the century, loosened ideological control and large scale industry reform intended to emancipate the industry from state monopolies in production, distribution, and exhibition gradually transformed a state-controlled and ideologically censored institution for the masses into a director/writer-centered and studio-owned popular medium for an urban audience. As a result, the early 2000s finally witnessed the prosperity of a popular cinema that not only proved irresistible to filmmakers from diverse backgrounds, but also gained a certain degree of support from film officials through new film policies and legislation. Meanwhile, the more democratic atmosphere also allowed more freedom for filmmakers in choosing the subjects of their films. The renaissance of the social criticism and cynicism of Feng's early works would not have been possible without such changes in the film industry and ideology. Still targeting urban audiences, Feng's films in this century began to place a stronger emphasis on the negative effects of rapid economic reform, including the decline in moral values, the often ludicrous extent of materialism and commercialization, and the irredeemable depravity and decadence of the rich. In the meantime, however, as a participant in a highly materialistic world, Feng inevitably fell victim to the drive for profits. Although pressure from film officials regarding film ideology was reduced, the demand to maximize profits forced him to insert as many as possible tie-ins to satisfy his investors, while still attempting to maintain the integrity of the narrative.

Made under the hegemonies of Party ideology and globalized economics, but with an increasing sense of the need to shift from implicit criticism to explicit commentary, Feng's films demonstrate a kind of "compromised equilibrium," a concept used by Gramsci to describe the media that are seen as the place of competition between different social forces.² According to Gramsci, this "compromised equilibrium" is marked by both "resistance and incorporation."³ In the case of Feng Xiaogang, his popular cinema is restricted by Party art policy and demands of profits, yet it also serves as a "voice" for the masses. Therefore, on the one hand, while his films do not overtly challenge any Party policy or official rhetoric, on the other hand, the explicit and implicit social commentary of his films can be seen as a subversive countercurrent to the dominant mainstream. In other words, in contemporary Chinese cinema, Feng's filmmaking is a process of "negotiation," which, according to Christine Gledhill "implies the holding together of opposite sides in an ongoing process of give-and-take....Meaning is neither imposed, nor passively imbibed, but arises out of a struggle or negotiation between competing frames of reference, motivation and experience."⁴

As for how to situate Feng's cinema in the larger context of Chinese film history, Feng's own views on the difference between his films and those of other Chinese film directors is revealing. In a conference held at the Beijing Film Academy in November 2001, Feng gave a metaphorical review of the history of Chinese cinema:

> After the emergence of Chinese cinema, through their hard work and diligence, the first three generations of directors erected a Sacred Hall of Chinese Cinema. After its establishment, one day, a group of people rushed in and took over the Hall and then established their own style of filmmaking and rules for other filmmakers to follow. In this way, the Fourth Generation directors, represented by Xie Fei, sealed the door of the Hall of Chinese cinema.
>
> When the Fourth Generation directors were carefully guarding the door of the Sacred Hall and enjoying a stable life and career there, suddenly a gang of people entered the Hall. Rather than going through the door, they entered through the window and then established their own way of filmmaking. These are the Fifth Generation directors, represented by Zhang Yimou and Chen Kaige. Like the Fourth Generation directors, as soon as they entered the Hall, the Fifth Generation closed and sealed the windows.
>
> Now that both the door and windows were sealed, it became very difficult for other directors to get in. But, out of all expectation, the Sixth Generation still found their way into the Hall—they entered through neither the door nor the window, but from the underground.
>
> As a result, it is now very crowded in the Hall of Chinese Cinema— someone guards the door, another the window, and even the underground tunnel is blocked by the Sixth Generation. I realized that it was impossible for me to get in, and that there wouldn't be any place

left for me in any case. So, I decided to build a side room (*erfang* 耳房) beside the Hall. Now I am surprised that my life here is not just comfortable, but also more and more prosperous. Now when I am peeping inside the Hall, it seems so crowded that I really don't want to be there.[5]

This quote vividly depicts the place that Feng claims for himself in the history of Chinese cinema. Within the edifice of socialist cinema, there is no place for Feng's non-political entertainment films or his films of social criticism. His films produced by private production entities are definitely outsiders to the Party-controlled film industry. At the same time, designed to satisfy the needs of ordinary urban audiences, his films do not fit the expectations of the internationally famous art cinema of the Fifth and Sixth Generation directors. Like a side room attached to a larger building, Feng's films are by no means a major part of any history of Chinese cinema, at least insofar as they have never been recognized by either the government's Golden Rooster Awards, or major international film festivals. However, this neglect and indifference is contradicted by the growing popularity and influence of his films in current Chinese cinema. In the past two to three years, even established filmmakers such as Zhang Yimou and Chen Kaige have begun to abandon their elitist styles and join the vogue for profit-oriented and urban entertainment films. Therefore, though it is perhaps unwise to overemphasize the role of one filmmaker in changing the whole course of Chinese cinema, especially when he lacks political status in an allegedly socialist country, it is still safe to say that the popularity of Feng's cinema at least indicates the significance of a popular cinema that both challenges the hegemonic notion of cinema as a tool of political propaganda, and attests to the importance of an alternative path for a national cinema targeting the needs of ordinary audiences and operating on the basis of market demand.

There are many possible avenues that one can adopt for a scholarly study Feng Xiaogang, a filmmaker who has such diverse experiences in his career. For example as the creator of New Year comedies, Feng has succeeded in elevating the comedic genre into a position of unprecedented importance. The question of how to situate Feng's New Year comedies in the history of Chinese comedic film and an examination of the specificities of Feng's, as well as other Chinese comedies, would a fascinating topic for a further research. Although Feng's films demonstrate many characteristics that are unique to Chinese cinema in an age of social flux, they, in many ways, are shared by films of the late Soviet Union, which also experienced a period when cinema faced both ideological liberation and pressures from industry reform. A comparative study of Feng's films and similar trends in Soviet cinema, for example, the satirical and comedic films produced by writer/director Eldar Ryazanov (b. 1950) before the collapse of the USSR, would situate contemporary Chinese cinema in a larger context of socialist/post-socialist cinema. This would demonstrate that Feng's cinema is not an isolated cultural phenomenon, and that the problems he faced are not unique to China but, instead, reflect developments that occurred in other socialist national cinemas. All of these questions, though beyond the scope of this work, offer potential for a further study of Feng's cinema.

Notes

Chapter 1

1. Yin Hong 尹鸿, *Xin Zhongguo dianying shi* 新中国电影史 (History of new China's cinema) (Changsha: Hunan meishu chubashe, 2002), p. 175.
2. Ni Zhen 倪震, "Dianying xushi: leixing he chuanbo kongjian de kuozhan", *Dianying yishu* 电影艺术 (Film art) 2006, no. 4, p. 58; 沙蕙 " 'Tianxia wuzei' he 'zei han zhuo zei': Feng Xiaogang dianying de beilun," *Wenyi yanjiu* 文艺研究 (Literature and art studies), 2005, no. 5, pp.18-25. Similar works include Su Yuewu 苏越武, "Feng Xiaogang gechang you qian ren," *Dianying tongxu* 电影通讯 (Film newsletter), 2000, no. 5 pp. 21-22 and Wang Nan 王楠, "Jiegou Feng Xiaogang," *Dianying* 2004, no. 12.
3. Stuart Hall, "Notes on Deconstructing the 'Popular'," in *People's History and Socialist Theory*, ed. Raphael Samuel (London: Routledge and Kegan Paul, 1981), p. 228.
4. *DYYS* (Film art) [hereafter *DYYS*], 2000, no. 3. 2001, no, 3, 2002, no. 3, 2003, no. 3 and 2004, Issue 3.
5. Chen Kaige 陈凯歌, *Shao nian Kaige* 少年凯歌 (Young Kaige) (Taibei: Yuanliu, 1991).
6. Feng Xiaogang 冯小刚, *Wo ba qingchun xian gei ni* 我把青春献给你 (I dedicated my youth to you) (Beijing: Changjiang wenyi, 2003), pp. 35-40.
7. Wang Zheng 王铮, "Yishu rensheng kai kou shuohua" 艺术人生开口说话 (*Art and Life* speaks), August 7, 2004, official website of China Central Television, http://www.cctv.com/entertainment/yishurensheng/erji/0809fxg.html
8. Feng seldom mentioned his father in his autobiography or other occasions. We just know that he lived with his mother and sister since he was little. But it is not clear whether it was because his parents were divorced or his father passed away.

9. Feng, *Wo ba qingchun xiangei ni*, pp. 25-35.
10. Keane and Tao, "Interview with Feng Xiaogang," *Positions* 7.1 (Spring, 1999): 194-195.
11. Ibid., p. 196.
12. Shuqin Cui, *Women Through the Lens: Gender and Nation in a Century of Chinese Cinema* (Honolulu: University of Hawaii Press, 2003), p. 246.
13. Zhang, *Screening China*, pp. 317-320.
14. Ibid, p. 318.
15. Ibid, p. 320.
16. Jason McGrath, "Culture and the Market in Contemporary China: Cinema, Literature, and Criticism of the 1990s" (University of Chicago, August, 2004), p. iv.
17. Stephen Short, "As Sex Scenes Are Banned, We Need to Be Creative," (Web-only interview with director Feng Xiaogang) *Time Asia, http://cgi.cnn.com/ASIANOW/time/features/interviews/2000/10/26/int.feng_xiaogang.html*; Wendy Kan, "Big Shot doesn't win over locals," *Variety* 387:2 (May 27, 2002 - June 02, 2002)? FILM, p. 8; Patrick Tyler, "In China, Letting a Hundred Films Wither," *New York Times*, December 1, 1996; Erik Eckholm, "Leading Chinese Filmmaker Tries for a Great Leap to the West," *New York Times* June 21, 2001. Scarlet Cheng, "There's Nothing Like Being There," *Los Angeles Times*, November 2, 1998, etc.
18. Patrick Tyler, "In China, Letting a Hundred Films Wither," *New York Times*, December 1, 1996.
19. Examples of the former include Wang Guangyi 王广宜, "Cong *bu Jian bu ban kan Feng Xiaogang de daoyan yishu*" 从《不见不散》看冯小刚的导演艺术 (Feng Xiaogang's art of directing in *Be There or Be Square*), DYYS, 1999, no. 3, pp. 58-59; Su Yuewu 苏越武, "Feng Xiaogang gechang you qian ren" 冯小刚歌唱有钱人 (Feng Xiaogang glorifies rich people), *Dianying tongxu* 电影通讯 (Film newsletter), 1995, no. 5, pp. 21-22 and Xiang Nan 向楠, "Feng Xiaogang, Ge You, sidu hesui xing" 冯小刚、葛优四度贺岁行 (Feng Xiaogang and Ge You are on their forth New Year films," *Dianying tongxu*, 2001, no. 3, pp. 8-11. Example of the latter are Wang Xiaofeng 王晓峰, "Feng Xiaogang kan hesuipian: wo de dianying jiangjiu chuanqixing he renminxing" 冯小刚侃贺岁片：我的电影讲究传奇性和人民性 (Feng Xiaogang on New Year films: my films focus on legends and serve the mass peole), *Sanlian shenhuo zhoukan*, 2003, no. 2 and Wang Nan 王楠, "Jiegou Feng Xiaogang" 解构冯小刚 (Deconstuct Feng Xiaogang), *Dianying*, (December, 2004).
20. Examples of such works are Wang Guangyi, "Cong *Bu Jian Bu San* kan Feng Xiaogang de daoyan yishu," DYYS, (1999, 03) pp. 58-59, and Xiang Nan, "Feng Xiaogang, Ge You, sidu hesui xing", *Dianying tongxu*, 2001, no. 3, pp. 8-11.
21. Yin Hong 尹鸿, *Xin Zhongguo dianying shi* 新中国电影史 (History of new China's cinema) (Changsha: Hunan meishu chubashe, 2002), p. 175. Similar

works include Su Yuewu, "Feng Xiaogang gechang you qian ren," *Dianying tongxu* 电影通讯 (Film newsletter), (2000, 05) pp. 21-22 and Wang Nan, "Jiegou Feng Xiaogang," *Dianying* 2004, no. 12.

22. Ni Zhen 倪震, "Dianying xushi: leixing he chuanbo kongjian de kuozhan," *DYYS*, 2006, no. 4, p. 58.

23. 沙蕙 "'Tianxia wuzei' he 'zei han zhuo zei': Feng Xiaogang dianying de beilun," *Wenyi yanjiu* 文艺研究 (Literature and art studies), 2005, no. 5, pp.18-25.

24. Andrew Sarris, "Toward a Theory of Film History", in *The American Cinema: Directors and Directions* (New York, E. P. Dutton, 1968), p. 30.

25. John Caughie, *Theories of Authorship* (London and New York: Routledge), 1993, p.9.

26. Andrew Sarris, "Toward a Theory of Film History", p. 30.

27. Janet Staiger, "Authorship Approaches," in *Authorship and Films*, ed. David A. Gerstner and Janet Staiger (New York and London: Routledge, 2003), p. 27.

28. Fredric Jameson, "Reification and Utopian of Mass Culture," *Social Text*, 1, p. 134.

29. Ibid., p. 144.

30. Stuart Hall, "Notes on Deconstructing the 'Popular,'" in *People's History and Socialist Theory*, ed. Raphael Samuel (London: Routledge and Kegan Paul, 1981), p. 228.

31. Ibid.

32. Janet Gaines, "Dream/Factory," in *Reinventing Film Studies*, ed. Christine Gledhill and Linda Williams (New York: Oxford University Press, 2000), p. 108.

33. Christine Gledhill, "Pleasurable Negotiations," in *Cultural Theory and Popular Culture*, ed. John Storey (Hemel Hempstead: Prentice Hall,1988), p. 244.

Chapter 2

1. Wang Yongwu 王永午 and Weng Li 翁立, "1988 Zhongguo dianying shichang beiwanglu" 1988 中国电影市场备忘录 (1988: Memoir of Chinese film market), Zhongguo dianying nianjian 中国电影年鉴 (China Film Year Book) [hereafter *ZGDYNJ*] (Beijing: Zhongguo dianying chubanshe, 1989), p. 297.

2. Qiang Ma, "Chinese Cinema in the 1980s: Art and Industry," in *Cinema and Cultural Identity*, ed. by Wimal Dissanayake (Lanham, MD: University Press of America, 1988), p. 167.

3. Wang Yongwu and Weng Li, "1988 Zhongguo dianying shichang beiwanglu," p. 295.

4. Ibid., p. 295.

5. Ibid., p. 294.

6. Zhong Chengxiang 仲呈祥, "1988: Zhongguo yingtan de liangge remen huati: 'yulepian' yu 'huxuanlu' zhi wo jian" 1988 中国影坛的两个热门话题：
"娱乐片"与"主旋律"之我见 (1988: Two hot topics in Chinese Cinema—my opinions on 'entertainment films' and 'main melody film'), *RMRB* (People's daily) [hereafter *RMRB*], January 13, 1989.

7. For more about this debate see: Li Xingye 李兴叶, "Bingtai shehui bingtai jingshen de zhenshi xiezhao: Wang Shuo dianying de jiazhi yu shiwu" 病态社会病态病态精神的真实写照：王朔电影的价值与失误 (Realistic representation of a morbid spirit in a morbid society—the value and failure of Wang Shuo films) *ZGDYNJ*, 1989, pp. 285-288. Shao Mujun 邵牧君, "Wang Shuo dianyingre yuanhe er qi" 王朔电影从何而起 (Where does the Wang Shuo Fever come from), *Zhongguo dianying bao* (China film newspaper), March 25, 1989. Jiashan Mi, "Discussing The Troubleshooters," *Chinese Education and Society* 31.3 (Jan-Feb): 8-14.

8. Esther Yao, "International Fantasy and the 'New Chinese Cinema,'" *Quarterly Review of Film and Video* 14. 3 (1995): 100-105, quoted in Zhang, *Screening China*, p. 291.

9. Paul Clark, *Chinese Cinema: Culture and Politics since 1949* (New York: Cambridge University Press, 1987), p. 35.

10. Central Committee of the CCP document, "Guanyu jingji tizhi gaige de jueding" 关于经济体制改革的决定 (Decisions on reform of the economic system), issued on October 12, 1984.

11. For more about Chinese economic reforms see: Barry Naughton, *Growing Out of the Plan: Chinese Economy Reform, 1978-1993* (Cambridge: Cambridge University Press, 1995); Ying Zhu, *Chinese Cinema During the Reform Era: The Ingenuity of the System* (Westport, Conn.: Praeger, 2003) and Paul Clark, *Chinese Cinema*.

12. Wang Yongwu and Weng Li, "1988 Zhongguo dianying shichang beiwanglu", p. 294.

13. Ying Zhu, *Chinese Cinema During the Reform Era*, p. 74.

14. Ibid., p.74.

15. Zhong Chengxiang, "1988: Zhongguo yingtan de liangge remen huati: 'yulepian' yu 'zhuxuanlu' zhi wo jian," p. 263.

16. Teng Jinxiang 腾进贤, "Wei tigao yingpian de yishu zhiliang er nuli" 为提高影片的艺术思想质量而努力 (Strive for improving artistic and ideological quality of films), *ZGDYNJ*, 1989, p. 13.

17. Chen Haosu 陈昊苏, "Guanyu yule pian benti lun ji qita" 关于娱乐片主体论及其它 (On dominance of entertainment film and others), *ZGDYNJ*, 1989, p. 8.

18. For more about the construction and operation of the systems of socialist film production, distribution and exhibition, see Paul Clark, *New Chinese Cinema* (New York: Cambridge University Press, 1987), pp. 35-37.

19. Greg Merritt, *Celluloid Mavericks: A History of American Independent Film* (New York: Thunder's Mouth Press, 2000), p. 38.

20. Garth Jowett, "A Significant Medium for Communication of Ideas—the Miracle Decision and Decline of Motion Picture Censorship," in *Censorship and American Culture*, ed. Francis G. Couvares (Washington and London: Smithsonian Institution Press, 1996), pp. 258-277.

21. Ministry of Radio, Film and TV, "Dianying shencha tiaoli" 电影审查条例 (Regulations of film censorship), January 1997.

22. For an English translation of Mao's Yan'an talks, see Bonnnie S. McDougall, *Mao Zedong's "Talks at the Yan'an Conference on Literature and Art": A Translation of the 1943 Text with Commentary, Michigan Papers in Chinese Studies, no. 39* (Ann Arbor: University of Michigan Center for Chinese Studies, 1980).

23. Editorial, "Xuexi Jiang Zemin lun Yan'an jingshen de zhongyao jianghua," 学习江泽民论延安精神的重要讲话 (Study Jiang Zemin's important talk on Yan'an spirit), *RMRB*, April 20, 2002.

24. Liu Qiong 刘琼, "Jinian 'Zai Yan'an Wenyi zuotan hui shang de jianghua, fabiao 60 zhou nian: zhongzhi yuan tuan zhengti chuji" 纪念'在延安文艺座谈会上的讲话发表60周年: 中直院团整体出击 (Celebrate the 60 years anniversary of the Yan'an Talks: All the central art institutions act now), *RMRB*, April 18, 2002.

25. For such activities, see "Meishu jie renshi jinian 'jianghua' fabiao 60 zhounian" 美术界人士纪念"讲话"发表60 周年 (The art circle celebrates the 60th anniversary of the "Talk"), *RMRB*, May 15, 2002, "Qiushi zaizhi he shanxi shengwei juxing zuotan hui jinian 'jianghua' fabiao 60 zhounian" 求是杂志和山西省委举行座谈会纪念"讲话"发表60周年 (*Qiushi* magazine and the Shanxi Provincial Administration held a conference to celebrate the 60 years anniversary of Yan'an Talk), *RMRB*, May 16, 2002, "Beijing yishu yanjiu suo chengli 50 zhiji, xuexi 'jianghua' fazhan yishu zhice" 北京艺术研究所成立50 年之际，学习"讲话"发展艺术之策 (As Beijing Art Research Center celebrates its 50th anniversary, it also celebrates the 60th anniversary of the "Talk"), *RMRB*, May 21, 2002.

26. State Council of PRC, document No. 14 (1988), "Yao jianli dui yingshipian de shencha dingji zhidu, dui zhongxiaoxuesheng buyi guankan de yingshi zuopin zuochu mingque guiding" 要建立对影视片的审查定级制度，对中小学生不宜观看的影视作品作出明确规定 (To establish a censorship of rating system of film and TV works, to specify films and TV works that are not appropriate for students of high, middle and primary schools).

27. Ministry of Radio, Movie and TV, document No. 201 Guangfayingsi (1989), No. 201.

28. "Ningde shi dazhong yingyuan bufu mingde diqu gongshang xingzheng guanli ju yiqi dianying guanggao neirong huangdan yuyi xingzheng chufa jueding an" 宁德市大众影院不服宁德地区工商行政管理局以其电影广告内容荒诞予以行政处罚决定案 (Case of Ningde Dazhong movie theater's appeal to

administrative penalty imposed by *Ningde* Regional Administration for Industry and Commerce for its absurd content in film advertisement), Fujian Province Supreme Court, May. 15, 1990. http://www.legalinfo.gov.cn/pfzx/2003-10/20/content_54144.htm/.

29. Li Li 李力, "Shouer buyi de youhuo he sikao" 少儿不宜的诱惑和思考 (Temptation and thinking of 'Not Appropriate for Children'), *RMRB*, February 28, 1989.

30. "Ningde shi dazhong yingyuan bufu Ningde diqu gongshang xingzheng guanli ju yi qi dianying guanggao neirong huangdan yuyi xingzheng chufa jueding an," http://www.legalinfo.gov.cn/pfzx/200310/20/content_54144.htm/.

31. Ibid.

32. Tian Congming 田聪明, "Dianying 'bawu' de huigu, 'jiuwu' de shexiang ji 1996 nian de gongzuo"电影 "八五" 的回顾、 "九五" 的设想及1996 年的工作 (Review of the cinema's 'Eight Five Year Plan'; envision of the 'Ninth Five Year Plan' and work in 1996—a talk at a meeting of film studio directors), *ZGDYNJ* (1996), p. 35.

Chapter 3

1. For a detailed introduction to film industry reform in the early 1990s, please see Ying Zhu, *Chinese Cinema During the Reform Era* (Westport, Conn.: Praeger, 2003).

2. Deng Xiaoping 邓小平, "Zai Wuchuang, Shenzhen, Zhuhai, Shanghai deng di de tanhua yaodian (1/8/1992-2/21/1992)" 在武昌、深圳、珠海、上海等地的谈话要点 (Highlights of talks given in Wuchang, Shenzhen, Zhuhai and Shanghai), in *Deng Xiaoping wenxuan* 邓小平文选 (Selected works of Deng Xiaoping) (Beijing: Renmin chubanshe, 1993), vol. 3, p. 370.

3. Ibid., p. 371.

4. Deng Xiaoping, "Women you xinxin ba Zhongguo de shiqing zuo de geng hao" 我们有信心把中国的事情做得更好 (We are confident that we can make China better), ibid., p. 324.

5. Deng Xiaoping, "Gao zichan jieji ziyouhua jiushi zou ziben zhuyi daolu" 搞资产阶级自由化就是走资本主义道路 (Insisting bourgeois liberation is following the capitalist road), ibid., p.123.

6. For a detailed discussion of production, investment and box office of the main melody film, see research by Zhongguo yishu yanjiu yuan dianying yanjiu suo (Film art research institute of Chinese art research academy), "Jiushi niandai zhongda geming lishi ticai yingpian chuangzuo diaocha baogao" 九十年代重大革命历史题材影片创作调查报告 (Survey of "films of significant revolutionary and historical subjects in the 1990s)," *DYYS*, 2002, no. 3.

7. Editorial, "Bixu qizhi xianming di fandui dongluan" 必须旗帜鲜明地反对动乱 (Must resolutely oppose an unrest), *RMRB*, April 26, 1989. Jiang Zemin,

"Zai shisa jie sizhong quanhui shang de jianghua" 在十三届四中全会上的讲话 (Talk on Fourth Meeting of Thirteenth Party Congress), Shisan da yilia zhongyao wenxian xuanbian 十三大以来重要文献选编 (Selections of important documents after the Thirteenth Party Congress) (Beijing: Renmin chubanshe, 1991), volume 2, p. 551. Also see Wushi tian de huigu yu fansi 五十天的回顾与反思 (Review and retrospection of the fifty days) edited by Guojia jiaowei shehui kexue yanjiu yu yishu jiaoyu si, Guojia jiaowei sixiang zhengzhi gongzuo si deng (Department of Social Science Research and Art Education of National Education Committee, Department of Political Works of National Education Committee and est.) (Beijing: Gaodeng jiaoyu chubanshe, 1989), pp. 2–22.

8. Four Modernizations was a slogan proposed by former Prime Minister Zhou Enlai after the Cultural Revolution and later became part of Deng Xiaoping's reform program. The initial goal of the "Four Modernizations" was to achieve modernization in agriculture, industry, science, and defense in the 21st century.

9. Liu Cheng 柳城, "Dui 1989 nian gushipian chuangzuo de huigu" 对1989年故事片创作的回顾 (Review of production of feature films of 1989), *ZGDYNJ*, 1990, p. 19.

10. Ibid.

11. Zhong Chengixang 仲呈祥, "1988 Zhongguo yingtan de liang ge remen huati—'yule pian' yu 'zhuxuan lu' zhi wo jian" 1988中国影坛的两个热门话题－"乐片"与"主旋律"之我见 (1988: Two hot topics in Chinese cinema—my opinions on 'entertainment films' and 'main melody film'), *ZGDYNJ*, 1991, p. 263.

12. Paul Clark, *Chinese Cinema: Culture and Politics since 1949*, pp. 94–95.

13. Wei Lian 韦廉, "*Pingjin zhanyi* pinge quisuo" 《平津战役》品格求索 (Stylistic exploration of *Pingjing Campaign*), *ZGDYNJ*, 1993, pp. 86–87.

14. Ibid.

15. "1992 nian ge chang faxing gushipian shouzhi yingkui mingxibiao" 1992年各长发行故事片收支盈亏明细表(Charts of lose and gain of distributed films of film studios in 1992), *ZGDYNJ*, 1993, p. 225.

16. Ying Zhu, *Chinese Cinema During the Reform Era*, p. 77.

17. http://news.163.com/40926/9/116RJSFE0001124L.html

18. http://www.people.com.cn/GB/jiaoyu/8216/36635/36640/2786267.html/.

19. http://www.chinasarft.gov.cn/manage/publishfile/35/2294.html/.

20. Film Art Research Institute of Chinese Art Research Academy, "Jiushi niandai zhongda geming lishi ticai yingpian chuangzuo diaocha bogao" 九十年代重大革命历史题材影片创作调查报告 (Survey of "films of significant revolutionary and historical subjects in the 1990s)," *DYYS*, 2002, no. 3, p. 55.

21. Wang Shushun 王树舜, "Nanwang de 1991 nian—1991 nian gushipian chuangzuo qingkuang gaishu" 难忘的1991年－1991年故事片创作情况概述 (Unforgettable 1991—review of feature film productions of 1991), *ZGDYNJ*,1992, p. 51.

22. "1992 nian ge chang faxing gushi pian shouzhi yingkui mingxi biao" 1992 年各长发行故事片收支盈亏明细表 (Table of gain and loss of distributed films of studios in 1992), *ZGDYNJ*, 1993, pp.226-228.

23. Ying Zhu, *Chinese Cinema During the Reform Era*, p. 77.

24. Liu Cheng, "Dui 1989 nian gushipian chuangzuo de huigu," *ZGDYNJ*, 1990, p. 22.

25. Ibid., p. 23.

26. Li Ruihuan 李瑞环, "Fanrong you Zhongguo tese de shehuizhuyi dianying yishu" 繁荣有中国特色的社会主义电影艺术 (Let the art of socialist cinema with Chinese specificities flourish), *Dianying tongxun* (Film Newsletter) 1990, no. 4, pp. 1-2 and no. 5, pp. 1-3. Ai Zhisheng 艾知生, "Duanzheng zhidao sixiang, mingque chuangzuo fangxiang" 端正指导思想，明确创作方向 (Correct the leaders' thinking, clarify directions of production), *ZGDYNJ*, 1990, pp. 5-10.

27. For more detailed discussions of industry reform in the early 1990s, please see Ying Zhu, *Chinese Cinema During the Reform Era* and Ni Zhen, *Gaige yu Zhongguo dianying* (Reform and Chinese cinema) (Beijing: Zhongguo dianying chubanshe, 1994).

28. *Guanyu dangqian shenhua dianying jizhi gaige de ruogan yijian* 关于当前深化电影机制改革的若干意见, also known as Document No. 3.

29. MRFT Document (1993) No. 3, "Guanyu dangqian shenhua dianying hangye jizhi gaige de ruogan yijian" 关于当前深化电影行业机制改革的若干意见 (Suggestions on the deepening of Chinese film industries institutional reform), Guang fa ying zi (1993) No. 3（广发影字[1993]3号.）

30. This figure is for 1990.

31. Li Ruihuan, "Fanrong you zhongguo tese de shehui zhuyi dianying yishu", *ZGDYNJ*, 1990, p.3.

32. According to MRFT's regulations, all films shot and distributed in China are required to get a shooting license from the MRFT and the only film entities that are qualified to apply for such a license are state-film studios. So, if a non-state film studio or company wants to make a film in China, which will also be distributed in China, it has to "corporate" with a state-studio in order to get such a license. In most cases, the state-studios would charge these companies a certain amount of money as the license fee. For more about the co-production between state and non-state film studios, see Ying Zhu, *Chinese Cinema During the Reform Era*, p. 77.

33. *ZGDYNJ*, 1993, p. 27.

34. Wang Zhiqiang 王志强, "1993 nian quanguo dianying shichang pingshu" 1993 年全国电影市场评述(Review of China's film market of 1993), *ZGDYNJ*, 1994, p. 202.

35. For such articles, see Liu Cheng, "Dui 1989 nian gushipian de huigu" 对1989年故事片的回顾 (Review of feature film productions in 1989), *ZGDYNJ*, 1990, pp. 18-24; Wang Shushun, "Nanwang de 1991 nian—1991 nian

gushipian chuangzuo zhuangkuang" 难忘的1991年—1991年故事片创作
状况 (Unforgettable 1991—feature film production in 1991), ZGDYNJ
(1992), pp. 49-51; Teng Jinxian, "Jianchi gaige kaifang, chuangzao dianying
xin de fanrong" 坚持改革，创造电影新的繁荣 (Continue reform for
cinema's new prosperity), *ZGDYNJ*, 1993, pp.13-19; Ai Zhisheng,"Jiaqiang
lingdao, nuli tigao yingpian zhiliang"加强领导，努力提高影片质量
(Reinforce leadership—improve quality of film), ZGDYNJ, 1994, pp.13-15
and Shi Ming,"Tiejin shidai pingzhong jianqi" 贴近时代，平中见奇
(Reflecting the time, presenting significance from usual), ZGDYNJ, 1995,
pp. 25-30.

36. "Xinwen beijing: wo guo de liuxue zhengce shi ruhe zouxiang chengshu de"
新闻背景： 我国留学政策是如何走向成熟的 (News background: how
does the policy of studying abroad has been formed), *Website of Central Committee
of China Zhi Gong Party.* http://www.zg.org.cn/zcfg/2004-02/17/
content_1639600.htm/.

37. An edited version of the script was published at the same time. See Wang Shuo
and Feng Xiaogang, *Bianjibu de gushi* 编辑部的故事 (Story of editorial board)
(Beijing: Zhongguo guangbo dianshi chubanshe, 1992).

38. Feng Xiaogang, *Wo ba qingchun xiangei ni*, p. 44.

39. *Wang Shuo, Wang Shuo wenji: suibiji* 王朔文集: 随笔集 (Selection of Wang
Shuo: volume of collection of essays) (Kunming: Yunnan chubanshe, 2004),
p. 115.

40. Feng Xiaogang, *Wo ba qingchun xiangei ni*, p. 43.

41. Ibid., p. 105.

42. Among scholarship on Wang Shuo, Geremie Barme's "Wang Shuo and
Liumang ('Hooligan') Culture," in *The Australian Journal of Chinese Affairs* 28
(1992): 23-66, is a groundbreaking and pioneering study, which provides both
an introduction of the social context from which Wang came from, and an
elaborate analysis of his styles. Yomi Braester's "Memory at a Standstill: From
Mao History to Hooligan History," in *Witness Against History: Literature, Film,
and Public Discourse in Twentieth-Century China* (Stanford: Stanford University
Press, 2003) and Harry Kuoshu's "Filming Marginal Youth: The 'Beyond'
Syndrome in the Postsocialist City," in *Lightness of Being in China: Adaptation
and Discursive Figuration in Cinema and Theater,* ed. by Harry Kuoshu (NY: Peter
Lang, 1999), pp. 123-152, deal with the influences of Wang's writing on
Chinese culture and cinema. Jonathan Noble's "Wang Shuo and the
Commercialization of Literature," in *Columbia Companion to Modern East Asian
Literatures,* ed. Joshua Mostow and Kirk A. Denton (NY: Columbia University
Press, 2003), pp. 598-603, focuses on Wang's activity as a commercialized writer
in recent years.

43. Geremie Barme, "Wang Shuo and Luimang (Hooligan) Culture," p. 23.

44. Beijing Industry and Commerce Administration (BICA) document.

45. Feng Xiaogang, *Wo ba qingchun xiangei ni*, p. 84.

46. Ibid., pp. 47–96.
47. BICA document.
48. Published on *Dangdai*, no. 6, 1989.
49. Published on *Dangdai*, no. 2, 1986.
50. Geremie Barme, "Wang Shuo and Hooligan Culture," p. 27.
51. Ying Zhu, *Chinese Cinema During the Reform Era*, p.155.
52. Xiaoming Wang, "The Mysterious Other: Postpolities in Chinese Film," trans. by Kang Liu and Anbin Shi, in *boundary 1*, vol. 24, no. 3, Postmodernism and China, pp. 123–124.
53. Geremie Barme, *In the Red: On Contemporary Chinese Culture* (New York: Columbia University Press, 1999), p. 96.
54. Wang Shuo's many works, including "Dongwu xiongmeng" 动物凶猛 (Furious animals), "Kongzhou xiaojie" 空中小姐 (Flight attendant) and "Kanshang qu henmai" 看上去很美 (Seemingly beautiful), all place in Beijing.
55. "Shoudu zhi chuang" 首都之窗 (Windows to Beijing), Website of Beijing municipal government. http://www.beijing.gov.cn/zw/ghxx/qtgh/t20040215_115265.htm/.
56. Shu Kewen 舒可文, quotes Qin Youguo 秦佑国 in "Beijing guoji jianzhu shuangnian zhan yinchu de lishi huati" 北京国际建筑双年展引出的历史话题 (Historical issues brought by Beijing Architecture Biennale), *Sanlian shenghuo zhoukai* (Sanlian life weekly) 305, September 24, 2004, p. 27.
57. First published on *Shouhuo* 收获 (Harvest), 1991, no.6.
58. The full term in Chinese reads "zhishi qingnian 知识青年" which means literally "youth with knowledge" refers to the educated youth aged between 14 and 20 who were sent down to the countryside for reeducation during the Cultural Revolution.
59. Jinhua Dai, "Imagined Nostalgia," trans. Judy T. H. Chen, *boundary 2*, vol. 24, no. 3, (Autumn, 1997): 154.
60. Interestingly, TV drama distributors succeeded in working around the ban and issued the work in VCD format several years later.
61. Feng Xiaogang, *Wo ba qingchun xiangei ni*, p. 99.

Chapter 4

1. Wang Shuo, "Wo kan dazhong wenhua gangtai wenhua ji qita" 我看大众文化港台文化及其它 (My opinions on popular culture, Hong Kong and Taiwan culture and others), in *Wang Shuo wenji: suibiji*, p.162.
2. Yin Hong 尹鸿, *Xin Zhongguo dianying shi*, p. 152.
3. Lao Mei 老梅, "Guochan dianying: shuguang he yinying—1995 nian Zhongguo dianying shichang yipie" 国产电影：曙光和阴影—1995年中国电影市场一瞥(Domestic films: dawn and shadow—a glance at Chinese film market of 1995), *ZGDYNJ*, 1996, p. 199.

4. Ibid., p. 200.
5. Ibid., p. 200-201.
6. For more on how the studios operated in the 1990s, see Ying Zhu, *Chinese Cinema During the Reform Era: The Ingenuity of the System*, p. 79-90.
7. Wang Zhiqiang, "1993 nian quanguo dianying shichang pingshu," *ZGDYNJ*, 1994, p. 203.
8. "Guanyu gaige gushipian shezhi guanli gongzuo de guiding" 关于改革故事片摄制管理工作的规定 (Policy and regulation on reforming production and administration of feature films), MRFT, Order No. 1995, 001.
9. Tian Congming, "Dianying 'bawu' de huigu, 'jiu wu' de shexiang ji 1996 nian de gongzuo—zai dianying zhipian chang changzhan zuotan hui shang de jianghua," *ZGDYNJ*, 1996, p. 34.
10. Sun Jiazheng 孙家正, "Duochu youxiu zuopin, fanrong dianying shiye" 多出优秀作品，繁荣电影事业(Produce more excellent works, let the film industry prosper), *ZGDYNJ*, 1997, p. 8.
11. Feng Xiaogang, *Wo ba qingchun xiangei ni*, p. 89.
12. "1996 nian Guangdianbu zhongdian yingpian" 1996年广电部重点影片 (Important films of MRFT in 1996), *Dianying tongxun* 电影通讯 (Film newsletter) January 1996, p. 16.
13. Gao Jun 高军 and Zhang Shuyu 张书煜, "96 guochan dianying shichang yingjia shu shui" 九六国产电影市场赢家属谁 (Who were the winners at the domestic film market in 1996), *DYYS*, 1997, no. 3, pp. 15-17.
14. Ying Xu, "A 'New' Phenomenon of Chinese Cinema: Happy-New-Year Comic Movie," *Asian Cinema 13*, no. 1 (Spring/Summer, 2002): 114-115.
15. Shi Ming 石明, "Tiejin shidai, pingzhong jianqi—1994 nian gushipian gaiguan," *ZGDYNJ*, 1995, pp. 25-30.
16. Liu Yantao 刘言韬, "*Jingtao Hailang* gaokeji suo jiangshu de zhenshigan de zai chuangzao he xiangmuyunzuo de gaoxiaoxing" 惊涛骇浪高科技所讲述的真实感的再创作和项目运作的高效性 (Recreation of realism and efficiency of project operation of high technology in *A Stormy Sea*), *DYYS*, 2003, no. 3, p. 57.
17. *Zhongguo dianying bao*, December 20, 2000.
18. *ZGDYNJ*, 2001, p.173.
19. Feng Xiaogang, *Wo ba qingchun xiangei ni*, pp. 87-88.
20. Feng Xiaogang, *Wo ba qingchun xiangei ni*, p. 99.
21. Ibid., p. 91.
22. Eric Eckholm, "Leading Chinese Filmmaker Tries for a Great Leap to the West," *New York Times*, April 21, 2001.
23. Scarlet Cheng, "There's Nothing Like Being There," *Los Angeles Times*, November 1, 1998.
24. Jane M. Gaines, "Dream/Factory," in *Reinventing Film Studies*, ed. Christine Gledhill and Linda Williams (New York: Oxford University Press, 2000), p. 107.

25. Although, according to Marx, "proletariats" are the industrial workers who lack their own means of production and have to sell their labor to live, the Chinese Communist Party uses this term with a broader definition, which includes not only workers, but also peasants and soldiers—the lowest socio-economic classes in Chinese society.

26. The Great Leap Forward 大跃进 (da yuejin) was an economic plan launched by Mao Zedong in 1958 that was designed to increase farm and industrial output through the creation of commune. This movement, based on Mao's belief that human willpower and effort could overcome all obstacles, resulted in economic disaster and widespread starvation.

27. Sun Jiazheng, "Duochu youxiu zuopin, fanrong dianying shiye," *ZGDYNJ* (1997), p. 8.

28. Ibid.

29. For detailed discussion of this book, please see Xiaomei Chen, *Occidentalism: A Theory of Counter-Discourse in Post Mao China* (Oxford: Oxford University Press, 1995), pp. 157-167.

30. Chen, *Occidentalism*, p. 157.

31. Ibid., p. 159.

32. Mao Zedong 毛泽东, *Mao Zedong xuanji* 毛泽东选集 (The collected works of Mao Zedong) vol. 5 (Beijing: Renmin chubanshe, 1977), pp. 289-292.

33. Quoted in Hannah Beech, "Keeping It Reel," *Time Asia*, July 23, 2001. http://www.time.com/time/asia/arts/magazine/0,9754,167619,00.html#/.

34. Thomas Schatz, "Film Genre and the Genre Film," in *Film Theory and Criticism*, ed. Leo Braudy and Marshall Cohen (New York: Oxford University Press, 1999), p. 646.

35. Jane M. Gaines, "Dream/Factory," p. 107.

Chapter 5

1. Zhao Shi, "Quanmian guanche shiliu da jingshen jiakuai tuijin dianying chanye de gaige fazhan chuangxin" 全面贯彻十六大精神加快推进电影产业的改革发展创新 (To fully implement the essence of the Sixteenth National Congress and to foster and promote the film industry's reforms, developments and innovations), *Official Website of SARFT*, http://www.sarft.gov.cn/manage/publishfile/11/873.html/.

2. "China and the WTO—Will Its Entry Unleash New Prosperity or Further Destabilize the World Economy?" Website of *Business Week*. http://www.businessweek.com/magazine/content/01_43/b3754126.htm/.

3. Jack Valenti, "Valenti urged senate to grant PNRT to China," April 11, 2000. Official Website of Motion Pictures Association of America. http://www.mpaa.org/jack/2000/00_04_11a.htm/.

4. Jack Valenti, "Statement of Jack Valenti, Chairman and Chief Executive Officer, Motion Picture Association, before the Committee on Ways and Means Subcommittee on Trade, Regarding US-China Trade Relations and the Possible Accession of China to the World Trade Organization," ibid. June 8, 1999. http://www.mpaa.org/jack/99/99_6_8a.htm/.

5. Ying Xu, "A 'New' Phenomenon of Chinese Cinema: Happy-New-Year Comic Movie," *Asian Cinema 13*, no. 1 (Spring/Summer, 2002): 114-115.

6. "2003 nian guochan, jinkou yingpian pai zuoci" 2003年国产、进口影片排座次 (2003 top ten domestic and imported films), *Changjiang ribao*, January 7, 2004.

7. Sun Liping 孙丽萍, "Haolaiwu dapian fenfen birang zhongguo dianying" 好莱坞大片纷纷避让中国国产电影 (Hollywood blockbusters are "avoiding" Chinese domestic films), *Xinhua wang* 新华网 (Xinhua net), http://news.xinhuanet.com/ent/2005-01/06/content_2424245.htm/.

8. Yin Hong and Zhan Qing Sheng 詹庆生, "2005nian Zhongguo dianying chanye beiwanglu" 2005年中国电影产业备忘录 (Memo of Chinese film industry in 2005), *2006 nian: Zhongguo chuanmei chanye baogao*, ed. Cui Baoguo 崔保国, (Beijing: shenhui kexue chubanshe, April, 2006), p. 329.

9. "Meinian guobai dianying shizong zhimi" 每年过百电影失踪之谜 (Mystery of over a hundred missing films every year), *Guangzhou Daily*, April 7, 2006, page B1.

10. Document number (guofa [2000] 41), "Guanyu zhichi wenhua shiye fazhan ruogan jingji zhengce de tongzhi" (国务院关于支持文化事业发展若干经济政策的通知）. http://www.ccdy.cn/pubnews/450273/20060316/482828.htm/.

11. Quote on the website of Xinhua News on February 20, 2004. http://news.xinhuanet.com/newmedia/2004-02/20/content_1323651.htm/.

12. Wang Xiaoshan 王小山, "Yuanqu de quangying: Zhongguo guoyou dianying zhipianchang shengcun zhuangkuang diaocha" 远去的光影：中国国有电影制片厂生存状况调查 (Fading lights and shadows: reports on current situations of Chinese state-owned film studios), *Xin jing bao*, April 14, 2005.

13. Liu Jianghua 刘江华 and Zheng Ye 郑叶, "Guoji chuanmei jutou fenfen daju jinjun zhongguo yingshi ye" 国际传媒巨头纷纷大举进军中国影视业 (International media moguls enter china's movie and TV industry), *Beijing qingnian bao*, November 26, 2004.

14. Ibid.

15. Wang Xiaoshan, "Yuanqu de quangying: zhongguo guoyou dianying zhipianchang shengcun zhuangkuang diaocha."

16. Ibid.

17. Zhang Yue 张悦, "Shanghai dianying jituan: dongfang Haolaiwu he ri jun zai lai" 上海电影集团：东方好莱坞何日君再来 (Shanghai Film Group Corporation: When will the Hollywood in the East come back), *Xinwen wubao*, April 15, 2005.

18. Yu Liang, "Film Giant's New Sideline: Kodak's $4 million Theater to Open Soon," *Shanghai Star*, January 08, 2001.

19. Shi Yan 师琰, "Huana shouci konggu guonei yingyuan" 华纳首次控股国内影院 (Warner priorities domestic movie theater for the fist time), *Zhongguo wenhua bao*, December 15, 2003.

20. Li Guangyi 李光一, "Shanghai chouiian donghua pindao" 上海筹建动画频道 (Shanghai is about to open a cartoon channel), *Jiefang ribao*, April 6, 2004.

21. Wang Xiaoshan, "Yuanqu de quangying: zhongguo guoyou dianying zhipianchang shengcun zhuangkuang diaocha".

22. Ibid.

23. Ibid.

24. Zhang Ling 张凌, "Dianyingju guanyuan qujing ruhe feiji" 电影局官员取经如何分级 (Film officials learn how to rate films), *Fazhi wanbao*, April 19, 2005.

25. Jiang Wei 姜薇, "Zhongguo dianying fenji ye buhui you san ji pian" 中国电影分级也不会有三级片(Chinese movie rating system won't have X ratings), *Beijing qingnianbao*, November 21, 2003.

26. Zhang Ling, "Dianying ju guanyuan qujing ruhe feiji."

27. Liu Yi 刘毅, "Dianying shencha zhidu zhongkounantiao" 电影审查制度众口难调 (Film censorship could not appeal to everyone), *Xinxi shibao*, January 12, 2005.

28. Yin Hong, "Damokelisi zhi jian—Zhongguo minzu dianying ye xianzhuang guankui" 达摩克利斯之剑：中国民族电影业现状管窥 (Sword of Damocles: Overview of the situation of Chinese national cinema), *Wenhua yuekan* 1999, No. 3, pp. 22-23 and no. 4, pp. 16-17.

29. Zeng Jiaxin 曾家新, "Shoujia difang dianying shencha zhongxin chengli" 首家地方电影审查中心成立(First local film censorship center was established), *Jinghua shibao*, August 23, 2004.

30. Xie Xiao 谢晓, "Bendi dianying zhijian zhongxin jiemi" 本地电影质检中心解密 (Quality control center of local films), *Nanfang dushi bao*, August 30, 2004.

31. Wang Peng 王鹏, "200 yu daoyan yu dianyingju gaoceng duihua" 200 余导演与电影局高层对话 (Over 200 film directors had a talk with high-ranking officials from SARFT), *Nanfang dushi bao*, January 11, 2005. Huang Bin 黄斌, "Dianying fenji niannei nanchan" 电影分级年内难产 (Film rating won't be issued before the end of this year), *Xiwen chenbao*, June 16, 2004. Tong Gang, "Dianying hangye de gaige yu guanli wenti" 电影行业的改革与管理问题 (Problems of reform and administration of film industry), Online Interview on the Official Website of SARFT, (December 15, 2004). http://www.sarft.gov.cn/downstage/zxdh/zxdh_4/zxdh_4.jsp/.

32. Wu Yueling, "Sida yinsu daidong guochan dianying chanliang chuang xin gao."

33. Ibid.

34. Valerie Jaffee, "An Interview with Jia Zhangke," *Senses of Cinema*, June 2004. http://www.sensesofcinema.com/contents/04/32/chinese_underground_film. html/.

35. Hou Ningning 侯柠柠, "Jia Zhangke bu qidai gao piaofang" 贾樟柯不期 待高票房 (Jia Zhangke doesn't expect high box-office revenue), *Beijing chenbao*, April 9, 2005.

36. Li Jun 李峻, "Wang Xiaoshuai *Qinghong* tongguo shencha, jisong Jiana dengdai cansai jieguo" 王小帅《青红通过审查　急送戛纳等待参赛结果》 (Wang Xiaoshuai's *Shanghai Dream* passed censorship and is waiting for result from Cannes), *Shanghai qingnian bao*, April 5, 2005.

37. The so-called "socialist advanced culture" (shehui zhuyi xianjin wenhua) is a notion promoted by China's former Chairman, Jiang Zeming, in 2002, as part of new orientations the China Communist Party should head in the future. The basic understanding of this policy is that CPC should remain successful and enjoy the heartfelt support of the people of China so long as the Party earnestly represents the development requirements of China's advanced social productive forces, the progressive course of China's advanced culture and the fundamental interests of the Chinese people,

38. Li Changchun (1944-) was Minister of SARFT in 2002.

39. Zhao Shi, "quanmian guanche shiliu da jingshen jiakuai tuijin dianying chanye de gaige fazhan chuangxin" 全面贯彻十六大精神加快推进电影产业的改 革发展创新 (To fully implement the essence of the Sixteenth National Congress and to foster and promote the film industry's reforms, developments and innovations), Official Website of SARFT, http://www.sarft.gov.cn/ manage/publishfile/11/873.html.

40. Official Document, SARFT, http://www.sarft.gov.cn/manage/publishfile/ 21/1569.htm/.

41. "Zhang Yimou changtan Xingfu shiguang" 张艺谋畅谈《幸福时光》 (Zhang Yimou on *Happy Times*), *Nanfang dushi bao*, July 24, 2002.

42. Chen Haini 陈海妮, "Zhang Yimou xiang shichang ditou *Xingfu shiguang* chongpai jieju" 张艺谋向市场低头 幸福时光重拍结局 (Zhang Yimou lowers his head to the market—*Happy Times* will have a new ending), *Yangcheng wanbao*, March 15, 2001.

43. Cai Ying 蔡颖, "Piaofang shouru jin shi ji wan, Zhang Yimou Shanghai zaoyu Huatielu" 票房收入仅十几万 张艺谋上海遭遇滑铁卢 (Only 10,000 at box office, Zhang Yimou Meets Waterloo in Shanghai), *Shanghai qingnian bao*, April 21, 2001.

44. Yang Zhanye 杨展业, "Dianying Xingfu shiguang: bianzao le de dushi tonghua" 电影幸福时光：编糟了的都市童话 (*Happy Times*, a lame urban fairytale), *Xinmin wanbao*, April 18, 2001. Dai Fang 戴方, "*Xingfu shiguang*, Zhang Yimou de bu jige zuopin" 幸福时光: 张艺谋的不及格作品 (*Happy Times*—Zhang Yimou's failed work), *Beijing wanbao*, January 4, 2001. Xia Ping 夏平, "*Xingfu shiguang*: yibu lingren shiwang de zuopin" 幸福时光：有没

有带失望的作品 (*Happy Times*: A disappointing work), *Hainan ribao*, January 5, 2001. He Long 何龙, "Xingfu shiguang you meiyou dai lai xingfu" 幸福时光有没有带来幸福 (Does *Happy Times* bring happiness), *Yangcheng wanbao*, January 4, 2001.

45. *DYYS* editorial, "2001 nian guochan yingpian piaofang shouru paihang" 2001 年国产影片票房收入排行榜 (List of box office revenues of domestic films of 2001), *DYYS* 2002, no. 3, pp. 12-13.

46. Elvis Mitchell, "Action Fans: Be Prepared for Heart and Feminism," *New York Times*, October 9, 2000.

47. For such reviews, see Yang Jisong 杨劲松 and Xie Xizhang 解玺璋, "Ni ba women xiang de tai jiandan le: gei Zhang Yimou de yi feng xin" 你把我们想得太简单了：给张艺谋的一封信 (We are not as naïve as you thought: a letter to Zhang Yimou), *Jinghua shibao*, December 12, 2002. "Ying Xiong xueye shouying baobian buyi" 英雄雪夜首映褒贬不一 (Both good and bad reactions from *Hero's* premier night), *Beijing wanbao*, December 12, 2002.

48. *Xinwen lianbo*, CCTV, December 15, 2002. http://www.cctv.com/news/xwlb/20021215/100198.shtml/.

49. Website of Ministry of Culture, http://www.ccm.gov.cn/mediaMovieChannel/main/yxdy-3o.jsp?lm=ywxw&id=233&type=null/.

50. Song Hong 宋虹, "*Maifu* yao yi kou chi cheng pang wawa" 埋伏要一口吃个胖娃娃 (*Flying Dagger* is about to get profitable), *Chengdu shangbao*, June 18, 2004.

51. Stephen Short, "Interview with director Feng Xiaogang," *Time Asia*, October, 2001.

52. Dai Jinhua 戴锦华, "Feng Xiaogang guilai" 冯小刚归来 (Return of Feng Xiaogang), Baijia jiangtan 百家讲坛 (Seminars of hundred schools), CCTV-10, (February 4, 2005). http://www.cctv.com/program/bjjt/20050204/100726.shtml/.

53. Feng Xiaogang, interview with Xinlangwang yuleban 新浪网娱乐版 (Sina Entertainment), "Zhuming daoyan Feng Xiaogang zuoke Xinlang fangtan shilu" 著名导演冯小刚作客新浪访谈实录 (Famous film director Feng Xiaogang is interviewed by Sina Entertainment", Sina.com.cn, December 21, 2001. http://ent.sina.com.cn/s/m/2001-12-22/67864.html/.

54. Thomas Schatz defines "genre film" as "on one hand, it is a familiar formula of interrelated narrative and cinematic components that serves to continually reexamine some basic cultural conflict....On the other hand, changes in cultural attitudes, new influential genre films, the economics of the industry, and so forth, continually refine any film genre." See Thomas Schatz, "Film Genre and the Genre Film," in *Film Theory and Criticism Introductory Readings*, ed. Leo Braudy and Marshall Cohen (New York, Oxford: Oxford University Press, 1999), pp. 642-653.

55. Erik Eckholm, "Leading Chinese Filmmaker Tries a Great Leap to the West: Will a Zany Satire Be a Breakthrough for a Popular Director?" *New York Times*, June 21, 2001.

56. Stephanie Donald, "Comedy and Affect: the Silkscreen Season and the Quiet Audience — Asian Cinema and Festival," *Metro Magazine*, winter 2003.

57. Jeff Vince, "Bury *Big Shot's Funeral*," *Deseret News (Salt Lake City)*, March 21, 2003.

58. Fredric Jameson, "Notes on Globalization as a Philosophical Issue," in *The Cultures of Globalization*, ed. Fredric Jameson and Masao Miyoshi (Durham, N.C.: Duke University Press, 1998), p. 63.

59. Jonathan Rosenbum, *Movie Wars: How Hollywood and the Media Limit What Movies We Can See* (Chicago: A Cappela Book, 2000), p. 114.

60. Liu Qing 刘清, "Shouji zhengyi de beihou" 《手机》争议的背后 (Behind the debate over Cell Phone), RMRB, February 11, 2004.

61. Yang Jinsong 杨劲松, "2003 nian jinkou dapian piaofang paihang" 2003 年进口大片票房排行 (Chart of box-office revenue of imported films of 2003), *Jinghua shibao*, December 20, 2003.

62. Zhong Yan 仲言, "Women shiqu yishu panduan li le ma?" 我们失去艺术判断力了吗 (Have we lost ability of artistic evaluation?), *RMRB*, March 31, 2005.

63. For such reviews, see, Feng Rui 冯睿, "Tianxia wuzei de yuanqi" 《天下无贼》的缘起 (The origin of *A World Without Thieves*), *Xin jingbao*, December 6, 2004 and Nie Wei 聂伟, "Chenggong de zhuanxing zhizuo" 成功的转型之作 (A successful work of transformation), *Jiefang ribao*, December 23, 2004.

64. Quote in Zhao Nannan 赵楠楠, "Feng Xiaogang jiantao Tianxia wuzei" 冯小刚检讨天下无贼 (Feng Xiaogang criticizes *A World Without Thieves*), *Jinghua shibao*, December 27, 2004.

65. Ibid.

66. Ibid.

67. Zhao Zheng 赵正, "Shouji+shangye=shoulei?" 手机+商业=手雷? (Cell Phone + Commercials=Grenade?), Zhongguo jingying bao, Dec. 22, 2003.

68. Quote in Ning Ling 宁玲, "Shouji cheng guanggao dianying: Feng Xiaogang shuo zhe bushi wo de cuo" 《手机》成广告电影：冯小刚说这不是我的错 (*Cell Phone* becomes a film of ads: Feng Xiaogang said it's not my fault), Shenyang jinbao, December 22, 2004.

70. Feng Xiaogang, interview with "Caifu gushi" 财富故事 (Story of wealth), CCTV-2, April 5, 2005, 12:40-13:10, http://news.xinhuanet.com/video/2005-04/05/content_2788597.htm/.

71. "Interview with Wang Zhonglei and Feng Xiaogang", April 25, 2006, website of sina.com.cn. http://ent.sina.com.cn/m/2006-04-25/ba1064400.shtml/.

72. Wang, Yichuan 王一川, "Feng Xiaogang and His Films in the Critics' Eyes" 众说冯小刚, *Dangdai dianying*, pp. 35-41.

73. "Xin zuo pingyi: Ye Yan" 新作评议：夜宴 (Discussion on New Movies: The Banquet), *Dangdai dianying*, 2006, 6, p. 67.

74. Feng, Xiaogang, "Feng Xiaogang zishu" 冯小刚自述 (Feng Xiaogang on Feng Xiaogang), *Dangdai dianying* (Contemporary Cinema), 2006, 06, p. 42.

75. Liu Jiaqi 刘嘉琪, "Wen Rui duihua Feng Xiaogang" 文睿对话冯小刚 (Wen Rui talks to Feng Xiaogang), *Dongfang zaobao*, November 18, 2004.

Chapter 6

1. Hou Ningning, "Liu Zhenyun xiaoshuo *Wengu 1942* zhengzai qiaoqiao yunzuo" 刘震云小说《温故1942》正在悄悄运作 (Liu Zhenyun's novel *Remembering 1942* is in production), *Beijing chenbao*, August 24, 2004.
2. Antonio Gramsci, *Selections from Prison Notebooks* (London: Lawrence and Wishart, 1971), p. 261.
3. Ibid.
4. Christine Gledhill, "Pleasurable Negotiations," in *Cultural Theory and Popular Culture*, ed. John Storey (Hemel Hempstead: Prentice Hall, 1988), p. 244.
5. Quoted in Wu Fei 吴菲, "Feng Xiaogang: wo mei juede gudu" 冯小刚：我没觉得孤独 (Feng Xiaogang: I don't feel lonely), *Beijing qingnian bao*, November 24, 2000.

Filmography

A Married Couple (Women fufu zhijian; dir. Zheng Junli 鄭君里, 1951)
A World Without Thieves (Tianxia wuzei; dir. Feng Xiaogang 冯小刚, 2004)
After Separation (Da sa ba; dir. Xiagang 夏刚, 1993)
All Men Are Brothers—Blood of the Leopard (Yingxiong bense; dir. Chang Hui-Ngai 陈会毅, 1993)
Back to Back, Face to Face (Liangkao liang, bei dui bei; dir. Huang Jianxin 黄建新, 1994)
Baise Rebellion (Baise qiyi; dir. Chen Jialin 陈家林, 1989)
Be There or Be Square (Bujian busan; dir. Feng Xiaogang, 1998)
Beautiful House (Meili de jia; dir. An Zhanjun 安占军, 2000)
Behind the Moon (Yueliang bei mian; TV drama, 10 episodes, dir. Feng Xiaogang, 1996)
Big Shot's Funeral (Da waner; dir. Feng Xiaogang, 2002)
Camel Xiangzi (Luotuo xiangzi; dir. Ling Zifeng 淩子风, 1983)
Cell Phone (Shou ji; dir. Feng Xiaogang, 2003)
Chicken Feathers on the Ground (Yidi jimao, TV drama; dir. Feng Xiaogang, 1995)
Choice Between Life and Death (Shengsi jueze; dir. Yu Benzheng 孙本正 and Zhang Ping 张平, 2000)
Commander Guan (Guan lianzhang; dir. Shi Hui 石挥, 1951)
Country Teacher (Fenghuang qin; dir. He Qun 何群, 1994)
Crane Kids (He tong; dir. Ge Xiaoying 葛晓英, 1997)
Creation of the World (Kaitian pidi; dir. Li Xiepu 李歇浦, 1991)
Crows and Sparrows (Wuya yu maque; dir. Zheng Junli, 1948-1949)
Dates Without Lei Feng (Likai Lei Feng de rizi; dir. Lei Xianhe 雷献禾, 1997)
Decisive Engagement (Da juezhan; dir. Cai Jiwei 蔡继渭, Yang Guangyuan 杨光远 and Wei Lian 韦廉, 1991)
Deep Gasping (Da chuanqi; dir. Ye Daying 叶大鹰, 1988)

Defense and Counterattack (Fangshou fanji; dir. Liang Tian 梁天, 2000)

Desperation (Zuihou de fengkuang; dir. Zhou Xiaowen 周晓文, 1987)

Elegy for Love (Qing shang; TV drama, 10 episodes, dir. Feng Xiaogang, ca. 1996)

Family Tie (Kaoshi yi jia qin; dir. Liu Xiaoguang 刘晓光, 2000)

Farewell My Concubine (Bawang bieji; dir. Chen Kaige 陈凯歌, 1993)

Fong Sai Yuk (Fang Shiyu; dir. Corey Yuen 元奎, 1993)

Founding of the Nation (Kaiguo dadian; dir. Li Qiankuan 李前宽 and Xiao Guiyun 肖桂云, 1989)

Gone Forever with My Love (Yongshi wo ai; dir. Feng Xiaogang, 1994)

Great Swordsman of the Yellow River (Huanghe da xia; dir. Zhang Xinyan张鑫炎 and Zhang Zien 张子恩, 1987)

Gua Sha Treatment (Gua sha; dir. Zheng Xiaolong 郑晓龙, 2001)

Guerrilla on the Plain (Pingyuan youjidui; dir. Su Li 苏里 and Wu Zhaodi 武兆堤, 1955)

Half Sea, Half Flame (Yiban shi haishui, yiban shi huoyan; dir. Xia Gang 夏刚, 1988)

Happy Times (Xingfu shiguang; dir. Zhang Yimou 张艺谋, 2000)

Harry Potter and the Chamber of Secrets (dir. Chris Columbus, 2002),

Her Smile Through the Candlelight (Zhuguang li de weixiao; dir. Wu Tianren 吴天忍, 1991)

Herdsman (Mu ma ren; dir. Xie Jin 谢晋, 1982)

Hero (Ying xiong; dir. Zhang Yimou, 2002)

Heroic Sons and Daughters (Yingxiong ernu, dir. Wu Zhaodi, 武兆堤, 1964)

House of Flying Daggers (Shimian maifu; dir. Zhang Yimou, 2004)

I Am Your Dad (Wo shi ni baba; dir. Wang Shuo, 1996)

In the Heat of the Sun (Yangguang canlan de rizi; dir. Jiang Wen 姜文, 1995)

Jianghu (Jianghu; dir. Huang Jingpfu 黄精甫, 2004)

Jiao Yulu (Jiao Yulu; dir. Wang Jixing 王冀邢, 1991)

Killing Me Softly (dir. Chen Kaige 陈凯歌, 2002)

King of Children (Haizi wang; dir. Chen Kaige, ca. 1985)

King of Lanling (Lanling wang, dir. Hu Xuehua 胡雪桦, 1995)

Kong Fansen (Kong Fansen; dir. Chen Guoxing 陈国星 and Wang Ping 王坪, 1995)

Legend of Tianyun Mountain (Tianyunshan chuanqi; dir. Xie Jin, 1980)

Liu Hulan (Liu Hulan, dir. Shen Yaoting 沈耀庭, 1997)

Live in Peace (An ju; dir. Hu Bingliu 胡柄榴, 1997)

Living Forever in Burning Flames (Liehuo zhong yongsheng; dir. Shui Hua 水华, 1965)

Living a Miserable Life (Guozhe langbeibukan de shenghuo; dir. Feng Xiaogang, aborted, 1996)

Long March (Changzheng; dir. Zhai Junjie 翟俊杰, 1998)

Love Story of the Yellow River (Huanghe juelian; dir. Feng Xiaoning 冯小宁, 1999)

Love Story in Lu Mountain (Lu shan lian; dir. Huang, Zumou 黄祖模, 1980)

Loyalty (Hai wai chi zi; dir. Ou Fan 欧凡 and Xing Jitian 邢吉田, 1979)

Mao Zedong and His Son (Mao Zedong he ta de erzi; dir. Zhang Jinbiao 张今标, 1991)

Murder Case No. 405 (Si ling wu mousha an; dir. Shen Yaoting 沈耀庭, 1981)

Mysterious Buddha (Shenmi de dafo; dir. Zhang Huaxin 张华欣, 1980)

Once Upon Time in China (Shiwang zhengba; dir. Tsui Hark 徐克, 1992)

Opium War (Yapian zhanzheng; dir. Xie Jin 谢晋, 1997)

Party A, Party B (Jianfang yifang; dir. Feng Xiaogang, 1997)

Postman in the Mountains (Nasha, naren, nagou; dir. Huo Jianqi 霍建起, 1998)

Red Cherry (Hong yingtao; dir. Ye Daying 叶大鹰, 1995)

Red Flush (Hong fen; dir. Li Shaohong 李少红, 1995)

Red River Valley (Hong hegu; dir. Feng Xiaoning 冯小宁, 1997)

Red Sorghum (Hong gaoliang; dir. Zhang Yimou, 1985)

Rumble in the Bronx (Hong fan qu; dir. Stanly Tong, 1995)

Samsara (Lun hui; dir. Huang Jianxin 黄建新, 1988)

Scouting Across the Yangzi River (Du jiang zhencha ji, dir. Tang Xiaodan, 汤晓丹, 1954)

Shanghai Triad (Yao a yao, yao dao waipo qiao; dir. Zhang Yimou, 1995)

Shaolin Temple (Shaolin si; dir. Zhang Xinya 张鑫炎, 1982)

Sigh (Yi sheng tanxi; dir. Feng Xiaogang, 2000)

Signal Right, Turn Left (Hongdeng ting, ludeng xing; dir. Huang Jianxin, 1996)

Smile (Weixiao; dir. Jeffery Kramer, 2005)

Soccer Heroes (Jingdu qiu xia; dir. Xie Hong 谢洪, 1987)

Sorry Baby! (Meiwan meiliao; dir. Feng Xiaogang, 1999)

Stage Sisters (Wutai Jiemei; dir. Xie Jin, 1965)

Stormy Sea (Jingtao hailing; dir. Zhai Junjie 翟俊杰, 2003)

Sun Yat-sen (Sun Zhongshan; dir. Tang Xiaodan 汤晓丹, 1987)

Sun on the Roof of the World (Shijie wuji de taiyang; dir. Wang Ping 王坪, 1991)

Surveillance (Maifu; dir. Huang Jianxin, 1996)

The Accused Uncle Shan Gang (Beigao Shangang ye; dir. Fan Yuan 范元, 1995)

The Case of Silver Snake (Yinshe mousha'an; dir. Li Shaohong, 1988)

The Grave Robbers (Dongling da dao; dir. Li Yundong, 李云东, five parts, 1984–1998)

The July Seventh Incident (Qi qi shibian; dir. Li Qiankuan 李前宽 and Xiao Guiyun 肖桂云, 1995)

The Life of Wu Xun (Wu Xun zhuan; dir. Sun Yu 孙瑜, 1950)

The Mahjong Incident (Feicui majiang; dir. Yu Xiaoyang 于晓洋, 1987)

The Nanpu Bridge (Qingsa pujiang; dir. Shi Xiaohua 石晓华, 1991)

The Red Detachment of Women (Hongse niangzijun; dir. Xie Jin, 1961)

The Tribulations of a Young Master (Shaoye de monan; dir. Wu Yigong 吴怡弓 and Zhang Jianya 张建亚, 1987)

The Unexpected Passion (Zaoyu jiqing; dir. Xia Gang, 1990)

The Village of Widows (Guaifu cun; dir. Wang Jin 王进, 1988)

Troubleshooter (Wan zhu; dir. Mi Jiashan 米家山, 1988)

Wu Dang (Wu dang; dir. Sun Sha 孙沙, 1983)

Yellow Earth (Huang tudi; dir. Chen Kaige, 1985)

Zhang Ga, the Soldier Boy (Xiaobing Zhangga; dir. Cui Wei 崔嵬 and Ouyang Hongying 欧阳红缨, 1963)

Zheng Chenggong (Zheng chenggong, dir. Lu Weiguo鲁卫国, 1997)

Zhou Enlai (Zhou Enlai; dir. Ding Yinnan 丁荫楠, 1991)

Selected Bibliography

BQB Beijing qingnian bao 北京青年报 (Beijing youth newspaper)
BWB Beijing wanbao 北京晚报 (Beijing evening newspaper)
DYTX Dianying tongxun 电影通讯 (Film newsletter)
DYYS Dianying yishu 电影艺术 (Film art)
JHSB Jinghua shibao 京华时报 (Beijing times)
RMRB Renmin ribao 人民日报 (People's daily)
XJB Xin jingbao 新京报 (New Beijing newspaper)
ZGDYNJ Zhongguo dianying nianjian 中国电影年鉴 (China film year book)
Ai Zhisheng 艾知生. "Duanzheng zhidao sixiang, mingque chuangzuo fangxiang" 端正指导思想，明确创作方向 (Correct the leaders' thinking, clarify directions of production). *ZGDYNJ* (1990), pp. 5-10.
Andrews, Julia F. *Painters and Politics of People's Republic of China* 1949-1979. Berkeley: University of California Press, 1994.
Arato, Andrew and Gebhardt, Eike, ed. *The Essential Frankfurt School Reader.* New York: Urizen Books, 1978.
Barme, Geremie. *In the Red: On Contemporary Chinese Culture.* New York: Columbia University Press, 1999.
____. "Wang Shuo and *Liumang* ('Hooligan') Culture." In *The Australian Journal of Chinese Affairs* 28 (1992): 23-66.
Bazin, André. *What Is Cinema? Vol. I.* Berkeley: University of California Press, 1967.
Beech, Hannah. "Keeping It Reel." *Time Asia,* July 23, 2001. http://www.time.com/time/asia/arts/magazine/0,9754,167619,00.html#/.
Berry, Chris. ed. *Chinese Film in Focus: 25 New Takes.* London: BFI publishing, 2003.
____, ed. *Perspectives on Chinese Cinema.* London: BFI Publishing, 1991.
____. "Suzhou River" (review). *Cinemaya* 49 (2000): 20-21.
____. "Xiao Wu: China 1997." *Cinemaya* (Winter 1998/99): 20.

____. "Towards a Postsocialist Cinema: The Representation of Cultural Revolution in Films from the People's Republic of China, 1976-1981." Ph.D. diss., University of California, Los Angeles, 1999.

Bordwell, David, Staiger, Janet and Thompson, Kristin. *The Classical Hollywood Cinema: Film Style and Mode of Production to 1960.* New York: Columbia University Press, 1985.

Bordwell, David. *Planet Hong Kong: Popular Cinema and the Art of Entertainment.* Cambridge, Mass,: Harvard University Press, 2000.

Braester, Yomi. *Witness Against History: Literature, Film, and Public Discourse in Twentieth-Century China.* Stanford: Stanford University Press, 2003.

Braudy, Leo and Cohen, Marshall, ed. *Film Theory and Criticism: Introductory Readings.* New York: Oxford University Press, 1999.

Browne, Nick, ed. *New Chinese Cinemas: Forms, Identities and Politics.* New York: Cambridge University Press, 1994.

Cai Ying 蔡颖. "Piaofang shouru jin shi ji wan—Zhang Yimou Shanghai zaoyu Huatielu" 票房收入仅十几万 张艺谋上海遭遇滑铁卢 (Only 10,000 at box office: Zhang Yimou's Waterloo in Shanghai). *Shanghai qingnianbao*, April 21, 2001.

Caughie, John. *Theories of Authorship.* London and New York: Routlege, 1986.

Central Committee of the CCP. "Guanyu jingji tizhi gaige de jueding" 关于经济体制改革的决定 (Decisions on reform of the economic system). Issued on October 12, 1984.

Chen Haini 陈海妮. "Zhang Yimou xiang shichang ditou *xingfu shiguang* chongpai jiejü" 张艺谋向市场低头 幸福时光重拍结局 (Zhang Yimou lowers his head to the market—*Happy Times* will have a new ending). *Yangcheng wanbao*, March 15, 2001.

Chen Haosu 陈昊苏. "Guanyu yule pian benti lun ji qita" 关于娱乐片主体论及其它 (On dominance of entertainment film and others). *ZGDYNJ* (1989), pp. 7-11.

Chen Huangmei 陈荒煤. "Guanyu dianying yishu de 'baihua qifang'" 关于电影艺术的 "百花齐放" (On "Let the hundred flowers bloom" in film art). *Zhongguo dianying*, 1956, no.1, pp. 10-11.

Chen Kaige 陈凯歌. *Shaonian Kaige* 少年凯歌 (Young Kaige). Taibei: Yuanliu, 1991.

Chen, Xiaomei. *Occidentalism: A Theory of Counter-Discourse in Post Mao China.* Oxford: Oxford University Press, 1995.

Chen Xihe 陈犀禾 and Shi Chuan 石川. *Duoyuan yujing zhong de xin sheng dai Zhongguo dianying* 多元语境中的新生代中国电影(New generation of Chinese cinema under multiple discourses). Shanghai: xuelin chubanshe, 2003.

Cheng, Scarlet. "There's Nothing Like Being There." *Los Angeles Times*, November 2, 1998.

Chow, Rey. *Primitive Passions: Visuality, Sexuality, Ethnography, and Contemporary Chinese Cinema.* New York: Columbia University Press, 1995.

Clark, Paul. *Chinese Cinema: Culture and Politics since 1949.* Cambridge and New York: Cambridge University Press, 1987.

———. "Two Hundred Flowers on China's Screen." In *Perspectives on Chinese Cinema,* edited by Chris Berry, pp. 42-61. London: BFI Publishing, 1991.

Couvares, Francis G., ed. *Censorship and American Culture.* Washington and London: Smithsonian Institution Press, 1996.

Cui, Shuqin. *Women Through the Lens: Gender and Nation in a Century of Chinese Cinema.* Honolulu: University of Hawaii Press, 2003.

Dai Fang 戴方. "*Xingfu shiguang,* Zhang Yimou de bu jige zhi zuo" 幸福时光: 张艺谋的不及格作品 (*Happy Times*—Zhang Yimou's failed work). *BJWB,* January 4, 2001.

Dai, Jinhua 戴锦华. *Cinema and Desire: Feminist Marxism and Cultural Politics in the Works of Dai Jinhua,* edited by Jing Wang and Tani E. Barlow. New York: Verson, 2002.

———. "Feng Xiaogang guilai" 冯小刚归来 (Return of Feng Xiaogang,), *Baijia jiangtan* 百家讲坛 (Seminars of hundreds schools). CCTV-10, February 4, 2005. http://www.cctv.com/program/bjjt/20050204/100726.shtml/.

———. "Imagined Nostalgia." Translated by Judy T. H. Chen, *boundary 2,* Vol. 24 No. 3 (Autumn, 1997): 143-161.

Deng Xiaoping 邓小平. *Deng Xiaoping wenxuan* 邓小平文选 (Selected works of Deng Xiaoping). Beijing: Renmin chubanshe, 1993.

Dianying yishu 电影艺术 (Film art). Periodical published by Association of Chinese Filmmakers, 1959-.

———. "2001 nian guochan yingpian piaofang shouru paihang" 2001年国产影片票房收入排行榜 (List of box office revenue of domestic films of 2001, (Editorial). *DYYS* 2002, no. 3, pp. 12-13.

Dianying tongxu 电影通讯 (Film newsletter). Periodical published by Chinese Cinema Research Center, 1979-.

Dirlik, Arif, and Zhang, Xudong, eds. *Postmodernism and China.* Durham: Duke University Press, 2000.

Dissanayake, Wimal, ed. *Cinema and Cultural Identity.* Lanham, MD: University Press of America, 1988.

Donald, Stephanie. "Comedy and Affect: The Silkscreen Season and the Quiet Audience — asian Cinema And Festival." *Metro Magazine* 2003, Winter.

Eckholm, Erik. "Leading Chinese Filmmaker Tries for a Great Leap to the West." *New York Times,* June 21, 2001.

Feng Rui 冯睿. "*Tianxia wuzei* de yuanqi" 《天下无贼》的缘起 (The origin of *A World Without Thieves*). *XJB,* Dec. 06, 2004.

Feng Xiaogang 冯小刚. *Wo ba qingchun xian gei ni* 我把青春献给你 (I dedicated my youth to you). Beijing: Changjiang wenyi, 2003.

Film Art Research Institute of Chinese Art Research Academy. "Jiushi niandai zhongda geming lishi ticai yingpian chuangzuo diaocha bogao" 九十年代重大革命历史题材影片创作调查报告 (Survey of ìfilms of significant revolutionary and historical subjects in the 1990s). *DYSY* 2002, no. 3, pp. 54-59.

Gaines, Jane M. "Dream/Factory." In *Reinventing Film Studies*, edited by Christine Gledhill, pp. 100-113. London: Oxford University Press, 2000.

Gao Jun 高军 and Zhang Shuyu 张书煜. "96 guochan dianying shichang yingjia shu shui" 九六国产电影市场赢家属谁 (Who won in the domestic film market in 1996). *DYYS* 1997, no. 3, pp. 15-17.

Gersner, David and Staiger, Janet, eds. *Authorship and Film*. New York: Routledge, 2003.

Gledhill, Christine and Williams, Linda. eds. *Reinventing Film Studies*. New York: Oxford University Press, 2000.

Gunning, Tom. "The Cinema of Attraction: Early Film, Its Spectator and the Avant-Garde." *Wide Angle* 8 (1986): 63-70.

He Long 何龙. "*Xingfu shiguang* you meiyou dai lai xingfu" 幸福时光有没有带来幸福 (Does *Happy Times* bring happiness). *Yangcheng wanbao*, January 4, 2001.

Hou Ningning 侯柠柠. "Jia Zhangke bu qidai gao piaofang" 贾樟柯不期待高票房 (Jia Zhangke doesn't expect high box-office revenue). *Beijing chenbao*, April 9, 2005.

_____. "Liu Zhenyun xiaoshuo *wengu 1942* zhengzai qiaoqiao yunzuo" 刘震云小说《温故1942》正在悄悄运作 (Liu Zhenyun's novel *Remembering 1942* is in production). *Beijing chenbao*, August 24, 2004.

Huang Bin 黄斌. "Dianying fenji niannei nanchan" 电影分级年内难产 (Film rating won't be issued with this year). *Xiwen chenbao*, June 16, 2004.

Huang Shixian 黄式宪. "Yu Haolaiwu 'boyi' Zhongguo dianying chanye jieguo chongzu de xin geju—jian lun 2004 nian xin zhuliu dianying 'san qiang' de pinpai xiaoying" 与好莱坞 "博弈" 中国电影产业结构重组的新格局 — 兼论 2004年新主流电影 "三强" 的品牌效应 (Gambling with Hollywood—new structure after Chinese film industry reform—also on brand effect of the top three new mainstream films in 2004). *Dangdai dianying* 2005, no. 2, pp. 11-17.

Jaffee, Valerie. "An Interview with Jia Zhangke." *Senses of Cinema*, June 2004.http://www.sensesofcinema.com/contents/04/32/chinese_underground_film.html/.

Jameson, Fredric. "Notes on Globalization as a Philosophical Issue." In *The Cultures of Globalization,* edited by Fredric Jameson and Masao Miyoshi, pp. 54-80. Durham, NC: Duke University Press, 1998.

_____. "Reification and Utopia in Mass Culture." *Social Text*, no. 1 (Winter, 1979): 130-148.

Jiang Wei 姜薇. "Zhongguo dianying fenji ye buhui you san ji pian" 中国电影分级也不会有三级片(Chinese movie rating system won't have X rate). *BJQNB*, Nov. 21, 2003.

Kan, Wendy. "Big Shot' doesn't win over locals." *Variety* 387:2 [May 27, 2002 - June 02, 2002]; *FILM*.

Keane, Michael, and Tao, Dongfeng. "Interview with Feng Xiaogang." *Positions* 7.1 (Spring, 1999): 192-200.

Kong, Shuyu. "Big Shot from Beijing: Feng Xiaogang's He Sui Pian and Contemporary Chinese Commercial Film." *Asian Cinema* 14 ,1 (Spring/ Summer 2003): 175-187.

Kraicer, Shelly. "Interview with Jia Zhangke." *Cineaction* 60, 1 (2003): 30-33.

____. "Review of Jia Zhangke's *Platform*." *Cineaction* 5, 2 (2001): 67-70.

____. "Review of *Unknown Pleasures*." *Cineaction* 61, 1 (2003): 65-66.

Kuoshu, Harry. "Filming Marginal Youth: The 'Beyond' Syndrome in the Postsocialist City." In *Lightness of Being in China: Adaptation and Discursive Figuration in Cinema and Theater*, edited by Harry Kuoshu, pp. 123-52. New York: Peter Lang, 1999.

Lao Mei 老梅. "Guochan dianying: shuguang he yinying—1995 nian zhongguo dianying shichang yipie" 国产电影：曙光和阴影 1995年中国电影市场一瞥 (Domestic films: dawn and shadow—a glance at the Chinese film market of 1995). *ZGDYNJ* (1996), pp.199-202.

Lau, Jenny. *Multiple Modernities: Cinemas and Popular Media in Transcultural Asia.* Philadelphia: Temple University Press, 2003.

Lee, Leo Ou-fan. "The Tradition of Modern Chinese Cinema: Some Preliminary Explorations and Hypothesis." In *Perspective on Chinese Cinema*, edited. Chris Berry, pp. 6-20. London: British Film Institute, 1997.

Leyda, Jay. *Dianying: An Account of Film and Film Audience in China.* Cambridge: The MIT Press, 1972.

Li Guangyi 李光一. "Shanghai choujian donghua pindao" 上海筹建动画频道 (Shanghai is about to open a cartoon channel). *Jiefang ribao*, April 06, 2004.

Li Jun 李峻. "Wang Xiaoshuai *Qinghong* tongguo shencha: jisong Jiana dengdai cansai jieguo" 王小帅《青红通过审查：急送戛纳等待参赛结果 (Wang Xiaoshuai's *Shanghai Dream* passed censorship and is waiting for result from Cannes). *Shanghai qingnianbao*, April 05, 2005.

Li Li 李力. "Shaoer buyi de youhuo he sikao" 少儿不宜的诱惑和思考 (Temptation and thinking of 'Not Appropriate for Children'). *RMRB*, February 28, 1989.

Li Ruihuan 李瑞环. "Fanrong you Zhongguo tese de shehuizhuyi dianying yishu" 繁荣有中国特色的社会主义电影艺术 (Let the art of socialist cinema with Chinese specificities flourish). *DYTX* 1990, no, 4 pp. 1–2 and no. 5 pp. 1-3.

Li Xingye 李兴叶. "Bingtai shehui bingtai jingshen de zhenshi xiezhao: Wang Shuo dianying de jiazhi yu shiwu" 病态社会病态病态精神的真实写照：王朔电影的价值与失误 (Realistic representation of a morbid spirit in a morbid society—the value and failure of Wang Shuo films). *ZGDYNJ* (1989), pp. 285-288.

Liang Yu. "Film Giant's New Sideline: Kodak's $4 million Theater to Open Soon". *Shanghai Star,* (January 8, 2001).

Liu Cheng 柳城. "Dui 1989 nian gushipian chuangzuo de huigu" 对1989年故事片创作的回顾 (Review of production of feature films of 1989). *ZGDNNJ* (1990), pp. 18-24.

Liu Jiaqi 刘嘉琪. "Wen Rui duihua Feng Xiaogang" 文睿对话冯小刚 (Wen Rui talks to Feng Xiaogang). *Dongfang zaobao,* Nov. 18, 2004.

Liu Qing 刘清. "*Shouji* zhengyi de beihou" 《手机》争议的背后 (Behind the debate over *Cell Phone*). *RMRB*, February 11, 2004.

Liu Qiong 刘琼. "Jinian 'zai Yan'an wenyi zuotan hui shang de jianghua' fabiao 60 zhou nian: zhongzhi yuan tuan zhengti chuji" 纪念"在延安文艺座谈会上的讲话"发表60周年: 中直院团整体出击 (Celebrate the 60 Years anniversary of Yan'an Talks: all the central art institutions act now). *RMRB*, April 18, 2002.

Liu Yantao 刘言韬. "*Jingtao Hailang* gaokeji suo jiangshu de zhenshigan de zai chuangzao he xiangmuyunzuo de gaoxiaoxing" 惊涛骇浪高科技所讲述的真实感的再创作和项目运作的高效性 (Recreation of realism and efficiency of project operation of high technology in *A Stormy Sea*). DYYS 2003, no. 3, pp. 55-57.

Liu Yi 刘毅. "Dianying shencha zhidu zhongkounantiao" 电影审查制度众口难调 (Film censorship could not appeal to everyone). *Xinxi shibao*, January 12, 2005.

Liu Jianghua 刘江华 and Zheng Ye 郑叶. "Guoji chuanmei j,tou fenfen daj, jinjun Zhongguo yingshi ye" 国际传媒巨头纷纷大举进军中国影视业 (International media moguls enter china's movie and TV industry). *BJQNB*, November 26, 2004.

Lu, Sheldon H. *China, Transnational Visuality, Global Postmodernity.* Stanford: Stanford University Press, 2001.

Mao Zedong 毛泽东. *Mao Zedong Xuanji* 毛泽东选集 (The collected works of Mao Zedong). Beijing: Renmin chubanshe, 1977.

McGrath, Jason, "Culture and the Market in Contemporary China: Cinema, Literature and Criticism of the 1990s." Ph.D. diss., University of Chicago, 2004.

Merritt, Greg. *Celluloid Mavericks: A History of American Independent Film.* New York: Thunder's Mouth Press, 2000.

Mi, Jiashan. "Discussing *The Troubleshooters*". *Chinese Education and Society* 31.3 (January-February), pp. 8-14.

Mitchell, Elvis. "Action Fans: Be Prepared for Heart and Feminism." *New York Times*, October 9, 2000.

Naughton, Barry. *Growing Out of the Plan: Chinese Economy Reform, 1978-1993.* Cambridge: Cambridge University Press, 1995.

Nie Wei 聂伟. "Chenggong de zhuanxing zhizuo" 成功的转型之作 (A successful work of transformation). *Jiefang ribao* December 23, 2004.

Ning Ling 宁玲. "*Shouji* cheng guanggao dianying: Feng Xiaogang shuo zhe bushi wo de cuo" 《手机》成广告电影：冯小刚说这不是我的错 (*Cell Phone* becomes a film of ads: Feng Xiaogang says 'it's not my fault). *Shenyang jinbao*, December 22, 2004.

Noble, Jonathan. "Cultural Performance in China: Beyond Resistance in the 1990s." Ph.D. diss., Ohio State University, 2003.

———. "Wang Shuo and the Commercialization of Literature." In *Columbia Companion to Modern East Asian Literatures*, edited by Joshua Mostow and Kirk A. Denton, pp. 598-603, China section, NY: Columbia University Press, 2003.

Renmin ribao, editorial, "Bixu qizhi xianming di fandui dongluan" 必须旗帜鲜明地反对动乱 (Must resolutely oppose an unrest). *RMRB*, April 26, 1989.

———, editorial, "Xuexi Jiang Zemin lun Yan'an jingshen de zhongyao jianghua" 学习江泽民论延安精神的重要讲话 (Study Jiang Zemin's important talk on Yan'an spirit). April 20, 2002.

Rosenbum, Jonathan. *Movie Wars: How Hollywood and the Media Limit What Movies We Can See.* Chicago: A Cappela Book, 2000.

Sarris, Andrew. *The American Cinema: Directors and Directions 1929-1968.* New York: E. P. Dutton, 1968.

Schatz, Thomas. "Film Genre and the Genre Film." In *Film Theory and Criticism Introductory Readings,* edited by Leo Braudy and Marshall Cohen, pp. 642-653, New York and Oxford: Oxford University Press, 1999.

Shao Mujun 邵牧君. "Wang Shuo dianyingre yuanhe er qi" 王朔电影热缘何而起 (Where does the Wang Shuo Fever come from). *Zhongguo dianyingbao*, March 25, 1989.

Shi Hui 石挥. "Wo dui 'zhengming' de yixie kanfa" 我对争鸣的一些看法 (My opinions on the "debate"). *Zhongguo dianying* 1956, no. 1, pp. 20-21.

Shi Ming 石明. "Tiejin shidai, pingzhong jianqi—1994 nian gushipian gaiguan" 贴近时代 平中见奇1994 年故事片概观 (Overview of feature films of 1994). *ZGDYNJ* (1995), pp. 25-30.

Shisan da yilia zhongyao wenxian xuanbian 十三大以来重要文献选编 (Selection of important documents after the Thirteenth Party Congress). Beijing: Renmin chubanshe, 1991.

Shi Yan 师琰. "Huana shouci konggu guonei yingyuan" 华纳首次控股国内影院 (Warner priorities domestic movie theater for the first time). *Zhongguo wenhua bao*, December 15, 2003.

Silbergeld, Jerome. *China into Film: Frames of Reference in Contemporary Chinese Cinema.* London: Reaktion, 1999.

Short, Stephen. "As Sex Scenes Are Banned, We Need to Be Creative." (Web-only interview with director Feng Xiaogang) *Time Asia*. http://cgi.cnn.com/ASIANOW/time/features/interviews/2000/10/26/int.feng_xiaogang.html.

———. "Interview with Director Feng Xiaogang." *Time Asia*, October 2001.

Song Hong 宋虹. "*Maifu* yao yi kou chi cheng pang wawa" 埋伏要一口吃个胖娃娃 (*Flying Dagger* is about to get profitable). *Chengdu shangbao*, June 18, 2004.

Staiger, Janet. "Authorship Approaches." In *Authorship and Films*, edited by David A. Gerstner and Janet Staiger, pp. 27-60. New York and London: Routledge, 2003.

Storey, John. *Cultural Studies and the Study of Popular Culture*. Edinburgh: Edinburgh University Press, 2003.

Su Yuewu 苏越武. "Feng Xiaogang gechang you qian ren" 冯小刚歌唱有钱人 (Feng Xiaogang glorifies rich people). *DYTX* 2000, no. 05, pp. 21-22.

Sun Jiazheng 孙家正. "Duochu youxiu zuopin, fanrong dianying shiye" 多出优秀作品，繁荣电影事业 (Produce more excellent works and let the film industry prosper). *ZGDYNJ* (1997), pp.10-15.

Sun Liping 孙丽萍. "Haolaiwu dapian fenfen birang Zhongguo guochan dianying" 好莱坞大片纷纷避让中国国产电影 (Hollywood blockbuster are "avoiding" Chinese domestic films). *Xinhua wang* 新华网 (Xinhua net). http://news.xinhuanet.com/ent/2005-01/06/content_2424245.htm/.

Teng Jinxiang 腾进贤. "Wei tigao yingpian de yishu zhiliang er nuli" 为提高影片的艺术思想质量而努力 (Strive for improving artistic and ideological quality of films). *ZGDYNJ* (1989), pp. 12-16.

Teo, Stephen. "Cinema with an Accent: Interview with Jia Zhangke, Director of *Platform*." *Senses of Cinema*, no. 15, July/August 2001. http://www.sensesofcinema.com/contents/01/15/zhangke_interview.html/.

Tian Congming 田聪明."Dianying 'bawu' huigu, 'jiuwu' de shexiang ji 1996 nian de gongzuo" 电影 "八五" 的回顾、 "九五" 的设想及1996年的工作 (Review of the "Eight Five Year Plan" of film; envision of the "Ninth Five Year Plan" and work in 1996—a talk at a seminar of film studio directors). *ZGDYNJ* (1996), pp. 33-41.

Tong Gang 童刚. "Dianying hangye de gaige yu guanli wenti" 电影行业的改革与管理问题 (Problems of reform and administration of film industry). *Online Interview on the Official Website of State Administration of Radio, Film and Television*, December 15, 2004. http://www.sarft.gov.cn/downstage/zxdh/zxdh_4/zxdh_4.jsp/.

Tyler, Patrick. "In China, Letting a Hundred Films Wither." *New York Times*, December 1, 1996.

Valenti, Jack. "Statement of Jack Valenti, Chairman and Chief Executive Officer, Motion Picture Association, Before the Committee on Ways and Means Subcommittee on Trade, Regarding US — China Trade Relations and the Possible Accession of China to the World Trade Organization, June 8, 1999." *Official Website of Motion Picture Association of America*. http://www.mpaa.org/jack/99/99_6_8a.htm/.

_____. "Valenti Urged senate to Grant PNRT to China", April 11, 2000. http://www.mpaa.org/jack/2000/00_04_11a.htm/.

Vince, Jeff. "Bury 'Big Shot's Funeral.'" *Deseret News (Salt Lake City)*, March 21, 2003.

Wang, David Der-wei, ed. *From May Fourth to June Fourth: Fiction and Film in Twentieth-Century China*. Cambridge, Mass.: Harvard University Press, 1993.

Wang Guangyi 王广宜. "Cong *Bu Jian Bu San* kan Feng Xiaogang de daoyan yishu" 从《不见不散》看冯小刚的导演艺术 (Feng Xiaogang's art of directing in *Be There or Be Square*). *DYYS* 1999, no. 03, pp. 58-59.

Wang Lanxi 王阑西. "Dianying gongzuo zhong de jige wenti" 电影工作中的几个问题 (Several problems in cinema). *Zhongguo dianying* 1956, no. 1, pp. 3-4.

Wang Nan 王楠. "Jiegou Feng Xiaogang" 解构冯小刚 (Deconstruct Feng Xiaogang). *Dianying* 2004, no. 12, pp. 8-10.

Wang Peng 王鹏. "200 yu daoyan yu dianying gaoceng duihua" 200 馀导演与电影局高层对话 (Over 200 film directors had a talk with high-ranking officials from SARFT). *Nanfang dushibao*, January 11, 2005.

Wang Shuo and Feng Xiaogang. *Bianjibu de gushi* 编辑部的故事 (Story of editorial board). Beijing: Zhongguo guangbo dianshi chubanshe, 1992.

Wang Shuo. *Wang Shuo wenji* 王朔文集 (Selection of Wang Shuo). Kunming: Yunnan chubanshe, 2004.

Wang Shushun 王树舜. "Nanwang de 1991 nian—1991nian gushipian chuangzuo qingkuang gaishu" 难忘的1991年－1991年故事片创作情况概述 (Unforgettable 1991—review of feature film productions of 1991). *ZGDYNJ* (1992), pp. 49-51.

Wang Xiaofeng 王晓峰. "Feng Xiaogang kan hesuipian: wo de dianying jiangjiu chuanqixing he renminxing" 冯小刚侃贺岁片：我的电影讲究传奇性和人民性 (Feng Xiaogang on New Year films: my films focus on legends and serve the mass people). *Sanlian shenhuo zhoukan*, February 2003.

Wang Xiaoshan 王小山. "Yuanqu de quangying: zhongguo guoyou dianying zhipianchang shengcun zhuangkuang diaocha" 远去的光影：中国国有电影制片厂生存状况调查 (Fading lights and shadows: reports on current situations of Chinese state-owned film studios). *XJB*, April 14, 2005.

Wang Yongwu 王永午 and Weng Li 翁立. "1988 Zhongguo dianying shichang beiwanglu" 1988 中国电影市场备忘录 (1988: Memoir of Chinese film market). *ZGDYNJ* (1989), pp. 294-299.

Wang Zhiqiang 王志强. "1993 nian quanguo dianying shichang pingshu" 1993 年全国电影市场评述 (Analysis on film market of 1993). *ZGDYNJ* (1994), pp. 202-204,

Wei Lian 韦廉. "*Pingjin zhanyi* pinge quisuo" 《平津战役》品格求索 (Stylistic exploration of *Pingjing Campaign*). *ZGDYNJ* (1993), pp. 86-87

Wu Fei 吴菲. "Feng Xiaogang: wo mei juede gudu" 冯小刚：我没觉得孤独 (Feng Xiaogang: I don't feel lonely). *BJQNB*, November 24, 2000.

Wushi tian de huigu yu fansi 五十天的回顾与反思 (Review and retrospection of the fifty days). Edited by Guojia jiaowei shehui kexue yanjiu yu yishu jiaoyu si, Guojia jiaowei sixiang zhengzhi gongzuo si deng (Department of Social Science Research and Art Education of National Education Committee, Department of Political Works of National Education Committee and est.) Beijing: Gaodeng jiaoyu chubanshe,1989.

Xia Ping 夏平. *"Xingfu shiguang:* yibu lingren shiwang de zuopin" 幸福时光：一部令人失望的作品 (*Happy Times:* A disappointing work). *Hainan ribao,* January 5, 2001.

Xiang Nan 向楠. "Feng Xiaogang, Ge You, sidu hesui xing" 冯小刚、葛优四度贺岁行 (Feng Xiaogang and Ge You are working on their fourth New Year film). *DYTX,* 2001, no. 3, pp. 8-11.

Xie Xiao 谢晓. "Bendi dianying zhijian zhongxin jiemi" 本地电影质检中心解密 (Demystifying quality control center of local films). *Nanfang dushibao,* August 30, 2004.

Xu, Ying. "A 'New' Phenomenon of Chinese Cinema: Happy-New-Year Comic Movie". *Asian Cinema* 13, no. 1 (Spring/Summer, 2002): 114-115.

Yang Jinsong 杨劲松. "2003nian jinkou dapian piaofang paihang" 2003 年进口大片票房排行 (Chart of box-office revenue of imported films of 2003). *JHSB,* Dec. 20,2003.

_____, and Xie Xizhang 解玺璋. "Ni ba women xiang de tai jiandan le: gei Zhang Yimou de yi feng xin" 你把我们想得太简单了：给张艺谋的一封信 (We are not as naïve as you thought: A letter to Zhang Yimou). *JHSB,* December 12, 2002.

Yang Zhanye 杨展业. "Dianyng *Xingfu shiguang:* bianzao le de dushi tonghua" 电影幸福时光：编糟了的都市童话 (*Happy Times:* A lame urban fairytale). *Xinmin wanbao,* April 18, 2001.

Yau, Esther. "International Fantasy and the 'New Chinese Cinema'." *Quarterly Review of Film and Video,* 14. 3: 100-105.

Yin Hong 尹鸿. *Xin Zhongguo dianying shi* 新中国电影史 (History of new China's cinema). Changsha: Hunan meishu chubashe, 2002.

_____. "Damokelisi zhi jian—Zhongguo minzu dianying ye xianzhuang guankui" 达摩克利斯之剑：中国民族电影业现状管窥 (Sword of Damocles: overview of the situation of Chinese national cinema). *Wenhua yuekan* 1999, no.3, pp. 22-23 and no. 4, pp. 16-17.

_____. and Xiao Zhiwei 萧志伟. "Haolaiwu quanqiu hua celuo yu zhongguo dianying de fazhan" 好莱坞全球化策略与中国电影的发展 (Globalization of Hollywood and the development of Chinese film). *Dangdai dianying,* April 2001.

Zeng Jiaxin 曾家新. "Shoujia difang dianying shencha zhongxin chengli" 首家地方电影审查中心成立 (First local film censorship center was established in Zhejiang province). *JHSB,* August 23, 2004.

Zhang Ling 张凌. "Dianying ju guanyuan qujing ruhe feiji" 电影局官员取经如何分级 (Film officials learning how to rate films). *Fazhi wanbao,* April 19, 2005.

Zhang, Yingjin. *Screening China: Critical Interventions, Cinematic Reconfigurations and the Transnational.* Ann Arbor: University of Michigan, 2002.

Zhang Yue 张悦. "Shanghai dianying jituan: Gdongfang Haolaiwu he ri jun zai lai" 上海电影集团：东方好莱坞何日君再来 (Shanghai Film Group Corporation: When will the Hollywood in the east come back). *Xinwen wubao,* April 15, 2005.

Zhang, Xudong. *Chinese Modernism in the Era of Reforms: Culture Fever, Avant-garde Fiction, and the New Chinese Cinema.* Durham: Duke University Press, 1997.

Zhao Zheng 赵正. "*Shouji*+shangye=shoulei?" 手机+商业=手雷？(*Cell Phone* + Commercials=Grenade?). *Zhongguo jingying bao*, December 22, 2003.

Zhong Chengxiang 仲呈祥. "1988 Zhongguo yingtan de liang ge remen huati— 'yule pian' yu 'zhuxuan lu' zhi wo jian" 1988 中国影坛的两个热门话题－ "娱乐片"与"主旋律"之我见 (1988: two hot topics in Chinese cinema—my opinions on 'entertainment films' and 'main melody film'). *ZGDYNJ* (1989), pp. 263-264.

Zhong Yan 仲言. "Women shiqu yishu panduan li le ma?" 我们失去艺术判断 力了吗 (Have we lost ability of artistic evaluation?). *RMRB*, March 31, 2005.

Zhongguo dianying nianjian 中国电影年鉴 (China film yearbook). Beijing: Zhongguo dianying chubanshe, 1983.

Zhou, Shaoming. "Making Money Can Be Funny." *Cinemaya* 52, 2001: 13-18.

Zhu, Ying. *Chinese Cinema During the Reform Era: The Ingenuity of the System.* Westport, Conn.: Praeger, 2003.

Index